Tried and tested

What people across the UK are saying about the **Law Express** and **Law Express Q&A** series:

'...is focused, concise and precise. It provides express and effective revision material and techniques without compromising the depth of your understanding.'

Avis Whyte, Senior Research Fellow, University of Westminster

'An accessible quick revision guide with all the essential information in one place, which makes a good addition to textbooks and other study material.'

Joanne Atkinson, Director of Postgraduate Law Programmes, University of Portsmouth

'... excellent companion for students. It is to be used as a revision guide and will be useful for students who are conversant with the principles and case law of each topic.

Alison Poole, Teaching Fellow, University of Portsmouth

'This series is great - after having revised everything, it showed me a way to condense all the information and gave me an idea of how I would go about structuring my essays.'

Arama Lemon, Student, Coventry University

'The Law Express Q&A series is perfect as it targets different learning styles - it includes diagrams and flowcharts that you can follow for easy application with confidence. It's perfect for anyone who wants to receive an extra boost with their revision!'

Mariam Hussain, Student, University of Westminster

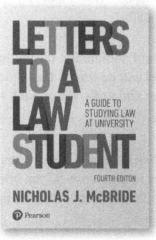

Law Express Q&A

Question&Answer

EQUITY
AND TRUSTS

5th edition

John Duddington
Former Head of the Law School, Worcester College of Technology
Lecturer in Property Law, University of Worcester

Pearson

Harlow, England • London • New York • Boston • San Francisco • Toronto • Sydney • Dubai • Singapore • Hong Kong
Tokyo • Seoul • Taipei • New Delhi • Cape Town • São Paulo • Mexico City • Madrid • Amsterdam • Munich • Paris • Milan

PEARSON EDUCATION LIMITED
KAO Two
KAO Park
Harlow CM17 9SR
United Kingdom
Tel: +44 (0)1279 623623
Web: www.pearson.com/uk

First published 2012 (print)
Second edition published 2014 (print and electronic)
Third edition published 2016 (print and electronic)
Fourth edition published 2018 (print and electronic)
Fifth edition published 2019 (print and electronic)

Contains public sector information licensed under the Open Government Licence (OGL) v3.0.
http://www.nationalarchives.gov.uk/doc/open-government-licence/version/3/

Contains Parliamentary information licensed under the Open Parliament Licence (OPL) v3.0.
http://www.parliament.uk/site-information/copyright/open-parliament-licence/

Pearson Education is not responsible for the content of third-party internet sites.

ISBN: 978-1-292-25379-4 (print)
       978-1-292-25380-0 (PDF)
       978-1-292-25381-7 (ePub)

British Library Cataloguing-in-Publication Data
A catalogue record for the print edition is available from the British Library

Print edition typeset in 10/13pt Helvetica Neue LT W1G by Pearson CSC

NOTE THAT ANY PAGE CROSS REFERENCES REFER TO THE PRINT EDITION

Contents

Acknowledgements   vi

Guided tour   xi

Table of cases and statutes   xiii

What you need to do for every question in Equity and Trusts   xix

Chapter 1   Nature of equity and trusts   1

Chapter 2   Equitable remedies and doctrines   17

Chapter 3   The three certainties   35

Chapter 4   Formalities   57

Chapter 5   Constitution of trusts   71

Chapter 6   Secret and half-secret trusts; mutual wills   93

Chapter 7   Resulting trusts   115

Chapter 8   Constructive trusts and estoppel   129

Chapter 9   Charitable trusts   159

Chapter 10   The beneficiary principle and purpose trusts   191

Chapter 11   Trusteeship and variation of trusts   213

Chapter 12   Remedies for breach of trust   235

Chapter 13   A mixture of questions   253

Bibliography   279

Index   283

Acknowledgements

To my father, Walter Duddington, who first encouraged me to become a lawyer, and who would, I think, have been an equity enthusiast; to my wife Anne, for her constant support, loyalty and technical expertise now over many years and without which my books would never begin to be written; to my daughter Mary, for her seemingly faultless proofreading and sense of fun which keeps me going; and to my son Christopher for just being himself.

I would also like to thank the staff of Pearson for their encouragement, cheerfulness and practical guidance, and all the reviewers who sent in such helpful comments on preliminary drafts of this book. I have considered them all and adopted most of them. I would indeed have adopted more had space permitted.

A word to students who may think of buying a (doubtless) cheaper previous edition of this book. Examiners often base questions on recent cases and statutes and this book contains new questions reflecting decisions of the courts on the three certainties (Chapter 3); resulting trusts (Chapter 7); constructive trusts (Chapter 8) political trusts and charity law (Chapter 9) and trustee exclusion clauses (Chapter 13). All of these are very likely topics for examination questions and a study of the questions on them in this book will, I hope, repay your investment in it. In addition, there is new material in every chapter, whether it is incorporating new cases, the throwing of new light on old cases or looking at a topic in a new light.

Finally, I still continue to visit the ground of Worcestershire County Cricket Club where, during quiet passages of play, many of the ideas for the questions in this book first come to my mind!

Readers should know that this book is based on sources available to me on 28th October 2018.

John Duddington

Publisher's acknowledgements

Text Credit(s):

4 Crown copyright: *Springett* v *Defoe* (1992) 2 FLR 388 **5 Crown copyright:** *Springett* v *Defoe* **6 Crown copyright:** *Oxley* v *Hiscock* (2004) EWCA Civ. 546 CA Chadwick LJ **6 New Zealand Government Open Access and Licensing:** *Carly* v *Farrelly* (1975) 1 NZLR 356 **6 Crown copyright:** *Bristol and West Building Society* v *Mothew* [1996] EWCA Civ 533 **10 Crown copyright:** *Gee* v *Pritchard* 2 Swan 402 HC **10 Crown copyright:** *Eves* v *Eves* [1975] 3 All ER 768 CA **10 Crown copyright:** Denning MR in *Hussey* v *Palmer* [1972] 3 All ER 744 CA **11 Crown copyright:** *Cowcher* v *Cowcher* [1972] 1 All ER 943 HC **14 LexisNexis:** Browne, D. (ed.) (1933) Ashburner's Principles of Equity (2nd edn). London: Butterworths. **14 Thomson Reuters:** Millett, P.J. (1998) Equity's place in the law of commerce. Law Quarterly Review, 114: 214. **19 Parliamentary Copyright:** *Co-operative Insurance Society* v *Argyll Stores Ltd* [1998] **20 Crown copyright:** *Wilson* v. *Northampton and Banbury Junction Railway Co.* (1874) L.R. 9 Ch.App. 279 CA **21 Crown copyright:** *Vercoe and others* v *Rutland Fund Management Ltd and others* (2010) EWHC 424 Ch **23 Parliamentary Copyright:** *Co-operative Insurance Society* v *Argyll Stores Ltd* **26 Crown copyright:** *Giles (CH) & Co Ltd* v *Morris* [1972] 1 WLR 307 HC **30 Crown copyright:** *Royal Bank of Scotland* v *Etridge* (No 2) [2001] UKHL 44 Lord Nicholls **31 Lord Nicholls:** Lord Nicholls **32 Crown copyright:** *HSBC Bank* v *Brown* [2015] EWHC 359 Ch. HC **38 Lindley LJ:** Re Hamilton [1895] 2 Ch 370 CA **38 Crown copyright:** *Suggitt* v *Suggitt* [2011] EWHC 903 (Ch) **39 Crown copyright:** *Anthony* v *Donges* [1998] 2 FLR 775 HC **39 Crown copyright:** Re Golay [1965] 1 WLR 969 HC **39 Parliamentary Copyright:** *McPhail* v *Doulton* [1971] AC 424 HL **39 Crown copyright:** Re Baden's Deed Trusts (No 2) [1973] Ch 9 CA **40 Parliamentary Copyright:** *McPhail* v *Doulton* [1971] AC 424 HL **40 Crown copyright:** *R* v *District Auditor ex parte West Yorkshire -Metropolitan County Council* [1986] RVR 24 HC **43 Crown copyright:** Re Adams and the Kensington Vestry [1884] 27 Ch D 394 HC **43 Crown copyright:** *Vucicevic* v *Aleksic* [2017] EWHC 2335 (Ch) HC **43 Crown copyright:** *Day* v *Harris* (2013) EWCA Civ. 191 CA **44 Crown copyright:** Re Barlow's Will Trusts [1979] 1 WLR 278 HC **45 Crown copyright:** *Comiskey* v *Bowring-Hanbury* [1905] AC 84 HL **45 Crown copyright:** *Sprange* v *Barnard* [1789] 2 Bro CC 585 **48 Crown copyright:** *Pearson* v *Lehman Brothers Finance SA* [2010] EWHC 2914 **49 Crown copyright:** *Hunter* v *Moss* [1994] **50 Crown copyright:** *Lehman Brothers (Europe) (in Administration)* v *CRC Credit Fund Ltd.* [2010] EWCA Civ 917 **53 Crown copyright:** *Morice* v *Bishop of Durham* [1804] 10 Ves 522 HC **54 Parliamentary Copyright:** *McPhail* v *Doulton* [1971] AC 424 HL **54 Crown copyright:** Re Baden Megaw LJ **61 Crown copyright:** Section 53(1)(b) of the LPA 1925 **62 Crown copyright:** Section 60(3) of the LPA 1925 **62 Crown copyright:** section 53(2) of the LPA 1925 **74 Lord Edon:** *Ellison* v *Ellison* [1802] 31 ER 1243 HC **75 Crown copyright:** *Richards* v *Delbridge* [1874] LR 18 Eq 11 HC **75 Crown copyright:** *Richards* v *Delbridge* [1874] LR 18 Eq 11 HC **75 Crown copyright:** *Vallee* v *Birchwood* [2013] EWHC 1449 (Ch) **80 Crown copyright:** *Vallee* v *Birchwood* [2013] EWHC 1449 (Ch) **80 Crown copyright:** *Woodard* v *Woodard* [1995] 3 All ER 580 CA **83 Crown copyright:** *Pennington* v *Waine* [2002] EWCA Civ 227 **85 Crown copyright:** *Pennington* v *Waine* **87**

ACKNOWLEDGEMENTS

Crown copyright: *Walter* v *Hodge* [1818] 2 Swans 92 **88 Crown copyright:** *Vallee* v
Birchwood [2013] EWHC 1449 (Ch) **88 Crown copyright:** *Thompson* v *Mechan* [1958] OR
357 HC **88 Crown copyright:** *Vallee* v *Birchwood* **89 Crown copyright:** *King* v *Dubrey*
[2014] EWHC 2083 (Ch) HC **89 Oxford University Press:** Baker, J.H. (2002) Introduction to
English Legal History (4th edn). Oxford: Oxford University Press. **101 Crown copyright:**
Ottaway v *Norman* [1972] Ch 698 HC **101 Crown copyright:** *Suggitt* v *Suggitt* [2011] EWHC
903 **101 Crown copyright:** Re Rees' Will Trusts [1950] Ch 204 HC **102 Crown copyright:**
Re Freud [2014] EWHC 257 **106 Parliamentary Copyright:** *McCormick* v *Grogan* [1869] 4
App Cas 82 HL **106 Parliamentary Copyright:** *Blackwell* v *Blackwell* [1929] AC 318 HL **106
Parliamentary Copyright:** *Blackwell* v *Blackwell* [1929] AC 318 HL **117 Thomson Reuters:**
Swadling, W. Explaining Resulting Trusts (2008) 124 LQR 72 **118 Parliamentary Copyright:**
Vandervell v *IRC* [1966] Ch 261 **119 Parliamentary Copyright:** *Westdeutsche Landesbank
Girozentrale* v *Islington BC* [1996] AC 669 HL **121 Thomson Reuters:** Swadling, W.
Explaining Resulting Trusts (2008) 124 LQR 72 **124 Crown copyright:** Lord Sumption , in *M*
v *M* and others [2013] EWCH 2534 **125 Crown copyright:** *Barclays Bank Ltd* v *Quistclose
Investments Ltd* [1970] AC 567 HL **125 Parliamentary Copyright:** *Twinsectra* v *Yardley*
[2002] UKHL **131 Crown copyright:** Lord Browne-Wilkinson in *Westdeutsche Landesbank
Girozentrale* v *Islington BC* [1996] **132 Crown copyright:** Denning MR in *Hussey* v *Palmer*
[1972] 3 All ER 744 **133 Crown copyright:** *Bray* v *Ford* [1896] AC 44 HL **135 Crown
copyright:** *Neste Oy* v *Lloyd's Bank* [1983] **137 Crown copyright:** Millett LJ in *Bristol and
West Building Society* v *Mothew* [1998] **138 Crown copyright:** *BCCI (Overseas) Ltd* v
Akindele [2001] **139 Crown copyright:** *Boardman* v *Phipps* [1966] UKHL 2 **140 Crown
copyright:** *Boardman* v *Phipps* [1966] UKHL 2 **142 Crown copyright:** *Bristol and West
Building Society* v *Mothew* [1998] **142 Oxford University Press:** Finn, P. (1992) Fiduciary
law and the modern world, in E. McKendrick
(ed.), Commercial Aspects of Trusts and Fiduciary Obligations. Oxford: Oxford University
Press. **142 University of Western Australia:** Birks, P. (1996) Equity in the modern law: an
exercise in taxonomy. University of Western Australia Law Review, 26: 18. **142 The Law
Book Company Limited:** Mason, A. (1985) Themes and prospects, in P. D. Finn (ed.), Essays
in Equity. Sydney: The Law Book Company. **142 Crown copyright:** *Lloyds Bank Ltd* v *Bundy*
[1975] QB 326 CA **142 The Law Book Company Limited:** Mason, A. (1985) Themes and
prospects, in P. D. Finn (ed.), Essays in Equity. Sydney: The Law Book Company. **143 Oxford
University Press:** Chambers, R. (1997) Resulting Trusts. Oxford: Oxford University Press.
143 Crown copyright: *Bristol and West Building Society* v *Mothew* **143 Parliamentary
Copyright:** *Boardman* v *Phipps* [1967] AC 46 HL **143 Parliamentary Copyright:** *Boardman* v
Phipps [1967] AC 46 HL **144 Parliamentary Copyright:** *Boardman* v *Phipps* [1967]
AC 46 HL **149 Crown copyright:** In *Daraydan Holdings Ltd* v *Solland International Ltd*
[2004] EWHC 622 (Ch).119, **151 Parliamentary Copyright:** *Boardman* v *Phipps*
153 Thomson Reuters: Hicks, A. (2011) Constructive trusts of fiduciary gain: Lister revived?
Conveyancer and Property Lawyer, 1: 62. **155 Thomson Reuters:** Hanbury, H.G. (2015)
Modern Equity (20th edn). London: Sweet & Maxwell. **156 Parliamentary Copyright:**
Yeoman's Row Management Ltd v *Cobbe* [2008] UKHL 55 HL, Lord Scott **163 Crown
copyright:** Charities Act 2011 Section 4(3) **163 Francis Bacon:** Bacon; Shakespeare **164**

Crown copyright: Charities Act 2011 **165 Crown copyright:** Campaigning and Political Activity by Charities: CC9 **167 Crown copyright:** Charities Act 2011 Section 4(3) **168 Crown copyright:** Re Coulthurst [1951] Ch 661 CA **169 Crown copyright:** Charities Act 2011 **169 Crown copyright:** *R. (on the application of Hodkin)* v *Registrar General of Births, Deaths and Marriages* [2013] UKSC 77 HL **170 Crown copyright:** *R. (on the application of Hodkin)* v *Registrar General of Births, Deaths and Marriages* [2013] UKSC 77 HL **172 Crown copyright:** Charities Act 2011 **174 Parliamentary Copyright:** *Oppenheim* v *Tobacco Securities Trust Co Ltd* [1951] AC 297 HL **174 Parliamentary Copyright:** *McPhail* v *Doulton* [1971] AC 424 HL **175 Parliamentary Copyright:** *McPhail* v *Doulton* [1971] AC 424 HL **176 Parliamentary Copyright:** Post-legislative scrutiny of the Charities Act 2006 by the Public Administration Committee [2012] **177 Parliamentary Copyright:** Charities Act 2006 **177 Parliamentary Copyright:** Charities Act 2006 **177 Thomson Reuters:** Hackney, J. (2008) Charities and public benefit. Law Quarterly Review, 124: 347. **178 Parliamentary Copyright:** *Oppenheim* v *Tobacco Securities Trust Co Ltd* [1951] AC 297 HL **180 Crown copyright:** Slade J. in *McGovern* v *A-G* [1982] Ch 321 HC **181 Crown copyright:** Slade J. in *McGovern* v *A-G* [1982] Ch 321 HC **181 Amnesty International:** Amnesty International **182 Crown copyright:** Re Bushnell [1975] 1 All ER 721 HC **183 Crown copyright:** Re Bushnell [1975] 1 All ER 721 HC **184 Crown copyright:** Re Bushnell [1975] 1 All ER 721 HC **184 Crown copyright:** Charities Act 2011 **188 Wilberforce J:** Re Roberts Wilberforce J **193 Crown copyright:** Goff J in Re Denley's Trust Deed [1969] 1 Ch 373 HC **193 Crown copyright:** Goff J in Re Denley's Trust Deed [1969] 1 Ch 373 HC **194 Crown copyright:** s.115 (l) (c) Charities Act 2011 **194 Crown copyright:** *Morice* v *Bishop of Durham* [1804] 10 Ves 522 **196 Parliamentary Copyright:** *McPhail* v *Doulton* [1971] AC 424 HL **196 Crown copyright:** Re Denley's Trust Deed [1969] 1 Ch 373 HC **196 Crown copyright:** Re Denley's Trust Deed [1969] 1 Ch 373 HC **197 Crown copyright:** *Schmidt* v *Rosewood Trust Ltd* [2003] AC 709 **200 Crown copyright:** Re Hetherington [1989] 2 All ER 129 HC **201 Crown copyright:** Brightman J in Re Recher's Will Trusts [1972] Ch 526 at 536 **203 Crown copyright:** Re Wood [1949] Ch 498 HC **204 Crown copyright:** Re Denley's Trust Deed [1969] 1 Ch 373 HC **208 Crown copyright:** Re Gillingham Bus Disaster Fund [1958] 2 All ER 749 HC **208 Crown copyright:** Re Gillingham Bus Disaster Fund [1958] 2 All ER 749 HC **209 Crown copyright:** *Hanchett-Stamford* v *Attorney General* [2008] EWHC 30 (Ch) **225 Crown copyright:** *Pitt* v *Holt* [2013] UKSC 26 **225 Parliamentary Copyright:** *McPhail* v *Doulton* [1971] AC 424 **227 Crown copyright:** Re Londonderry's Settlement **227 Crown copyright:** *Schmidt* v *Rosewood Trust Ltd* [2003] AC 709 PC **228 Crown copyright:** (Mummery LJ in *Goulding* v *James* [1997] 4 All ER 239 CA) **230 Crown copyright:** *Goulding* v *James* [1997] 2 All ER 239 **231 Crown copyright:** Re Steed's Will Trust [1960] Ch 407 **231 Crown copyright:** Re Remnant's Settlement Trusts [1970] Ch 560 **232 Parliamentary Copyright:** section 57 of the Trustee Act 1925 **238 Crown copyright:** *Baden Delvaux Lecuit* v *Société Générale pour Favoriser le Développement du Commerce et de l'Industrie en France* [1983] BCLC 325 HC **238 Crown copyright:** Re Montagu's Settlement Trust [1987] Ch 264 HC **239 Crown copyright:** Re Montagu's Settlement Trust [1987] Ch 264 HC **245 Crown copyright:** *Foskett* v *McKeown* [2001] 1 AC 102 **248 Crown copyright:** *Ultraframe (UK) Ltd* v *Fielding* [2007] WTLR 835 **250 Supreme Court of Canada:** *Canson Enterprises Ltd* v *Broughton & Co* [1991]

85 DLR (4th) 129 **256 Crown copyright:** section 53(1)(b) of the LPA 1925 **261 Crown copyright:** *Armitage* v *Nurse* [1998] Ch 221 HC **261 Crown copyright:** *Armitage* v *Nurse* [1998] Ch 221 HC **261 Crown copyright:** *Armitage* v *Nurse* [1998] Ch 221 HC **262 Crown copyright:** *Armitage* v *Nurse* [1998] Ch 221 HC **262 Crown copyright:** Law Commission's Consultation Paper No 124, Fiduciary Duties and Regulatory Rules (1992) **264 Oxford University Press:** Virgo, G. (2018) The Principles of Equity and Trusts.3rd. edn. Oxford: Oxford University Press. **265 Bloomsbury Publishing:** Watt, G. (2009) Equity Stirring: The Story of Justice Beyond Law. Oxford: Hart Publishing. **265 Thomson Reuters:** Hanbury, H.G. (2015) Modern Equity (20th edn). London: Sweet & Maxwell. **266 Crown copyright:** *Tinsley* v *Milligan* [1994] 1 AC 340 **267 Parliamentary Copyright:** *Midland Bank Trust Co Ltd* v *Green* (No 1) [1981] AC 513 HL **268 Crown copyright:** *Paul* v *Constance* [1977] 1 All ER 195 CA **268 Crown copyright:** *Paul* v *Constance* [1977] 1 All ER 195 CA **268 Crown copyright:** Arden LJ in *Pennington* v *Waine* **269 State of New South Wales (Department of Justice):** Lord Neuberger, President of the Supreme Court, giving the Lehane Lecture 2014, Supreme Court of New South Wales, Sydney 4 August 2014 **271 Crown copyright:** *Jones* v *Kernott* **271 Parliamentary Copyright:** *Stack* v *Dowden* **271 Parliamentary Copyright:** *Stack* v *Dowden* **271 Crown copyright:** *Jones* v *Kernott* **272 Crown copyright:** *Jones* v *Kernott* **273 Crown copyright:** *Paragon Finance Plc* v *DB Thakerar & Co* [1999] 1 All E.R. 400 CA **273 Crown copyright:** *Novoship (UK) Ltd* v *Nikitin* [2014] EWCA Civ 908 CA **274 J. R. Smith:** Table-Talk of John Selden, 1856 **275 Crown copyright:** *Royal Brunei Airlines Sdn Bhd* v *Tan Kok Ming* [1995] 2 AC 378 at 392 HL **276 Commonwealth of Australia:** *Commonwealth of Australia* v *Verwayen* (1990) 170 CLR 394

Guided tour

How to use features in the book 📖 and on the companion website 🖱️

What to do for every question – Identify the key things you should look for and do in any question and answer on the subject, ensuring you give every one of your answers a great chance from the start.

How this topic might come up in exams – Understand how to tackle any question on this topic by using the handy tips and advice relevant to both essay and problem questions. In text, symbols clearly identify each question type as they occur.

Before you begin – Visual guides to help you confidently identify the main points covered in any question asked. You can also download them from the companion website to pin on your wall or add to your revision notes.

Answer plans and Diagram plans – A clear and concise plan is the key to a good answer and these answer plans and diagram plans support the structuring of your answers.

Answer with accompanying guidance – Make the most out of every question by using the guidance; recognise what makes a good answer and why. The length of the answers reflect what you could realistically achieve in an exam and show you how to gain marks quickly when under pressure.

Make your answer stand out – Impress your examiners with these sources of further thinking and debate.

Don't be tempted to – Spot common pitfalls and avoid losing marks.

Try it yourself – Compare your responses with that of the answer guidance on the companion website.

Visit **www.pearsoned.co.uk/lawexpressqa** for a wealth of additional resources to support your revision, including:

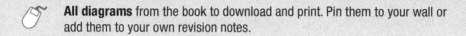 **All diagrams** from the book to download and print. Pin them to your wall or add them to your own revision notes.

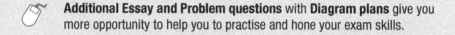 **Additional Essay and Problem questions** with **Diagram plans** give you more opportunity to help you to practise and hone your exam skills.

You be the marker Evaluate sample exam answers and understand how and why an examiner awards marks.

Table of cases and statutes

■ Cases

Abbot v Abbot [2007] UKPC 53 PC 271
Abou-Rahmah v Abacha [2006] EWCA Civ 1492 240
Adams and the Kensington Vestry, Re [1884] 27 Ch D 394 43, 46
Agip (Africa) Ltd v Jackson [1990] Ch 265 245
AIB Group (UK) Plc v Mark Redler & Co Solicitors [2014] UKSC 58 SC 246, 250
Aid/Watch Incorporated v Commissioner of Taxation [2010] 241 CLR 539 165, 184
Air Jamaica Ltd v Charlton [1999] 1 WLR 1399 210
American Cyanamid Co v Ethicon Ltd [1975] AC 396 HL 28
Angove's Pty Ltd v Bailey [2016] UKSC 47 131–2, 134–5
Anthony v Donges [1998] 2 FLR 775 39
Armitage v Nurse [1998] Ch 241 260–2
Ashburn Anstalt v Arnold [1989] Ch 1 CA 135, 147
Astor's Settlement Trusts, Re [1952] Ch 534; [1952] 1 All ER 1067 193–6, 199
Attorney General for Hong-Kong v Reid [1994] 1 AC 324 134, 142, 149–53, 263
Attorney General v Charity Commission for England and Wales [2012] UKUT 420 (TCC) 166, 168, 176–8
Austerberry v Oldham Corporation [1885] 29 Ch D 750 15

Babanaft International Co SA v Bassatne [1989] 1 All ER 433 28
Baden, Delvaux and Lecuit v Société Général pour Favoriser le Développement du Commerce et de l'Industrie en France SA [1983] BCLC 325 238–9
Baden's Deed Trusts (No 2), Re [1973] Ch 9 39, 54
Bahin v Hughes [1886] 31 Ch D 390 218
Baldrey v Feintuck [1972] 2 All ER 183

Bank of Credit and Commerce International (Overseas) Ltd v Akindele [2001] Ch 437; [2000] 4 All ER 221 138, 238, 240
Barclays Bank Ltd v Quistclose Investments Ltd [1970] AC 567 123, 125, 205
Barclays Bank Plc v O'Brien [1995] 1 All ER 438 28–9, 31–33
Barlow Clowes International Ltd (in liquidation) v Eurotrust International Ltd [2005] UKPC 37 241
Barlow Clowes International Ltd (in liquidation) v Vaughan [1992] 4 All ER 22 244
Barlow's Will Trusts, Re [1979] 1 WLR 278 44, 46, 56
Baumgartner v Baumgartner [1988] 62 ALJR 29 10
Beaumont, Re [1902] 1 Ch 889 80
Beloved Wilkes' Charity, Re [1851] 3 Mac & G 440 225
Benjamin, Re [1902] 1 Ch 723 55
Besterman's Will Trusts, Re [1980] The Times, 21 January 164
Beswick v Beswick [1968] AC 58 113
Binions v Evans [1972] 2 All ER 70 133, 135, 147
Blackwell v Blackwell [1929] AC 318 96, 105–6, 148
Blathwayt v Baron Cawley [1976] AC 397 195
Boardman v Phipps [1967] 2 AC 46 139, 143–4, 150, 153
Boston Deep Sea Fishing and Ice Co v Ansell [1888] 39 Ch D 339 144, 262
Bourne v Keane [1919] AC 815 200
Bray v Ford [1896] AC 44 133
Breakspear v Ackland [2008] EWHC 220 (Ch) 108
Brink's-MAT Ltd v Elcombe [1988] 3 All ER 188 27
Bristol and West Building Society v Mothew [1998] Ch 1 6, 137, 142–3
Bucks Constabulary Widows' and Orphans' Fund Friendly Society (No 2), Re [1979] 1 WLR 936 209
Burns v Burns [1984] Ch 317 11

Canson Enterprises Ltd v *Broughton & Co* [1991] 85 DLR (4th) 129 250

Capehorn v *Harris* [2015] EWCA Civ 955 271

Carly v *Farrelly* [1975] 1 NZLR 356 6

Central London Property Trust v *High Trees Houses Ltd* [1947] KB 130 155

Chapman v *Chapman* [1954] AC 429 232

Choithram (T) International SA v *Pagarani* [2001] 2 All ER 492 82, 84, 90

Churchill, Re [1909] 2 Ch 431 223

Clayton's Case [1816] 35 ER 781 243–5

Cleaver, Re [1981] 1 WLR 939 112

Co-operative Insurance Society Ltd v *Argyll Stores (Holdings) Ltd* [1998] AC 1 7, 19, 22–3

Coatsworth v *Johnson* [1886] 55 LJQB 220 6

Cohen v *Roche* [1927] 1 KB 169 22

Comiskey v *Bowring-Hanbury* [1905] AC 84 35, 45–6, 101

Commissioner of Stamp Duties (Queensland) v *Livingston* [1965] AC 694 49

Commonwealth of Australia v *Verwayen* [1990] 170 CLR 394 276–7

Cook v *Fountain* [1676] 3 Swans 585 275

Cook v *Thomas* [2010] EWCA Civ 227 157

Coulthurst, Re [1951] Ch 661 168

Cowcher v *Cowcher* [1972] 1 All ER 943 10

Craven's Estate, Re [1937] Ch 423 87

Cresswell v *Cresswell* [1868] LR 6 Eq 69 97

Curran v *Collins* [2015] EWCA Civ 404 271

Curtis v *Pulbrook* [2011] EWHC 167 (Ch) 83

Dale, Re [1994] Ch 31 113

Daraydan Holdings Ltd v *Solland International Ltd* [2004] EWHC 622 (Ch) 119 149

Daventry District Council v *Daventry & District Housing Ltd* [2011] EWCA Civ 1153 8

Davis v *Richards and Wallington Industries Ltd* [1990] 1 WLR 1511 210

Day v *Harris* [2013] EWCA Civ 191 CA 43

Dean, Re [1889] 41 Ch D 552 195, 199

Denley's Trust Deed, Re [1969] 1 Ch 373 173, 192–3, 196, 202, 204–5

Diggles, Re [1889] 39 Ch D 253 HC 45

Dillwyn v *Llewelyn* [1862] 4 De GF & J 517 156

Dingle v *Turner* [1972] AC 601 168, 175

Diplock, Re [1948] Ch 465 245

Donoghue v *Stevenson* [1932] AC 562 15, 225

Drummond, Re [1914] 2 Ch 90 189, 193

Ellison v *Ellison* [1802] 31 ER 1243 74, 83

Evans (deceased), Re [1999] 2 All ER 777 219

Eves v *Eves* [1975] 3 All ER 768 10, 148

EVTR, Re [1987] BCIC 646 CA 123, 125

Faraker, Re [1912] 2 Ch 488 187

FHR European Ventures LLP v Cedar Capital Partners LLC [2014] UKSC 45 SC 134

FHR European Ventures LLP v *Cedar Capital Partners LLC* [2014] UKSC 45 SC 149, 152, 263–4

Finger's Will Trusts, Re [1972] Ch 286 173, 203

Foskett v *McKeown* [2001] 1 AC 102 245

Freud, Re [2014] EWHC 2577 (Ch) 97, 102

Gale v *Bennett* [1772] Amb 681 9

Gee v *Pritchard* [1818] 2 Swan 402 10

Giles (CH) & Co Ltd v *Morris* [1972] 1 WLR 307 26

Gillett v *Holt* [2001] Ch 210 156

Gillingham Bus Disaster Fund, Re [1958] 2 All ER 749 208, 210

Gilmour v *Coats* [1949] AC 426 10, 170, 177

Gissing v *Gissing* [1971] AC 886 HL 119

Golay, Re [1965] 1 WLR 969 39, 41

Goldcorp Exchange Ltd (in receivership), Re [1995] 1 AC 74 49

Gonin (Deceased), Re [1979] Ch 16; [1977] 93 LQR 448 79, 81, 257, 259

Goulding v *James* [1997] 2 All ER 239 228, 231

Grant's Will Trusts, Re [1979] 3 All ER 359 205

Grey v *Inland Revenue Commissioners* [1960] AC 1 60, 67, 258

Gulbenkian's Settlement Trusts (No 1), Re [1970] AC 508 55

Gunton v *Richmond-upon-Thames LBC* [1981] Ch 448 28

Hagger, Re [1930] 2 Ch 190 112

Haines, Re, [1952] The Times, 7 November 199

Halifax Building Society v *Thomas* [1996] Ch 217 135

Hallett's Estate, Re [1880] 13 Ch D 696 243

Halloran v *Minister Administering National Parks and Wildlife Act* 1974 [2006] 80 AJLR 519 68

Hamilton, Re [1895] 2 Ch 370 38, 44

Hanchett-Stamford v *Attorney General* [2008] EWHC 30 (Ch) 209–10

Harwood, Re [1936] Ch 285 189
Hastings-Bass, Re [1975] Ch 25 225
Hawkesley v *May* [1956] 1 QB 226
Hay's Settlement Trusts, Re [1982] 1 WLR 202 40
Healey v *Brown* [2002] EWHC 1405 (Ch); [2002] All ER
   (D) 249 (Apr) 110, 112
Hedges v *Hedges* [1708] Prec. Ch. 269 87
Hetherington, Re [1989] 2 All ER 129 200–1
Holt's Settlement, Re [1969] 66
Hooper, Re [1932] 1 Ch 38 195, 199
Hopkins' Will Trusts, Re [1964] 3 All ER 46 163
Horley Town Football Club, Re [2006] EWHC 2386 (Ch)
   204–5
HSBC Bank v *Brown* [2015] EWHC 359 Ch. 32
Hunt v *McLaren see Horley Town Football Club, Re*
   [2006] EWHC 2386 (Ch) 204
Hunter v *Moss* [1994] 1 WLR 452 46–50
Hussey v *Palmer* [1972] 3 All ER 744 10, 132

Independent Schools Council v *Charity Commission for
   England and Wales* [2011] UKUT 421 178
Inland Revenue Commissioners v *McMullen* [1981]
   AC 1 172
Inwards v *Baker* [1965] 2 QB 29; [1965] 1 All ER 446
   5, 6, 276
Irani v *Southampton and South West Hampshire Health
   Authority* [1985] ICR 590 26
Isaac v *Defriez* [1754] Amb 595 168

James, Re [1935] Ch 449 79
Jenkins' Will Trusts, Re [1966] 2 WLR 615 196 188
*Jonathan Bishop on Behalf of Crocels Community
   Media Group* v *The Charity Commission for England
   and Wales* [2016] WL 03947469 183
Jones, Re [1932] 1 Ch 642 222
Jones v *Kernott* [2011] UKSC 53 269–73
Jones v *Lock* [1865] 1 Ch App 25 77, 268

Kane v *Radley-Kane* [1999] Ch 274 138
Kasperbauer v *Griffith* [2000] WTLR 333 96
Keech v *Sandford* [1726] Eq Cas Abr 741 132–4,
   139–40, 150
Keen, Re [1937] Ch 236 97, 107
Kelly, Re [1932] IR 255 185 193
Kershaw's Trusts, Re [1868] LR 6 Eq 322 221
King v *Dubrey* [2014] EWHC 2083 (Ch) 76, 86–90
Kings v *Bultitude* [2010] EWHC 1795 (Ch) 189

Klug v *Klug* [1918] 2 Ch 67 226
Koeppler Will Trusts, Re [1986] Ch 423; [1985] 2 All ER
   869 189
Koeppler's Will Trusts [1985] 2 All ER 869 HC 182
Koh Cheong Heng v *Ho Yee Fong* [2011] SGHC 48 77,
   86, 87, 89

Lehman Brothers (Europe) (in Administration) v *CRC
   Credit Fund Ltd.* [2010] EWCA Civ 917 50
Lillingston, Re [1952] 2 All ER 184 81
Lipinski's Will Trusts, Re [1976] Ch 235 173, 204
Lipkin Gorman v *Karpnale Ltd* [1991] 2 AC 548
   239, 245
Lister v *Stubbs* [1890] 45 Ch D 1 134, 143, 149–52,
   260, 263
Lloyds Bank Ltd v *Bundy* [1975] QB 326 142
Lloyds Bank Plc v *Rosset* [1991] 1 AC 107 271
Lohia v *Lohia* [2001] WTLR 101 HC 123
London Wine Co (Shippers) Ltd, Re [1986] PCC 121 33,
   46–8, 49
Londonderry's Settlement, Re [1965] Ch 918 226
Lysaght, Re [1966] Ch 191 189
Lyus v *Prowsa Developments Ltd* [1982] 1 WLR
   1044 146, 148

Mac-Jordan Construction Ltd v *Brookmount Erostin Ltd*
   [1992] BCLC 350 49
Macdonald v *Scott* [1893] AC 642 267
Manisty's Settlement, Re [1974] Ch 17 41
Mareva Compania Naviera v *International Bulk Carriers
   SA* [1975] 2 Lloyd's Rep 509 CA 27
Mascall v *Mascall* [1984] 50 P & CR 119 84
Matila Ltd v *Lisheen Properties Ltd* [2010] EWHC
   1832 (Ch) 23
McCormick v *Grogan* [1869] 4 App Cas 82 106
McGovern v *AG* [1982] Ch 321 HC 180–3
McGovern v *Attorney General* [1982] Ch 321 165
McPhail v *Doulton* [1971] AC 424 39–40, 51,
   54–5, 92, 174, 225, 258
Medlock, Re [1886] 55 LJ Ch 738 223
Midland Bank Trust Co Ltd v *Green (No 1)* [1981] AC
   513 145–7, 148, 267
Milroy v *Lord* [1862] 4 De GF & J 264 71, 74, 79,
   82, 84, 86
Montagu's Settlement Trusts, Re [1987] Ch 264 238, 239
Morice v *Bishop of Durham* [1804] 10 Ves 522 53, 194–5
Murad v *Al-Saraj* [2005] WTLR 1573 140

National Crime Agency v Dong [2017] EWHC 3116 (Ch) 130

National Westminster Bank plc v Amin [2002] UKHL 9 32

Nationwide Building Society v Davisons Solicitors [2012] EWCA Civ 1626 218

Neste v Lloyd's Bank [1983] 2 Lloyd's Rep 658 134

Neville Estates v Madden [1962] Ch 832 170, 208

Neville v Wilson [1997] Ch 144 68

Newgate Stud Co v Penfold [2008] 1 BCLC 46 138

Norbert v Wynrib [1992] 92 DLR (4th) 449 142

Novoship (UK) Ltd v Nikitin [2014] EWCA Civ 908 239, 273

Oatway, Re [1903] 2 Ch 356 245

Oldham, Re [1925] Ch 75 110

Oppenheim v Tobacco Securities Trust Co Ltd [1951] AC 297 HL 10, 174–5, 177–8

Ottaway v Norman [1972] Ch 698 96, 101

Oughtred v Inland Revenue Commissioners [1960] AC 206 22, 64–8

Oxley v Hiscock [2004] EWCA Civ 546 CA 6

Paragon Finance Plc v DB Thakerar & Co [1999] 1 All E.R. 400 273

Parkin, Re [1892] 3 Ch 510 111

Partington, Re [1887] 57 LT 654 219

Pascoe v Turner [1979] 1 WLR 431 156

Patel v Ali [1984] Ch 283 6, 14

Paul v Constance [1977] 1 All ER 195 268

Pauling's Settlement Trusts (No 1), Re [1964] Ch 303 221

Pearson v Lehman Brothers Finance SA [2010] EWHC 2914 (Ch) 48–9

Peffer v Rigg [1977] 1 WLR 285 147

Pennington v Waine [2002] EWCA Civ 227 77, 79, 81, 83, 85, 90, 258–9, 266, 268, 276

Picarda, Re [1982] 132 NLJ 223 210

Pinion, Re [1965] Ch 85 163

Pitt v Holt [2013] UKSC 26 224–7

Plumptre's Marriage Settlement, Re [1910] 1 Ch 609 267

Posner v Scott Lewis [1987] Ch 25 22, 26

Prest v Petrodel Resources Ltd. [2013] UKSC 34 SC 115, 122–5

Queensland Mines v Hudson [1978] 52 AJLR 399 144

R v District Auditor, ex parte West Yorkshire Metropolitan County Council [1986] RVR 24 40, 175

R v Registrar General, ex parte Segerdal [1970] 2 QB 697 169

R. (on the application of Hodkin) v Registrar General of Births, Deaths and Marriages [2013] UKSC 77 166, 169

Re Bushnell [1975] 1 All ER 721 HC 182

Re Resch's Will Trusts [1969] 1 AC 514 PC 178

Recher's Will Trusts, Re [1972] Ch 526 173, 202, 204–5

Rees' Will Trusts, Re [1950] Ch 204 101–2

Remnant's Settlement Trusts, Re [1970] Ch 560 231

Richards v Delbridge [1874] LR 18 Eq 11 75, 77

Roberts, Re [1963] 1 All ER 674 187–8

Robinson v Ommanney [1883] 23 Ch D 285 111

Rochefoucauld v Boustead [1897] 1 Ch 196 146, 148, 267

Roscoe v Winder [1915] 1 Ch 62 244, 245

Rose, Re [1952] Ch 499 79–80, 84, 258, 277

Royal Bank of Scotland v Etridge (No 2) [2001] UKHL 44 29–32

Royal Brunei Airlines Sdn Bhd v Tan Kok Ming [1995] 2 AC 378 6, 240, 275

Russell-Cooke Trust Co v Prentis (No 1) [2002] EWHC 2227 (Ch) 245

Ryan v Mutual Tontine Association [1893] 1 Ch 116 22

Rymer, Re [1895] 1 Ch 19 188

Saunders v Vautier [1841] 41 ER 482 229, 239

Scarisbrick, Re [1951] Ch 622 168

Schmidt v Rosewood Trust Ltd [2003] AC 709; [2003] 2 WLR 1442 197, 227–8

Sen v Headley [1991] 2 WLR 1308 75, 76, 81, 87

Sinclair Investments (UK) Ltd v Versailles Trade Finance (In Administration) [2011] EWCA Civ 347 142–3, 149–53, 250, 260, 263

Sky-Petroleum v V.I.P. Petroleum [1974] 1 All ER 954 22

Slevin, Re [1891] 2 Ch 236 188

Snowden, Re [1979] Ch 528 99

Southgate v Sutton [2011] EWCA Civ 637 223, 229, 230, 232

Southwood v AG [2000] WTLR 119 HC 182–4

Sprange v Barnard [1789] 2 Bro CC 585 45

Spread Trustee Co Ltd v Hutcheson [2011] UKPC 13 260–2

Springett v Defoe [1992] 2 FLR 388 CA 4, 5, 6

Stack v Dowden [2007] UKHL 17 HL 6, 11, 271

Stapylton Fletcher Ltd, Re [1994] 1 WLR 1181 49

Stead, Re [1900] 1 Ch 237 **100, 103–4**
Steed's Will Trust, Re [1960] Ch 407 **231**
Stewart, Re [1908] 2 Ch 251 **79, 257**
Strong v *Bird* [1874] LR 18 Eq 315 **72, 77, 79, 81, 255, 257**
Suggitt v *Suggitt* [2011] EWHC 903 (Ch) **38, 101**

Target Holdings Ltd v *Redferns* [1996] AC 421
   246–7, 249
Tate v *Hilbert* [1793] 30 ER 548 **80**
Tempest v *Lord Camoys* [1882] LR 21 Ch.
   D 571 **225**
Thompson, Re [1934] Ch 342 **140, 200**
Thompson v *Mechan* [1958] OR 357 **88**
Thorner v *Major* [2009] UKHL 18 **11, 76, 154, 157**
Thynn v *Thynn* [1684] 1 Vern 296 **106**
Tilley's Will Trusts, Re [1967] Ch 1179 **244–5**
Tinsley v *Milligan* [1994] 1 AC 340 **6, 266**
Tito v *Waddell (No 2)* [1977] Ch 106 **137**
TSB v *Camfield* [1995] 1 WLR 340 HC **32–3**
Tulk v *Moxhay* [1848] 1 H & Tw 105 **15**
Turner v *Turner* [1984] Ch.100 **226**
Twinsectra v *Yardley* [2002] UKHL 12; [2002] AC 164
   125–6, 240–1
Tyler's Fund Trusts, Re [1967] 1 WLR 269 **102**

Ultraframe (UK) Ltd v *Fielding* [2007] WTLR 835 **248**
United Bank of Kuwait plc v *Sahib* [1997] Ch 107 **67**
United Scientific Holdings v *Burnley Borough Council*
   [1978] AC 904 **14**

Vallee v *Birchwood* [2013] EWHC 1449 (Ch) **75, 76, 80,**
   81, 86–9
Vandervell v *Inland Revenue Commissioners*
   [1967] 2 AC 291; *affirming* [1966] Ch 261 **63,**
   118–20
Vandervell's Trusts (No 2), Re [1974] Ch 269 **118**
Vercoe and others v *Rutland Fund Management Ltd and*
   others [2010] EWHC 424 Ch **21**
Vinogradoff, Re [1935] WN 68 **61, 119, 123**

Wallgrave v *Tebbs* [1855] 20 JP 84 **97–8, 102**
Walsh v *Lonsdale* [1882] 21 Ch D 9 **12, 13**
Walter v *Hodge* [1818] 2 Swans 92 **87**
Webb v *O'Doherty* [1991] The Times, 11 February HC **183**
West, Re [1913] 2 Ch 345 **222**
West Sussex Constabulary's Benevolent Fund Trust, Re
   [1970] 1 All ER 544 **208**

Westdeutsche Landesbank Girozentrale v *Islington BC*
   [1996] AC 669 **118–9, 121**
Westdeutsche Landesbank Girozentrale v *Islington BC*
   [1996] AC 669 714-715 **131**
White v *Shortall* [2006] NSWSC 1379 **49**
Williams v *Central Bank of Nigeria* [2014] UKSC 10 SC
   269–93
Wilson v *Northampton and Banbury Junction Railway*
   Co [1874] LR 9 Ch App 279 CA **20**
Wood, Re [1949] Ch 498 **203**
Woodard v *Woodard* [1995] 3 All ER 580 **80, 87**
Wright v *Morgan* [1926] AC 788 **137**

X v *A* [2006] 1 WLR 741 **223**

Yeoman's Row Management Ltd v *Cobbe* [2008] UKHL
   154–7, 277
Young, Re [1951] Ch 344 **103–4**

Zeital v *Kaye* [2010] EWCA Civ 159 **84**

■ Statutes

Chancery Amendment Act 1858
   s. 2 **26, 251**
Charities Act 2006 **163, 171, 176**
   s. 4(2) **176**
   s. 4(3) **177**
Charities Act 2011 **159, 161–3, 169, 171, 174, 207**
   s. 1(1) **209**
   s. 2(1)(b) **162, 167**
   s. 3 **161, 162, 167, 176, 198, 200**
   s. 3 (1)(i) **164**
   s. 3(1) **183, 207**
   s. 3(1)(a) **168**
   s. 3(1)(b) **163, 174, 200**
   s. 3(1)(c) **169**
   s. 3(1)(d) **174**
   s. 3(1)(f) **158, 164, 199**
   s. 3(1)(g) **172, 173**
   s. 3(1)(h) **184**
   s. 3(1)(j) **168–9**
   s. 3(1)(k) **198**
   s. 3(2)(a) **169**
   s. 3(2)(d) **172**

s. 4 163, 169
s. 4(2) 157, 163, 167, 177, 178
s. 4(3) 163, 167, 174, 176, 178
s. 5 180
s. 17 157, 168, 178
s. 17(5) 157, 168
s. 62 188, 210
s. 62(1)(a)(ii) 188
s. 115(i)(c) 194
Contracts (Rights of Third Parties) Act 1999 111–2
s. 7(1) 112
Equality Act 2010
s. 199 121
Hunting Act 2004 201
Inheritance (Provision for Families and Dependants) Act 1975 90
Inheritance and Trustees' Powers Act 2014 220
Insolvency Act 1986 33
Judicature Acts *see* Supreme Court of Judicature Acts 1873 and 1875
Land Registration Act 1925 147
Land Registration Act 2002 74
Law of Property Act 1925 59–63
s. 52(1) 14, 59–63, 73, 74
s. 53 148
s. 53(1)(b) 59–63, 68, 74, 103, 146, 147, 256, 257, 267
s. 53(1)(c) 59–68, 258
s. 53(2) 59–68, 103, 139
s. 60(3) 59–63, 122–4
Law of Property (Miscellaneous Provisions) Act 1989
s. 2 110
Limitation Act 1980
s. 21 (1) (a) 272
s. 21 (3) 272
Perpetuities and Accumulations Act 1964 173, 175, 199, 203
s. 15(4) 173, 199, 203
Perpetuities and Accumulations Act 2009 40, 175, 203
s. 5 40
s. 5A 40
s. 18 175
Sale of Goods Act 1979
s. 52 22
Sale of Goods (Amendment) Act 1995
s. 20A 50
s. 20B 50

Statute of Frauds 1677 10, 87, 105, 106
s. 4 146
Supreme Court Act 1981
s. 49 13
Supreme Court of Judicature Act 1873 13, 14
s. 25(11) 13
Supreme Court of Judicature Act 1875 13, 14
Trade Union and Labour Relations (Consolidation) Act 1992
s. 236 25
Trustee Act 1925
s. 31 220–1
s. 31(1)(i) 222
s. 31(3) 222
s. 32 220–1
s. 32(1)(b) 221
s. 57 229, 232
s. 61 218
s. 62 218
s. 69(2) 221
Trustee Act 2000 215–6, 219, 264
s. 1 216–7
s. 3 216
s. 4 216–7
s. 5 217
s. 11 217
s. 23 217
Trusts of Land and Appointment of Trustees Act 1996
s. 11 226
Variation of Trusts Act 1958 228–33
s. 1 230
Wills Act 1837 106, 148
s. 1 107
s. 9 106
s. 15 103

■ International conventions

European Convention for the Protection of Human Rights and Fundamental Freedoms 1950
Article 9 170
Article 10 165, 184
Protocol 1
Article 1 209

What you need to do for every question in Equity and Trusts

Equity and trusts exams have a mixture of questions ranging from very technical questions on areas such as constitution of trusts to questions dealing with theoretical areas such as the nature of a resulting trust.

First, you need to have an appreciation of exactly what equity is about. If you have not, this will be obvious throughout your answer. Equity is not easy to pin down and it certainly cannot be defined with absolute precision. However, it is possible to acquire a feeling for a flavour of equity, such as the broad outlines of its history and the existence of the equitable maxims.

You will not go far, however, before you discover that many areas are controversial. One example is the extent to which equitable remedies are discretionary. A poor answer will simply say: 'Equitable remedies are discretionary.' A good answer will first ask: 'What is meant by discretion?' So the message is to avoid bland over-definite statements and instead ask questions as you go along.

You must also remember that equity needs to be seen in contrast to the common law and so just because you are studying equity does not mean that you should leave behind your knowledge of, for example, contract and tort. Questions in an equity exam may ask about the relationship between equity and the common law, one instance being the extent to which flexibility in the application of the law is unique to equity. If you can illustrate your answer by reference, for example, to the common law of negligence then this will immediately improve your marks.

You must also make sure that you are absolutely clear on the fundamental principles and concepts of equity. Make sure, for example, that you understand the nature of a resulting trust as compared to a constructive trust, and a charitable trust as compared with a non-charitable purpose trust. However, when you delve deeper you will find that there may be dispute about the exact nature of, for example, a resulting trust and it is here that you start to score marks. Remember that in the end you may have to say that a particular point remains uncertain. A good example of this is exactly who a fiduciary is and what are the duties a fiduciary owes. Do not feel that you should come to a black and white conclusion.

Above all ask questions, put your book down and *think* about the subject, and be adventurous in your reasoning!

Nature of equity and trusts

1

How this topic may come up in exams

This area will almost certainly prompt essay questions in your exam rather than problems but of course you must check in your own case. The nature of equity is a fertile area for general topics but in some cases answers on these areas have been left until later (see Chapter 13), as they require you to use material from particular topics to illustrate your answer and it is more appropriate to look at these questions when these topics have been covered.

Before you begin

It's a good idea to consider the following key themes of the nature of equity and trusts before tackling a question on this topic.

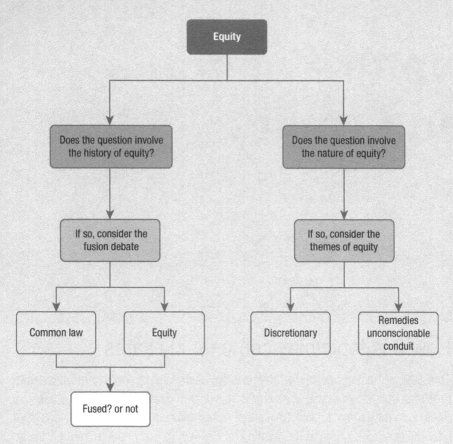

A printable version of this diagram is available from **www.pearsoned.co.uk/lawexpressqa**

 # Question 1

'But equity is not a sort of moral US fifth cavalry riding to the rescue every time a claimant is left worse off than he anticipated as a result of the defendants behaving badly, and the common law affords him no remedy.' Lord Neuberger 'The Stuffing of Minerva's Owl? Taxonomy and Taxidermy in Equity' (2008) 68 CLJ 537 at 540.

Critically evaluate this statement.

Answer plan

→ Put this statement in context: Lord Neuberger was referring to the idea that equity can be used in all situations where injustice is alleged and is not tied to principle. He is disagreeing with this.

→ Then go on at once to a clear concrete example of Lord Neuberger's point that equity may 'ride to the rescue' but only on grounds of principle.

→ Take the example of contracts for the sale of land and show how equity works here.

→ Then develop your answer by looking at the development of the common intention construct-ive trust by reference to two cases and show how the law has developed whilst remaining true to the principle stated by Lord Neuberger.

→ Then move on to equitable remedies and show how the grant of these is governed by an element of discretion but always within principle.

→ Mention briefly an important but often overlooked point: that in some cases there is really no room for discretion in equity.

→ Conclude by returning to the question and emphasising that equity does operate according to principles but exercised in accordance with discretion.

Diagram plan

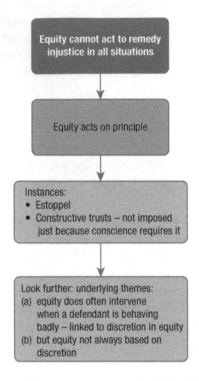

A printable version of this diagram is available from **www.pearsoned.co.uk/lawexpressqa**

Answer

[1] This is a good clear start encapsulating in one sentence the twin issues raised by the question.

In this quotation Lord Neuberger is explaining that equity does not act as some general corrective to injustices suffered by a rule of the common law but instead its intervention must be justified by principle.[1] Another way of putting this is the statement of Dillon LJ in **Springett v Defoe** (1992) 2 FLR 388 CA, that 'The court does not as yet sit, as under a palm tree, to exercise a general discretion to do what the man in the street, on a general overview of the case, might regard as fair.'

[2] This second paragraph is important, as elaborating on what the question says. Make it a habit to include this type paragraph in every essay answer.

Equity certainly does act in situations where a rule of the common law or statute law may result in injustice.[2] The real issue is whether equity will do so in any situation where injustice is claimed or whether, as Lord Neuberger would contend, the intervention of equity is only in situations defined by principle. Additionally, Dillon LJ referred above to the court not exercising 'a general discretion'. What he did not say is that equity does not exercise any discretion at all.

[3] Here it is essential to give a good, solid and well-researched example of exactly how equity does work. We have gone into some detail and used an example which often arises in a Land Law syllabus. This will impress the examiner as it shows that you are thinking across the whole area of law.

There are many instances where equity intervenes to correct a possible injustice caused by a legal rule. Suppose that a contract for the sale of land is made orally. It will not satisfy the requirements of section 2(1) of the Law of Property (Miscellaneous) Provisions Act 1989 which provides that these contracts must be in writing, signed by both parties and contain all agreed terms. However, it may still be enforceable in equity under the principles of constructive trusts and estoppel.[3]

Taking estoppel as an instance, its essential elements are a commitment or promise by one person (X) to another (Y), which X intends Y to rely on and where Y's actual reliance to his detriment is reasonable in the circumstances. In *Inwards v Baker* (1965), a father allowed his son to build a bungalow on land owned by the father but there was no written contract. If statute law only had applied then, because there was no writing, the son would have had no rights over the land and he would have received nothing in return for all his time and effort in building the bungalow. However, because the equitable doctrine of proprietary estoppel applied, he was granted a licence for life to occupy the bungalow. Equity did not simply say that the son had a licence for life; it did so on the basis that the above elements of proprietary estoppel were satisfied. So we see the truth of Lord Neuberger's statement that equity's intervention must be justified by principle.[4]

[4] It is vital to come back to the point of the question: the importance of principle in equity.

At the same time, we see the application of discretion in equity as the court had a discretion as to what remedy to award the son. It could have awarded him the fee simple of the bungalow but instead gave him a licence, albeit for life.

In *Springett v Defoe,* Dillon LJ was referring specifically to cases where property had been purchased in the name of one party but the other claimed a beneficial share. In this case the proportions of the initial contributions of the parties was 75/25 per cent,[5] but the trial judge awarded them each a half share under the principles of common intention constructive trusts. It was this that Dillon LJ criticised. He pointed out, 'The common intention must be founded on evidence such as would support a finding that there is an implied or constructive trust for the parties in proportions to the purchase price.' As there was no evidence of such discussions, Dillon LJ fell back on the

[5] Note that we have picked out the only fact in this case relevant to the present discussion. Make a habit of this in the exam.

principles of resulting trusts, where the parties are awarded a share in proportion to their contributions.

However, the law has moved on since **Springett v Defoe** and in more recent cases we see a greater willingness by the courts to take various factors into account in deciding if the parties did have any common intention and if so what their respective shares should be.[6] So in **Oxley v Hiscock** (2004) EWCA Civ 546 CA, Chadwick LJ said that, 'each is entitled to that share which the court considers fair having regard to the whole course of dealing between them in relation to the property'. This approach was approved by the House of Lords in **Stack v Dowden** [2007] UKHL 17 HL. It does not mean that the court is now awarding beneficial shares in property on the basis of complete discretion; there is still an underlying principle but how it is exercised has changed and the approach in **Oxley v Hiscock** gives room for a greater exercise of discretion.

What equity does not do is impose a constructive trust whenever justice requires.[7] Mahon J memorably observed in the New Zealand case of **Carly v Farrelly** (1975) 1 NZLR 356, 'No stable system of jurisprudence can permit a litigant's claim to justice to be consigned to the formless void of individual moral opinion.'

There is, however, an underlying theme running through equity that, although it does act according to principle, its intervention is often the result of the defendants behaving badly, and the common law affording no remedy.[8] One example is **Inwards v Baker,** mentioned earlier. The moral flavour of equity comes out strongly when considering the duties of a fiduciary. So in **Bristol and West Building Society v Mothew** [1996] EWCA Civ 533, Millett LJ said, 'The distinguishing obligation of a fiduciary is the obligation of loyalty.' Equity was originally conceived in terms of remedies to mitigate the harshness of the common law and in this way there are traces of the 'fifth US cavalry'.[9] Moreover, in order to fulfil this role, equity, when operating through its remedies, is a discretionary system. For example, the common law will grant a remedy if the claim is made out, but equity has discretion to refuse a remedy if, for example, the claimant has not come with clean hands.[10] In **Coatsworth v Johnson** [1886] 55 LJQB 220, a tenant who claimed equitable relief as he only had an agreement for a lease of land and not a deed had not looked after the land and was in breach of the covenants in the lease and so equity refused relief. Another example is **Patel v Ali** [1984] Ch 283, where the court used its equitable discretion to

[6] This is adding depth to your answer. An average answer would have ended at an account of *Springett* v *Defoe* but here we are adding to our marks by showing how the law has developed whilst still remaining within the parameters of Lord Neuberger's statement in the question.

[7] It is useful to 'anchor' your answer to fundamentals at this stage in your answer to show the examiner that you are aware of the main issue.

[8] There is an underlying moral flavour to equity and at some point in your answer the examiner will expect you to mention this.

[9] We are now going further and developing our answer, showing how there is some truth in the idea of equity 'riding to the rescue' where the common law affords no remedy.

[10] Now we need to develop our answer. We have made the point that equity is based on principle but now we need to show the distinctive character of equity: discretion and what this actually means.

decline to order the equitable remedy of specific performance for the sale of a house on the basis of the equitable principle that specific performance would not be awarded where to do so would amount to 'hardship amounting to injustice', which would have been the case here due to the personal circumstances of one of the sellers.

[11] This is an important point not often made. It will add value to your answer.

On the other hand, equity is not always a discretionary system.[11] Where, for example, the remedies for breach of trust are used, often involving tracing of assets on an insolvency, the system is anything but discretionary, as it would clearly be wrong if the rights of creditors were to depend on the whim of each judge.

Lord Neuberger is right that equity does not 'ride to the rescue' every time that an injustice is claimed, but we must not leave it there: equity is concerned to remedy injustice but only on the basis of equitable principles which are exercised on the basis of equitable discretion.

✓ Make your answer stand out

- Be selective in your use of examples. Concentrate on the main themes and bring in your examples to illustrate them.
- Look in more detail at the distinction between resulting and constructive trusts and contrast the way in which they operate by reference to the questions of equitable principles and discretion. You may prefer to do this when you have completed your studies of these areas.
- Read Watt (2009), especially pp. 26–45 on the character of equity. It has some really excellent and illuminating ideas which will add depth to your answer.
- Read Worthington (2006) especially her ideas on whether equity really does have distinctive features.

! Don't be tempted to . . .

- Just give a list of cases dealing with e.g. discretion in equity.
- Fail to ask what does equitable principle and equitable discretion mean?
- Give too much detail on the cases. For example, *Springett* v *Defoe* has some memorable facts but it is the precise point on how to decide the extent of the beneficial shares that we need here.
- Think of just one possible area and leave it at that. Instead, consider a number of areas as we have here.

Question 2

Critically evaluate the statement 'that a study of the history of equity can teach us valuable lessons for equity today'.

Diagram plan

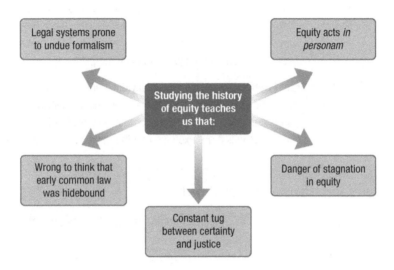

A printable version of this diagram is available from **www.pearsoned.co.uk/lawexpressqa**

Answer plan

→ Explain how equity originally developed and consider the lessons from this for today.

→ Now look at the later history of equity and show how to some degree there was a period of stagnation.

→ Explain that this is not entirely true and give examples.

→ Consider whether there is any evidence of stagnation in equity today.

Answer

[1] As ever, you could take the opposite view and argue that the history of equity is indeed just history but you would really be saying that the question is pointless! However, the argument would be interesting.

A study of the history of equity is not an end in itself but can teach us valuable lessons for today.[1]

The first lesson comes from the way in which equity originally developed. One could summarise[2] this by saying that, although the early history of equity is in parts obscure, it is true to say that there were increasing complaints about the ability of the common law courts to deal with a variety of matters and there is evidence of increasing rigidity by the mid-fourteenth century. Some examples were that juries were bribed or intimidated so that a litigant could not obtain justice; the writ system had become an obstacle to the proper development of the law; and the procedures of the common law courts were often unsatisfactory, ill-suited to deal with cases which required the personal attendance of the parties and witnesses and where it was necessary to command a party to actually do, or not do, something. The common law courts were far better suited to disputes concerning land where, rather than dealing with an individual directly, his land could be taken from him. For these, and other reasons, litigants took to petitioning the King's Council to do justice and by the mid-fourteenth century this practice was becoming increasingly common. It was by this means that what we now know as equity eventually developed.[3]

There are three lessons to be drawn from this. The first is the obvious one that legal systems are always prone to undue formalism and are there to serve the interests of justice. The second point is that, as we have seen, the common law courts acted against the litigant's land but equity acted against the person and this is still an indispensable feature of equity's jurisdiction today as it is the origin of the maxim that equity acts *in personam.* Thus this reminds us of the continuing importance of the equitable remedies of specific performance and injunction by which equity can command an act or restrain an individual. Recent examples of the importance of these are what were known as 'Mareva orders' (now known as freezing orders) and 'Anton Piller orders' (now known as search orders), both of which can be granted even before the issue of proceedings. Had equity not developed in response to the need for court orders to act against the person, these remedies might not have existed today. Finally, it is wrong to say that in this early period the common law was entirely hidebound as there is evidence, for example, from the early cases of the remedies of specific performance and injunction being granted by the common law courts. The contemporary moral here is that perhaps there is not as much difference today between equity and the common law as we think and that fusion might be possible.[4]

[2] This is vital, as the answer could go hopelessly wrong at this point. You could easily find yourself enmeshed in a lengthy account of how equity developed and leave yourself no time at all to actually answer the question. This is a good example of where, in an exam, you may have far more information than you can usefully use and you need to stop yourself and continually refer back to the question.

[3] This is all you need to say on this point, as what is important for us today is what equity did rather than the actual way in which it developed.

[4] This is a really good point which the examiner may not expect and for which you can expect due credit. It leads directly to the very topical question of whether there is really all that much that is distinctive about equity and, if you have time, you would do well to say more on this.

1 NATURE OF EQUITY AND TRUSTS

[5] The logic here is that we have moved on from early history and here again there are lessons to be drawn.

Another way in which the study of the history of equity teaches us lessons for today is by looking at the history of equity in the period of the late seventeenth to the mid-nineteenth centuries when equity began to examine itself.[5] This development was probably inevitable as far as trusts were concerned, as the actual administration of a trust needs to be governed by clear rules. But in addition there was a reluctance to extend equity into new fields as when, in **Gale v Bennett** [1772] Amb 681, the Court of Chancery declined to give relief against unfair terms in contracts. Much later, in 1818, Lord Eldon said, in **Gee v Pritchard** 2 Swan 402 HC, that nothing would give him greater pain 'quitting this place' than recollecting that he had done anything 'to justify the reproach that the equity of this court varies like the Chancellor's foot'.

[6] This is the kind of approach which sets a good answer out from a poor one. It is essential, in questions such as these, to stress that there is no simplistic answer.

Even so, equity at this date was by no means stagnant.[6] When the Statute of Frauds was passed in 1677, it quickly developed the doctrine of secret trusts and redeveloped the rules of *donatio mortis causa* to deal with cases where property had been left outside a will. Also this was the era when the maxims were developed as a guide to equitable jurisdiction. Nevertheless, it is difficult to avoid the impression that equity had lost its early vigour. It could be said that this phase lasted until fairly recent times with, for example, the restrictive decisions of Lord Simonds as Lord Chancellor in cases involving public benefit in charitable trusts such as **Gilmour v Coats** [1949] AC 426 HL and **Oppenheim v Tobacco Securities Trust Co Ltd** [1951] AC 297 HL.[7] What is clear is that, at present, there is renewed vigour in equity. In Australia, for example, there has been a revitalised interest in, and utilisation of, equitable doctrines, remedies and institutions. One example is the development of a jurisprudence based on unconscionability to resolve disputes over any beneficial entitlement to the family home (see e.g. **Baumgartner v Baumgartner** [1988] 62 ALJR 29).

[7] There is no time to go into this area in detail: you only need to give enough information to show that you understand the issue.

In England the courts have been less adventurous. In a series of cases in the 1970s, Denning MR sought to develop what he called 'a constructive trust of a new model' (**Eves v Eves** [1975] 3 All ER 768 CA). The existence of a fiduciary relationship was not required to found such a trust: instead, one would be imposed 'whenever justice and good conscience require it . . . it is an equitable remedy by which the court can enable an aggrieved party to obtain restitution' (Denning MR in **Hussey v Palmer** [1972] 3 All ER 744 CA). However, this idea was not approved by Bagnall J, who, in **Cowcher v Cowcher** [1972] 1 All

ER 943 HC, insisted that, 'In any individual case the application of [established rules of law] may produce a result which appears unfair. So be it: in my view that is not an injustice . . . in determining rights, particularly property rights, the only justice that can be attained by mortals . . . is justice that flows from the application of sure and settled principles . . . ' Since then, however, the idea of a remedial constructive trust, which is what Denning MR was referring to, has been taken up by Lord Scott in **Thorner v Major** [2009] UKHL 18, and in **Stack v Dowden** [2007] UKHL 17 the House of Lords[8] seems to some extent to have departed from the rule that, in determining the beneficial interests in the family home, the courts need to find the intentions of the parties. This had threatened to place the law on this area in a straight-jacket, as seen in such cases as **Burns v Burns** [1984] Ch 317 CA.

[8] This part of the answer began by saying that there was some stagnation in equity and then it described attempts by Denning MR, among others, to develop the law and how this did not meet with success in England. Now, finally, and to gain extra marks, you must show how more recently the picture has changed. In this way you have covered the whole topic.

What this really illustrates is the constant tug in equity between those who desire certainty and those who wish equity to strike out in pursuit of justice. This is true of all legal systems and not just of equity but it is still a lesson worth learning from history.

✓ Make your answer stand out

- Read more on the early history of equity – any standard textbook on equity will start you off but for more detail go to Baker (2002).
- To give a contemporary flavour to your answer, look in more detail at the debate on the remedial constructive trust and other areas. Begin with Etherton (2008).
- Look at the debate on whether equity and the common law should indeed in time converge. See, for example, Honoré (2003). He argues that one major creation of equity, the trust, could be introduced into other legal systems. One could then go on to argue that, if so, what is distinctively equitable about it?
- Mention that in *Capehorn v Harris* [2015] EWCA Civ 955, the CA may have gone back to the significance of intention in family home cases.

! Don't be tempted to . . .

- Give an account of the history of equity. This is not what is asked for and will earn you a very poor mark. The question is concerned with the lessons of history.
- Equally do not give too much detail on present-day developments. It would be easy to go right off the point by, for example, giving lengthy accounts of cases.

Question 3

'The so-called "fusion debate" is simply "old hat" and is only of historical interest.' Critically consider this statement.

Diagram plan

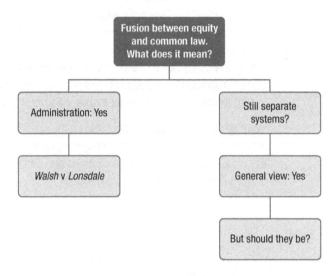

A printable version of this diagram is available from **www.pearsoned.co.uk/lawexpressqa**

Answer plan

→ Explain that the administration of common law and equity is fused as a result of the Judicature Acts.

→ Provide an example of this: *Walsh* v *Lonsdale*.

→ Set out the view that equity and the common law are fused as systems of law and then subject this to critical analysis.

→ Critically consider the view that integration between the common law and equity is possible in future.

→ Show briefly in conclusion how this last point shows that the fusion debate is not dead.

Answer

[1] This is an absolutely fundamental point, which you should make at the start and gain credit for a clear answer.

[2] This is the second point and this requires much more thought. In this first paragraph you have set out the main lines of this essay and so it is an ideal start.

[3] In this essay you need to mention just enough history to make your answer understandable but you must resist the temptation to mention too much, as the question is clearly about equity today.

[4] The facts of this case have been set out in detail as they are of such importance. Students often oversimplify this case and here we have gained extra marks by showing the interaction of common law and equity.

There is no doubt that the actual administration of equity and the common law are fused by the Judicature Acts[1] but are equity and the common law themselves fused[2] so that it is no longer correct to speak of equity and the common law as distinct systems? It is suggested that they are still separate systems and so the debate is not just of historical interest.

Prior to the Judicature Acts 1873–1875, equity and the common law were separate systems so that if one wanted an equitable remedy or if the case concerned a trust then it was necessary to bring the action in the Court of Chancery, which administered equity.[3] Since the enforcement of the Judicature Acts, that has changed and equitable remedies are available in all courts alongside common law remedies and, for example, a court may award common law damages and/or an injunction for breach of contract. Moreover, section 25(11) of the Judicature Act 1873 (the rule is now in section 49 of the Supreme Court Act 1981) recognised that equitable and common law rules are applied side by side by providing that where the rules of equity and common law conflict then equity shall prevail.

An example of administration of both systems in the same courts is **Walsh v Lonsdale** [1882] 21 Ch D 9 CA,[4] where the parties had agreed on a lease of a mill for seven years. Rent was payable quarterly in arrears but the landlord was entitled to demand a year's rent in advance. However, the agreement was not contained in a deed as required to make it binding in law (this requirement is now in section 52(1) of the Law of Property Act 1925). The tenant entered into possession and paid rent quarterly in accordance with the lease. The landlord then demanded a year's rent in arrears and when the tenant refused to pay he brought a common law claim for distress. The issue was whether the terms of the agreement for a lease could be relied on. The court held that equity could be applied and here the maxim 'equity looks on that as done which ought to be done' meant that, as the parties had agreed on a lease, equity would consider this as good as a lease. Thus as the agreement allowed the landlord to claim payment of rent in advance, the landlord's claim succeeded.

The vital point is that this result would have been the same before the passage of the Judicature Acts but the claim would have had to have been heard in two different courts:[5] the common law courts would have heard the distress claim and the courts of equity would have dealt with the equitable principles. Now the same court can deal with both. However, the actual principles were different and we must now examine whether this is still so.

The general view is that equity and common law have not fused. This was expressed in a well-known metaphor by Ashburner (Browne, 1933): 'the two streams of jurisdiction, though they run in the same channel, run side by side and do not mix their waters'. This view has been contradicted, most notably by Lord Diplock in **United Scientific Holdings v Burnley Borough Council** [1978] AC 904 HL, who said that this 'fluvial metaphor' is 'mischievous and deceptive' and that the two systems of law, common law and equity, were indeed fused by the Judicature Acts.

[6] This approach will gain you marks. A poor answer would just say that Lord Diplock was wrong as, of course, equity and the common law are different systems and otherwise, for example, this book would not have been written!

It is not entirely clear what Lord Diplock meant.[6] He may have been referring to the fact that we should now consider common law and equity as different streams of law which operate together rather in the way that, for example, one might use both contract and tort in one action. This is, of course, true. On the other hand, he may have meant that they are in fact one system so that the distinctive features of both can no longer be seen and they are merged into one. The truth is, however, that this is not so, as a moment's thought will make anyone realise. Equitable and common law remedies operate together but are not governed by the same principles, as shown by **Patel v Ali** [1984] Ch 283.[7] Here the court used its equitable discretion[8] to decline to order the equitable remedy of specific performance for the sale of a house as this, due to the personal circumstances of one of the sellers, would have amounted to 'hardship amounting to injustice'. The court did, however, award the buyers their remedy at common law – in this case, damages – on being satisfied that they would be paid.

[7] *Patel* v *Ali* is a really excellent and easily remembered case to illustrate this point. It is easy with a case with memorable facts like this one to let the facts crowd out your explanation of the legal principle. Do not let this happen!

[8] It is important that you mention this, as discretion in the grant of remedies is one of the characteristics of equity which distinguishes it from the common law.

[9] This is all the detail you need to give here, as you have shown that you are aware of the fundamental difference between the approaches of common law and equity.

Examples of the difference between legal and equitable rules are found throughout the law. For example, the rules on the running of the burden in freehold covenants differ in common law (see **Austerberry v Oldham Corporation** [1885] 29 Ch D 750 HL) from those in equity (see **Tulk v Moxhay** [1848] 1 H & Tw 105 HC), as at common law the burden does not run at all but in equity it does run where the covenant is negative.[9] On a broader level, Millett J (as he then was) wrote (1998): 'The common law insists on honesty, diligence and the due performance of contractual obligations. But equity insists on nobler and subtler qualities: loyalty, fidelity, integrity, respect for confidentiality, and the disinterested discharge of obligations of trust and confidence.' He was speaking in the context of equity and commerce but his words can, it is submitted, be applied to all areas in which equity engages, and are particularly relevant to the equitable concept of the fiduciary.

[10] We have outlined the obvious point that equity and common law do in fact have different characteristics but now we are taking the answer further by asking if this should always be so in future. If you are aiming for high marks then this is exactly what the examiner is looking for.

The fusion debate has been revived from another angle by Worthington (2006), who suggests that it is time that equity and the common law were fully integrated.[10] She points out that it is untrue to say that it is only equity which permits the exercise of discretion; so does the common law. She instances, for example, the discretionary element in deciding whether a duty of care exists in tort or if a consumer contract contains unfair terms. At times, on the other hand, equity has no discretion at all: for example, in deciding if equitable proprietary remedies should be awarded or not. She makes the telling point that, if there were discretion here, the law of insolvency would turn into a farce. Moreover, she rightly draws attention to the increased willingness of the common law to adjudicate according to the standard of reasonableness following *Donoghue* v *Stevenson* [1932] AC 562 HL.[11]

[11] Mention of a case from a completely different area, even one as celebrated as this, will gain you credit.

[12] Here you are linking the views quoted in the previous paragraph to the quotation in the question.

This in itself shows[12] that the fusion debate is not merely of historical interest but that, instead, the extent to which equity and the common law are fused is part of the ongoing debate on the relationship between these two complementary systems of law.

✓ Make your answer stand out

- Look at the article by Duggan (1996). He looks at whether both equity and the common law aim at 'efficient outcomes' and argues that they do. Nor does he consider that equity is 'motivated by altruistic concerns'. Look at some of the cases which he quotes and compare his view with that of Millett J mentioned in the article.
- Read Worthington (2006). It is not very long and is extremely useful on this area and on others.
- Look in detail at other cases and areas to evaluate the extent to which equity and the common law are fused – one possibility is the law on trusts of the home.

! Don't be tempted to . . .

■ Give a detailed historical account of how equity and the common law developed as separate systems of law.

■ Fail to distinguish between fusion of the administration of equity and the common law and fusion of them as actual systems of law.

■ Set out facts of cases and not link them to the fusion debate.

■ Fail to give examples of how equity and the common law are still separate systems.

■ Fail to mention the views of Worthington.

@ Try it yourself

Now take a look at the question below and attempt to answer it. You can check your response against the answer guidance available on the companion website (**www.pearsoned.co.uk/lawexpressqa**).

Is it possible to say that the terms 'equity' and 'justice' mean the same?

www.pearsoned.co.uk/lawexpressqa

 Go online to access more revision support including additional essay and problem questions with diagram plans, 'You be the marker' questions, and download all diagrams from the book.

Equitable remedies and doctrines

2

How this topic may come up in exams

This area is a familiar one in equity exams and a very common question is an essay on equitable remedies. This gives you the opportunity to gain extra marks by looking across the whole subject and looking at remedies in the context of trusts, as well as equitable remedies in general. You can also expect essay questions on the main equitable remedies such as specific performance and injunctions. In addition, there can be problem questions on areas such as specific performance and injunctions as well as on equitable doctrines. In this chapter you will also find a problem on undue influence.

■ Before you begin

It's a good idea to consider the following key themes of equitable remedies and doctrines before tackling a question on this topic.

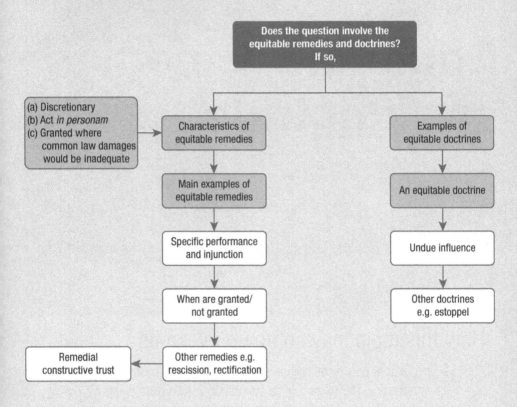

A printable version of this diagram is available from **www.pearsoned.co.uk/lawexpressqa**

 Question 1

'A decree of specific performance is of course a discretionary remedy . . . There are well-established principles which govern the exercise of the discretion but these, like all equitable principles, are flexible and adaptable to achieve the ends of equity.' Lord Hoffman in *Co-operative Insurance Society* v *Argyll Stores Ltd* [1998].

Critically examine in the context of this case the circumstances in which equity will examine its discretion to award the remedy of specific performance in the light of the 'ends of equity' to which Lord Hoffman referred.

Answer plan

→ Begin with a concise definition of specific performance and then unpick the quotation using this as the structure for your answer.

→ Pick up the phrase 'ends of equity' used in the question and explain what it means.

→ Note that you should only select those areas relevant to this case to illustrate your answer.

→ Consider *Co-operative Insurance Society* v *Argyll Stores Ltd* [1998] in detail to show how the courts deal with conflicting considerations in the grant of specific performance (SP).

→ Note that this is a fact-sensitive area due to the discretionary nature of equitable remedies.

→ Emphasise the fundamental principle that SP will not be granted where damages would be an adequate remedy – what are the implications of this?

→ Move on to consider the other relevant bar to SP: that an order must not require constant supervision.

→ Conclude by saying that the principles which govern the exercise of the courts' discretion are not absolute but have to be applied looking closely at the facts of each case to do 'more perfect equity'.

Diagram plan

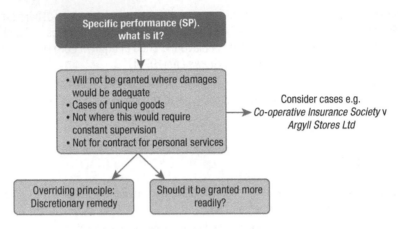

A printable version of this diagram is available from **www.pearsoned.co.uk/lawexpressqa**

Answer

[1] You need to give a concise definition of specific performance and then flesh out what the quotation is saying. This then gives a structure to your answer.

Specific performance (SP) is an equitable remedy which requires a party to perform a positive obligation, usually arising under a contract. It is granted instead of the common law remedy of damages. The quotation from the speech of Lord Hoffman makes three points:[1]

(a) As with all equitable remedies it is discretionary.

(b) There are well-established principles which govern the exercise of this discretion.

(c) These principles are themselves flexible and adaptable to serve the needs of equity.

[2] The quotation mentions this phrase and so you should explain what it means.

The 'ends of equity'[2] were described by Lord Selborne LC in **Wilson v Northampton and Banbury Junction Railway Co** (1874) LR 9 Ch App 279 CA, as to 'do more perfect and complete justice' than would be the result of leaving the parties to their remedies at common law. In effect equity, by awarding SP instead of the common law remedy of damages, is doing 'more perfect justice'.

We shall consider Lord Hoffman's three points by initially looking at the case where he made his speech: **Co-operative Insurance Society v Argyll Stores Ltd** [1998] AC 1 HL. SP was refused of an undertaking to keep a supermarket open during the usual hours of business in a lease which had still 19 years to run. The supermarket was an 'anchor store' in a shopping centre and its closure would badly affect the viability of the rest of the centre. The House of Lords, over-ruling the Court of Appeal, considered that if the store was ordered to be kept open, the loss to the tenant would exceed that suffered by the landlord if the supermarket closed. In addition, the principle that the court would need to supervise any order of SP remained important. Moreover, both parties were large, sophisticated organisations.

The fact that a grant of SP is discretionary is shown by the completely different stance taken by the Court of Appeal, which took a poor view of Argyll's conduct in closing the store in breach of the agreement and ordered SP to compel it to keep the store open.[3] It held that the terms of the covenant to keep open were clearly defined and Argyll was a substantial company that had undertaken to keep the premises open for a stipulated period.

Dowling (2011) points out that here the court is exercising its discretion to award or withhold the remedy of SP on the basis that the defendant can raise a defence, making it inequitable for the court to compel performance of his obligations, and instead to leave the claimant to seek compensation from the defendant.[4] The result is that in this case a grant of SP was held to be inequitable rather than equitable and so 'more perfect equity' would *not* be achieved by granting this remedy. Instead it would be equitable to leave the claimant to the common law remedy of damages.

Here we see the operation of discretion in the grant of equitable remedies in action. It is vital to emphasise that there are principles and that discretion is not absolute.[5] In ***Vercoe and others v Rutland Fund Management Ltd and others*** [2010] EWHC 424 Ch, Sales J said, 'Although in a certain sense the courts' decisions about these matters might be described as discretionary, in truth I think the courts are now seeking to articulate underlying principles which will govern the choices to be made as to the remedy or remedies available in any given case.' The principles governing the exercise of discretion in the grant of SP are known as bars to specific performance.

Where damages are an adequate remedy, then SP is unlikely to be granted,[6] and this was what the House of Lords held in ***Co-operative Insurance Society v Argyll Stores Ltd.*** The loss to the tenant if SP was granted was held to be likely to exceed that

[3] This is one of the cases where research into the decision of the court appealed from really will pay dividends. When you are studying equity, make a note of other cases where you might research different opinions in higher and lower courts to give examples of discretion in equity.

[4] This type of research will really boost your marks. Students often throw in a quote from an article or text book but do not explain it. Here you have shown that you have read the article, have understood the argument in it and related it to the question.

[5] We are now turning from the first point to the second one. Make sure that there is a degree of flow to your argument and avoid your essay being just a series of apparently disjointed points. Sentences like these two help.

[6] Note that we have said 'unlikely to be granted' and not 'will (or will not) be granted'. Be careful not to make definite statements about when equitable remedies will be granted as you are then giving the impression that there is no discretion in equity and so you will lose marks.

suffered by the landlord if the supermarket closed and so it was sufficient to leave the landlord to his remedy of damages. Although section 52 of the Sale of Goods Act 1979 empowers the court to grant SP of a contract for the sale of specific or ascertained goods, in practice it is unlikely to be granted as the buyer can normally obtain replacement goods elsewhere. It might be otherwise if the goods were unique but even here there seems a reluctance to grant SP. Thus, in **Cohen v Roche** [1927] 1 KB 169 HC, SP was refused of a contract to sell Hepplewhite chairs but a less restrictive attitude was taken in **Sky-Petroleum v V.I.P. Petroleum** [1974] 1 All ER 954 HC, where an injunction was granted restraining the defendants from withholding supplies of petrol which they had contracted to supply to the claimants. There was a petrol shortage and so if only damages had been awarded to the claimants they would have been unlikely to obtain supplies elsewhere. The effect of the injunction was to compel the defendants to continue to supply the petrol and so it was really an order of SP.[7] This pair of cases demonstrates the application of the principle that damages will not be awarded where damages will be an adequate remedy. In addition, taking Lord Hoffman's third point, it also shows that the principles governing the remedy of SP are 'flexible and adaptable to serve the needs of equity'.

[7] It is vital to explain this when you refer to this case, otherwise it is not clear, given that an injunction was sought, why it is relevant.

There are cases where there is less discretion in the grant of SP and it is routinely granted, such as in contracts for the sale of shares in a private company (**Oughtred v I.R.C.** [1960] AC 206) and contracts for the sale of land, land being regarded as unique. In **Matila Ltd v Lisheen Properties Ltd** [2010] EWHC 1832 (Ch) HC, the court granted SP of a contract for the sale of land and held that it was only in extraordinary cases that hardship can be a reason not to grant SP.[8] There was no evidence that it was impossible to obtain finance to complete the purchase, although it had become more difficult.

[8] Here is another example of discretion in equity but we have stressed that here discretion is limited.

A further instance of a bar to SP, referred to in **Co-operative Insurance Society v Argyll Stores Ltd,** is where an order would require constant supervision. The discretionary nature of equity makes this a fact-sensitive area.[9] In **Ryan v Mutual Tontine Association** [1893] 1 Ch 116, SP of a contractual obligation to provide a porter constantly in attendance at a service flat was refused, but in **Posner v Scott-Lewis** [1987] Ch 25, SP of a covenant to employ a resident porter

[9] Comments of this kind are useful in preventing essays on general areas such as SP from becoming mere recitals of cases.

[10] A poor answer would have simply gone through each possible bar to SP but the question asked you to consider this remedy in the context of a particular case. So you will not gain any marks by discussing other bars to SP, such as the extent to which it would require personal service, which are not relevant here. It is also a plus point that in your last words you have referred back to the exact words of the question.

for certain duties, although not to be constantly in attendance, was granted. The court felt that enforcing compliance would not involve it in an unacceptable degree of supervision. In **Co-operative Insurance Society v Argyll Stores Ltd**, the issue was the exact nature of the obligation: to 'keep the demised [i.e. leased] premises open for retail trade'. The Court of Appeal thought that this was sufficiently clear to be capable of an order of SP; the House of Lords thought not and their view prevailed.

There are other bars to SP but the above are relevant to the decision in **Co-operative Insurance Society v Argyll Stores Ltd**[10] and they show that whilst there are principles which govern the exercise of the courts' discretion, these are not absolute but have to be applied looking closely at the facts of each case to do 'more perfect equity'.

✓ Make your answer stand out

- Explain exactly what 'discretion' means in the context of the decision on whether or not to grant SP.
- Bring out the principles governing the exercise of discretion.
- Make sure that you contrast pairs of cases.
- Adopt a critical approach: research *Co-operative Insurance Society Ltd v Argyll Stores (Holding) Ltd* and critically assess which court, the CA or the HL, made the right decision.
- Read and refer to articles such as Luxton (1998) on *Co-operative Insurance Society Ltd v Argyll Stores (Holding) Ltd* and Dowling (2011) on *Matila Ltd v Lisheen Properties Ltd*.

! Don't be tempted to . . .

- Just write down as many cases as you can on SP.
- Give too much detail on the facts and not bring out the underlying issues.
- Leave out a discussion of the element of discretion in the grant of equitable remedies.
- Leave yourself no time for a conclusion, which is essential in a question like this.

❓ Question 2

Advise John, who owns a medium-sized hotel, on the following matters:

(a) He has engaged Fred on a self-employed basis for three months from 1 February to redesign the business's website and to assist with marketing the hotel for the summer season. Fred had worked on this project for two months but on 1 April he rang John and told him that he was not going to continue any longer as he had obtained a 'very lucrative job' in Germany which he felt that he could not turn down. John feels that it is too near to the summer season to engage anyone else and he wishes to obtain a court order to compel Fred to work for the remaining month.

(b) John is owed £10,000 by Rosemary, a guest who stayed at the hotel for a long time. He intends to bring proceedings against her to claim this sum but has learned that, very shortly, she intends to sell her stamp collection which he believes is her main asset. If it is sold then, even if John wins the case, Rosemary is likely to have no assets to satisfy the judgment. Is there any action which he can take to prevent the sale of the stamp collection?

Answer plan

→ Explain the general principles of equity which apply to enforcement of a contract for personal services.

→ Go on to link this to the point that equitable remedies are discretionary.

→ Apply these to the question and briefly mention the question of damages.

→ Explain the idea behind freezing orders.

→ Apply the guidelines for the grant of these orders to the question and in the process decide if one is likely to be granted in this case.

Diagram plan

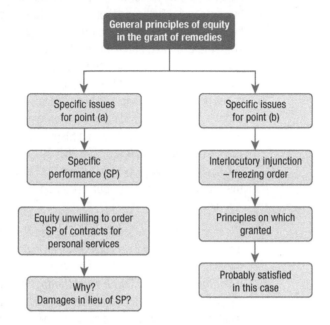

A printable version of this diagram is available from **www.pearsoned.co.uk/lawexpressqa**

Answer

(a) The contract which Fred has with John is one for personal services. We are told that John has engaged Fred on a 'self-employed basis', which means that Fred is not an employee but is an independent contractor. John wishes to obtain a court order to compel Fred to work for the remaining month of his contract and this means that he is seeking either an order of specific performance to directly compel performance of the contract or possibly a mandatory injunction to restrain its breach, which would have the same effect.[1] Section 236 of the Trade Union and Labour Relations (Consolidation) Act 1992 prohibits the courts from enforcing performance of contracts of employment either by SP or injunction but this will not apply to Fred as he is not an employee, unless the court finds on the facts that despite the description of Fred as self-employed, he is in fact an employee.[2] If Fred is self-employed, this means that the matter is governed by equity alone.

[1] Note the overlap between the two remedies. Later on in the answer you can develop this point and it will certainly earn extra marks.

[2] This is more of an employment law point than an equity one, but it flows from the point that, as all law students know, the label which the parties attach to their relationship is not decisive. It is certainly an excellent point for this answer.

[3] This is an important general point which you should always include in any question on equitable remedies.

[4] Although we are simply asked to advise John on whether he can obtain an order against Fred, it will add depth to your answer if you can explain the reasons why such an order cannot be obtained.

[5] This is the vital point. Do not be misled by a superficial glance at the cases into thinking that here equity literally enforced contracts for personal services.

The remedies of SP and injunction are equitable, and equitable remedies are discretionary. This means that although the court has a discretion in the grant of a remedy, its discretion is guided by certain principles.[3] In this case the principle is that equity has always refused to grant an order which would compel performance of a contract for personal services. This is based on a number of factors:[4] the difficulty of supervision; the undesirability of one person being compelled to submit to the orders of another; and the difficulty of deciding whether an employee was actually performing his contract. Thus, as Megarry J observed in *Giles (CH) & Co Ltd v Morris* [1972] 1 WLR 307 HC, 'if a singer sang flat, or sharp, or too fast, or too slowly . . . who could say whether the imperfections of performance were natural or self-induced?'

It is true that in some situations equity has appeared to enforce a contract for personal services where an injunction is sought by the employee to restrain dismissal by the employer, as in *Irani v Southampton and South West Hampshire Health Authority* [1985] ICR 590 HC, where an injunction restrained implementation of a dismissal notice until a disputes procedure had been complied with. However, in this case it was not sought to enforce the contract, so that, for example, his employers would not be expected to actually employ Irani.[5] In addition, in our case the order is sought by the employer and not the employee. Also in *Posner v Scott-Lewis* [1987] Ch 25 HC, SP was indeed granted of a contract to employ a resident porter at a block of flats; however, this was not strictly enforcement against the porter but enforcement of a contract to employ a porter.

The conclusion must be that John cannot obtain an order enforcing this contract. Section 2 of the Chancery Amendment Act 1858 (Lord Cairns Act) allows the court to grant damages in substitution for an order of SP, but as the remedy of SP is not available in this case, it seems likely that damages cannot be awarded under this Act. However, there is no reason why John cannot seek damages at common law against Fred for breach of his contract.

(b) The other question is whether John can take action to prevent the sale of Rosemary's stamp collection so that it is available to satisfy any damages which may be awarded against her for her breach of contract in failing to pay her hotel bill.

The appropriate remedy here is a freezing order, which is an interlocutory injunction designed to prevent the defendant from disposing of assets which would otherwise be available to meet the claimants' claim or removing them from the courts' jurisdiction. It was originally known as a Mareva order, from the case where it was first used: ***Mareva Compania Naviera v International Bulk Carriers SA*** [1975] 2 Lloyd's Rep 509 CA. The order is normally granted without notice to the other party (the previous term, still often used in practice, was *ex parte*) because of the need for speed and because if the other party knew that the order was being sought they would dissipate the assets.

John will need to check whether he can satisfy the guidelines, suggested by Lord Denning MR in the ***Mareva*** case, which the courts apply for the issue of a freezing order. The relevant ones[6] are as follows:

(i) The claimant must have a good arguable case. The court will therefore need to form a provisional view on the final outcome of the case on the evidence before it, and where there are substantial disputes of fact the requirement of a 'good arguable case' will be difficult to meet. Here John will need to check if there are any possible grounds on which Rosemary might dispute liability to pay the bill. One possibility would be if she had complained about the standard of service and/or accommodation at the hotel.[7]

(ii) The claimant should make full and frank disclosure of all material matters (see ***Brinks-MAT Ltd v Elcombe*** [1988] 3 All ER 188 HC), together with full particulars of his claim and its amount, and should state fairly the points made against it by the defendant. Thus John would need to produce any letter of complaint from Rosemary.

(iii) John, as the claimant, should normally give grounds for believing that the defendants have assets (here the stamp collection) in the jurisdiction.

[6] It is vital that you stress that you are only mentioning the *relevant* guidelines. You could waste time and valuable marks to list them all.

[7] Notice how we have not only stated the guidelines but also applied them to the specific facts of the question. This is what an examiner wants to see.

(iv) The claimant should normally give grounds for believing either that the assets will be removed from the jurisdiction before the claim is satisfied or that in some way they might be dissipated so that there will be a real risk that a judgment in the claimant's favour will not be satisfied (see ***Babanaft International Co SA v Bassatne*** [1988] 1 All ER 433 HC). Thus, John will have to bring evidence that Rosemary intends to sell the stamp collection and that it is her main asset.

[8] This is one of those areas where you need to decide which of a long list of points to mention. There would be no point in setting out all the guidelines, as if you did you would have no time to relate them to the question and so you would lose marks.

There are other guidelines,[8] such as the fact that the court should exercise caution before granting an order which would bring the defendant's business to a standstill, but they are not relevant here. What is clear is that John has no automatic right to a freezing order and that, in order to obtain it, he will need to collect evidence to satisfy the court on all the above points.

✓ Make your answer stand out

- Mention the idea behind an interlocutory injunction and the general principles which decide if it will be granted: *American Cyanamid Co v Ethicon Ltd* [1975] AC 396 HL.
- Mention other cases where the court has considered the question of possible enforcement of an employment contract: *Gunton v Richmond-upon-Thames LBC* [1981] Ch 448 HC.
- Consider whether there are sufficient safeguards for the defendant in an application for the grant of a freezing order. This will add some depth to your answer, although of course you will not have much time to consider this in detail.

! Don't be tempted to . . .

- Just say in the first part of the question that the contract cannot be enforced. Although this may be the conclusion in the end, you should consider the law fully.
- Forget to mention the possibility of damages where SP is not granted.
- Be too dogmatic and think of the guidelines for the grant of a freezing order as absolute rules.

❓ Question 3

Fred and Elsie jointly own their house, 12 High Road Westview. Fred also owns a building business which he wishes to expand. He asks his bank manager, Oliver, for a loan of £100,000 and Oliver says that this will be possible but only if the mortgage on the house is extended to provide security. Oliver tells Fred that Elsie will have to agree to this and, knowing that she will not be keen on the idea, Fred tells her that the loan is only for 'no more than £5,000' to cover some extensions to his workshop. Oliver says that Elsie can only sign once she has had advice from a solicitor and that a solicitor friend of Oliver's, Jake, can do this. Elsie almost always takes Fred's advice on financial matters and so, when Jake says 'There's nothing to worry about, it is all fine ', she willingly signs the mortgage deed.

Fred is now bankrupt and the bank is seeking to enforce its security.

Advise Elsie on whether she has any grounds to resist this.

Answer plan

→ Consider whether Elsie's signature was procured by undue influence.

→ Then move on to ask if it could also have been procured by misrepresentation.

→ If it was procured by either of these methods, then ask if the bank could be affected by this and apply the principles in *Barclays Bank* v *O'Brien* and *Royal Bank of Scotland* v *Etridge.*

→ Conclude by considering the effect on the bank if it was so affected.

Diagram plan

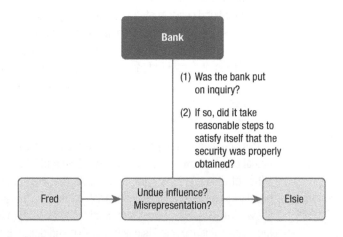

A printable version of this diagram is available from **www.pearsoned.co.uk/lawexpressqa**

Answer

[1] There is no point in discussing whether the bank is affected by undue influence or misrepresentation unless you have first considered if in fact there has actually been undue influence or misrepresentation. Many students miss this point altogether and so miss a lot of marks.

[2] It is vital to stress the significance of deciding into which category the particular type of undue influence falls. This does not decide if there has been undue influence or not but how it is proved. Make this clear.

[3] Link your conclusions clearly to Lord Nicholls' categories.

The first question is whether Fred used either undue influence or misrepresentation to procure Elsie's signature on the mortgage deed.[1]

Undue influence is a doctrine that, by its nature, is difficult to define precisely but in essence it aims to prevent the vulnerable from exploitation. It is really directed at the manner in which a transaction is entered into. In *Royal Bank of Scotland* v *Etridge (No 2)* [2001] UKHL 44, Lord Nicholls held that there is a distinction between:

(a) Cases of actual coercion.

(b) Cases where the undue influence arises from a particular relationship.

In (b) there is a subdivision between:

(i) Cases where there is a relationship of trust and confidence between two people. If it is established that there has been a transaction which calls for some explanation then the burden shifts to the person seeking to uphold the transaction to produce evidence to counter the inference of undue influence.

(ii) Certain types of relationship where one party has acquired influence over another who is vulnerable and dependent and by whom substantial gifts are not normally to be expected (e.g. parent and child, trustee and beneficiary and medical adviser and patient). In these cases there is a presumption of undue influence by the stronger party over the weaker. The effect is that, if (b) applies, it is for Fred, as the party seeking to uphold the transaction, to show that there was no undue influence because if there is undue influence then Elsie may not be bound and so the whole liability will fall on him.[2]

In this situation it is impossible on the facts to show that there was actual coercion exercised by Fred over Elsie and so we need to ask if either of the situations in (b) applies. All that we know is that Elsie usually takes Fred's advice on financial matters but this does not really show a relationship of trust and confidence as in (b)(i) above, nor is there any evidence that Elsie is vulnerable and dependent on Fred as in (b)(ii).[3] The conclusion must be that, if she is to rely on undue influence, Elsie will need to prove it as it will fall under the first category of actual coercion. On the facts there is no evidence of this. She may, however, be able to show that her signature was procured by the misrepresentation of Fred. Misrepresentation is an untrue statement of fact which induces a person to enter into a transaction and here Fred told Elsie that the amount which he was borrowing was 'no more than £5,000'. This is clearly untrue, as it was £100,000.

However, proving that Fred was guilty of misrepresentation will only enable Elsie to avoid the transaction as against Fred himself, but the document which she signed was in favour of the bank. Thus Elsie will need to show that the bank had notice of Fred's undue influence under the principles first laid down in ***Barclays Bank plc v O'Brien*** [1995] 1 All ER 438 HL, which have now been clarified by the House of Lords in ***Royal Bank of Scotland v Etridge (No 2)***.[4]

[4] Be careful not to use the law as set out in *O'Brien:* much of the detail has now been superseded by that in *Etridge*.

Here Lord Nicholls said that a lender, the bank in this case, is put on inquiry when one person offers to stand surety for the debts of:

(a)   his or her spouse;

(b)   a person involved in a non-commercial relationship with the surety and the lender is aware of this;

(c)   any company in which any of the above hold shares.

[5] This is a crucial point, as if Elsie also owned the business, the bank would not be under this duty.

In this case it is clear that (a) applies, as Elsie is standing surety for Fred's debts as the business does not belong to her.[5]

The House of Lords in ***Etridge*** then clarified the steps[6] which the creditor should reasonably be expected to take in satisfying itself that the security has been properly obtained:

[6] You must put this in the correct order. First decide if the bank is put on inquiry and only if it is do you need to consider the steps which it should take to satisfy itself that the security has been properly obtained.

(a)   The lender must contact the surety and request that it nominate a solicitor.

(b)   The surety must reply nominating a solicitor.

(c)   The lender must, with the consent of the surety, disclose to the solicitor all relevant information – both the debtor's financial position and the details of the proposed loan.

(d)   The solicitor must advise the surety in a face-to-face meeting at which the debtor is not present. The advice must cover an explanation of the documentation, the risks to the surety in signing and emphasise that the surety must decide whether to proceed.

(e) The solicitor must, if satisfied that the surety wishes to proceed, send written confirmation to the lender that the solicitor has explained the nature of the documents and their implications for the surety.

[7] The failure of the bank on this point alone is probably enough to make it impossible for it to enforce the security against Elsie but you should go through all the other points to pick up marks.

In this case the lender has not requested the surety, Elsie, to nominate a solicitor to advise but instead the lender in the person of the bank manager, Oliver, has himself nominated his friend, Jake.[7] In addition, there is no evidence that the lender has disclosed all relevant information to the solicitor. In **HSBC Bank v Brown** [2015] EWHC 359 Ch HC, it was emphasised that the bank must furnish the nominated solicitor, Jake here, with information that would enable the solicitor to explain the financial risks to be assumed by the surety, Elsie in this case, and there is no evidence that this has been done.

Moreover, it is not clear whether Jake advised Elsie when the debtor, Fred, was not present and it is obvious that Jake did not explain the risks to Elsie as all that he said was, 'There's nothing to worry about, it's all fine.' Finally, it appears that Jake did not send written confirmation to the lender that he has explained the nature of the documents and their implications for Elsie. In **National Westminster Bank plc v Amin** [2002] UKHL 9,[8] it was held that the solicitor must be expressly instructed to advise the surety on the nature and effect of the transaction and clearly this has not happened here.

[8] Students often quote the guidelines in *Etridge* and no more. Although these must of course be the main focus of your answer, it will add to your marks if you can quote a post-*Etridge* case.

[9] When you are coming to a conclusion on this point, try to come back to the phrases used by Lord Nicholls to set out what the lender must do: 'put on inquiry', 'take reasonable steps'.

In view of this, it is suggested that as the bank was 'put on inquiry' and it has failed to take steps to ensure that the security has been properly obtained,[9] it cannot enforce the security against Elsie, although of course it can do so against Fred. This will mean that the bank will be able to enforce its security against Fred's beneficial interest in the property but not that of Elsie and it may apply for a sale of the property.

Finally, there has been some discussion as to whether the surety should still be liable for the amount to which she consented, in this case, £5,000. In **TSB v Camfield** [1995] 1 WLR 340 HC, it was held that the mortgage so far as the surety is concerned should be entirely set aside. The question is probably whether Elsie agreed voluntarily to some liability and on the facts it is doubtful if she did.

Make your answer stand out

- Clear explanation of the O'Brien principle.
- Read Andrews (2002). This looks at the decision in *Royal Bank of Scotland* v *Etridge* (No 2).
- Read Thompson (2003). This gives a clear account of the law and of how it has developed, which many textbooks do not do.
- A brief reference to the possibility of the bank being able to force a sale of the property and the relevant provisions of the Insolvency Act 1986.

 Don't be tempted to . . .

- Assume that there has been undue influence. Check the facts of the question.
- Assume that just because the parties are married, this means that Elsie has trust and confidence in Fred so that undue influence is presumed.
- Talk of the lender 'having notice' of undue influence or misrepresentation. This term was used in *O'Brien* but not in *Etridge*, which talked of being 'put on inquiry'. The term 'notice' could lead to confusion with 'notice' in other areas.

@ Try it yourself

Now take a look at the question below and attempt to answer it. You can check your response against the answer guidance available on the companion website (**www.pearsoned.co.uk/lawexpressqa**).

Critically consider whether the rules governing the grant of freezing and search orders provide adequate safeguards for defendants.

www.pearsoned.co.uk/lawexpressqa

 Go online to access more revision support including additional essay and problem questions with diagram plans, 'You be the marker' questions, and download all diagrams from the book.

The three certainties

How this topic may come up in exams

This is a favourite topic for problem questions. The central points are reasonably clear, with lots of smaller points on which you can pick up vital extra marks too. Make this one of your main areas to revise for the exam. Essays can focus on why the courts require certainty in trusts, and on cases such as *Re London Wine Co.*

This topic can also come up in problem questions in any other area where the question is mainly on one area but you need to check if the certainties are present. Examples here are problem questions on formalities, constitution and secret trusts.

■ Before you begin

It's a good idea to consider the following key themes of the three certainties before tackling a question on this topic.

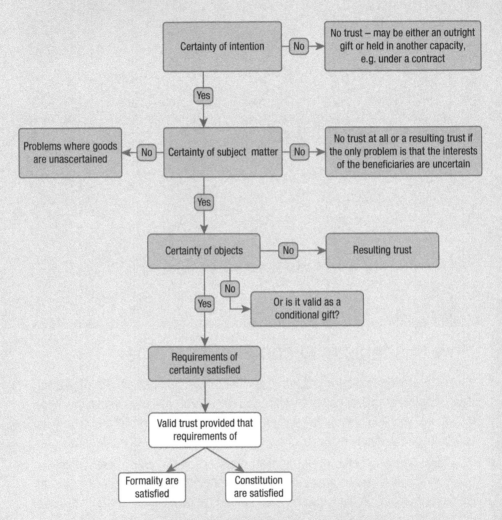

A printable version of this diagram is available from **www.pearsoned.co.uk/lawexpressqa**

❓ Question 1

Paul died in March 2019, leaving a will dated 7 April 2010 containing the following bequests:

(a) £50,000 to Tom, and it is my wish that he will hold this sum to provide a reasonable amount out of it to enable my girlfriend Eileen to keep up her present standard of living, and generally 'keep up appearances'.

(b) £1 million to my trustees Josephine and Maureen to distribute in their absolute discretion to any inhabitant of the County of Herefordshire who has attained the age of 21 years at the date of my death or any child of such an inhabitant on reaching the age of 21 years.

Advise on the validity of these gifts.

Would your answer differ if the will had been dated 5 April 2010?

Diagram plan

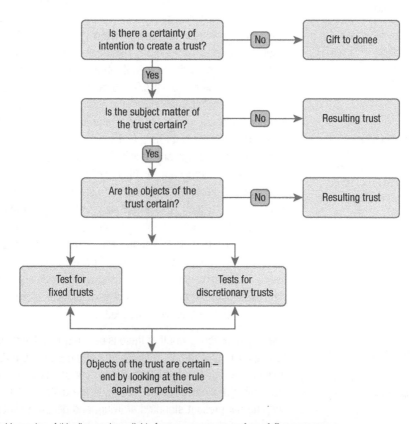

A printable version of this diagram is available from **www.pearsoned.co.uk/lawexpressqa**

Answer plan

→ In each part of the question you should check that the following are present and apply the relevant law:

Certainty of intention

Certainty of subject matter

Certainty of objects

→ Then consider the possible application of the rules against perpetuities.

→ If you decide that the gifts are not valid and will not go to the intended beneficiaries then you must decide where the property contained in the gifts will go – always find a home for the property.

Answer

[1] A mention of this general principle is an excellent way to begin an answer in certainties.

[2] There is no need at this stage to set out the terms of the bequest – this will waste time as you will come to this later. Just concentrate on the intention point.

[3] This point is always worth making – analyse the exact words of the gift and look at it as a whole and you will boost your marks!

[4] See how very close reading of the words of the question pays off: the key words are 'a reasonable amount out of it' and not the entire sum to be held for Eileen.

(a) The first question is whether there is certainty of intention to create a trust or just a request which Tom can comply with or ignore as he wishes. In **Re Hamilton** [1895] 2 Ch 370 CA, Lindley LJ said that the courts must look at all the words used by the testator or settlor to see if, on their true construction in the context of the particular gift, a trust was intended.[1] The test asks what the actual intentions of the person were, looking at the words as a whole, rather than concentrating only on particular words. Here the gift is 'to Tom, and it is my wish that he will hold this sum to provide Eileen'.[2] It is suggested that the words 'it is my wish' do not imply any intention by Paul to place Tom under an obligation to hold the £10,000 on trust for Eileen. However, it is important to look at the gift as a whole[3] (**Comiskey v Bowring-Hanbury** [1905] AC 84) and here the will goes on to say that Tom is to 'hold this sum', which looks like the language of trusts. This can be contrasted with **Suggitt v Suggitt** [2011] EWHC 903 (Ch), where the words used were: 'And I express the wish (without imposing a trust).' It was quite clear, looking at all the words, that no trust was intended.

The next question is whether there is certainty of subject matter as it appears that Tom is to take some of the £50,000 as a gift and that he only has to allocate a sum out of this to provide a reasonable amount out of it[4] to enable the girlfriend Eileen to keep up her present standard of living, and generally 'keep up appearances'. Is the phrase 'a reasonable amount' certain enough? In **Anthony v Donges** [1998] 2 FLR 775 HC, a widow was left 'such minimal part of (the) estate as she might be entitled to . . . for maintenance purposes'. This was held to be too uncertain, as no such minimal entitlement exists.

Where the trustees are given discretion, this may enable the court to declare that there is certainty of subject matter. This seems to be the explanation of **Re Golay** [1965] 1 WLR 969 HC, where the testator directed that a Mrs Bridgewater should 'enjoy one of my flats during her lifetime' and 'receive a reasonable income from my other properties'. It was held that the word 'reasonable' provided a sufficiently objective standard to enable the court if necessary to quantify the amount. The case must be regarded as borderline as there was no further assistance given in the will to guide the trustees or the court.[5] In this case Paul has also added the words 'and generally to keep up appearances'. This sounds very informal and may distinguish it from **Re Golay** and mean that there is no certainty. If the court finds that there is no certainty of subject matter at all and so the whole trust fails, then the property will also be held on a resulting trust for Paul's estate.

(b) The gift of '£1 million to my trustees Josephine and Maureen' obviously satisfies the test of certainty of intention as the word 'trustees' is used and certainty of subject matter as the gift is of £1 million. The problem is with certainty of objects. The words 'to distribute in their absolute discretion'[6] indicate a discretionary trust, and the test for certainty of objects was laid down in **McPhail v Doulton** [1971] AC 424 HL, where Lord Wilberforce in the House of Lords held that the test was: 'Can it be said with certainty that any given individual is or is not a member of the class?' (This is often known as the individual ascertainability test.) Thus it is open to anyone to come forward and show that they are an inhabitant of the County of Herefordshire.

Lord Wilberforce in **McPhail v Doulton** pointed out that trustees should not approach their duties in a narrow way but 'ought to make such a survey of the range of objects or possible beneficiaries as will enable them to carry out their fiduciary duty'. In **Re Baden's Deed Trusts (No 2)** [1973] Ch 9 CA, Sachs LJ said

[5] It is important to clarify this point. Too many students see the words 'reasonable income' etc. in a question and automatically apply *Re Golay* without any explanation.

[6] If you see these words remember that they indicate a discretionary trust and so if the question involves certainty of objects then you will have to apply *McPhail v Doulton*.

that the trustees must assess the size of the problem in 'a businesslike way'. In **Re Hay's Settlement Trust** [1982] 1 WLR 202 HC, Megarry V-C said that a trustee should first appreciate the 'width of the field' and the 'size of the problem' before considering whether a grant was appropriate in individual cases.[7]

The other point is that there are nearly 200,000 inhabitants of the County of Herefordshire and in **McPhail v Doulton** Lord Wilberforce said that even though a description of beneficiaries complied with the test he had laid down, it might be 'so hopelessly wide as not to form anything like a class', and gave as an example 'all the residents of Greater London'. This principle was applied in **R v District Auditor ex parte West Yorkshire Metropolitan County Council** [1986] RVR 24 HC, where a trust set up for the inhabitants of the County of West Yorkshire, of which there were about 2,500,000, was held void for administrative unworkability.[8] Lloyd LJ held, 'A trust with as many as 2½ million potential beneficiaries is . . . quite simply unworkable.' If the court decides that the trust is administratively unworkable then it will fail. As there is certainty of intention and subject matter, the trustees cannot treat the £1 million as an absolute gift but will hold it on a resulting trust for Paul's estate.

Assuming that there is a valid trust, there is also the question of whether it complies with the rule against perpetuities.[9] There are two perpetuity rules and the applicable one here concerns remoteness of vesting of interests. Section 5 of the Perpetuities and Accumulations Act 2009 provides that in these cases there shall be a perpetuity period of 125 years, but by section 5A the new period will not apply to a will executed before the 2009 Act comes into force, which was on 6 April 2010. Here the will is dated 7 April 2010 and so the 2009 Act will apply.[10] In the cases of the trusts for individuals, this period will clearly be satisfied but in the case of the trust for the inhabitants of the County of Herefordshire, the trustees must distribute the funds within 125 years. Any funds remaining will be held on a resulting trust for those entitled under Paul's estate.

If the will had been dated 5 April 2010 then my answer would differ[11] as the old law on perpetuities would apply and the gift

[7] Add to your marks by not just mentioning *McPhail* v *Doulton* but this point too.

[8] There is some debate on whether this is actually a separate point or not but most textbooks treat it separately and you would be unwise not to mention it.

[9] The perpetuity point is often missed: you should always mention it in a certainties question.

[10] Check in any question exactly when the will was executed.

[11] It is an (almost) infallible rule that if a question says: 'would your answer differ' then it will, but it may not so do not assume this! However, here it does.

[12] You could mention that the gift could have specified a period of 80 years but in fact it did not.

would have to vest within lives or lives in being plus 21 years.[12] Here the lives in being will be the inhabitants of the County of Herefordshire who have attained the age of 21 at the date of Paul's death and any child of such an inhabitant who clearly must reach the age of 21 years within 21 years of the date of their parents' death. Thus the gift satisfies the perpetuity period.

✓ **Make your answer stand out**

- Work your way through the three certainties, taking one at a time, and analysing the exact words of the question.
- Discussion of why the courts impose the requirements of certainty.
- Discussion of *McPhail* v *Doulton* and reference to academic criticism, e.g. Matthews (1984).
- Is there any need for the 'administratively unworkable' principle at all? See McKay (1974), who feels that this principle has no satisfactory basis. In *Re Manisty's Settlement* [1974] Ch 17 HC, Templeman J held that Lord Wilberforce's example of a class consisting of all the residents of Greater London showed that the settlor/testator had no sensible intention and was 'capricious'. However, in the West Yorkshire case there was no question of capriciousness and so the administrative unworkability principle may add something to the law.

! **Don't be tempted to . . .**

- Omit to mention in each case each of the three certainties even if it is obvious that there is certainty. If so, a brief mention will suffice.
- Fail to recall accurately *exactly* what Lord Wilberforce laid down in *McPhail* v *Doulton* on the requirement of certainty of objects in discretionary trusts.
- Miss the perpetuity point.
- Apply the decision in *Re Golay* uncritically.

❓ Question 2

Vincent, who has just died, left the following bequests in his will. You are asked to advise the trustees, Brian and Patrick, on their validity. Vincent had no known relatives.

(a) £20,000 to my old friend Bernard, the vicar of my local church, in full confidence that he will use it for Alice and Sarah, two old friends of mine.

(b) My collection of rare books to be held to enable any work colleague of mine or friend who wishes to buy one. (Vincent worked at a local supermarket).

(c) £20,000 to my neighbour Helen and I wish her to use it partly for herself and the rest, what she does not want, to go to all her children.

Diagram plan

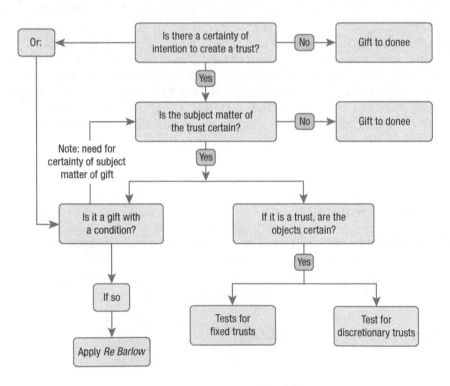

A printable version of this diagram is available from **www.pearsoned.co.uk/lawexpressqa**

Answer plan

→ Analyse exactly what the words of each bequest mean.

→ Then go on to analyse each bequest to see if there is certainty of intention, subject matter and objects.

→ Is there a gift with a condition rather than a trust in any of these cases?

→ If any of the certainties are not present, identify what the consequences will be and apply the relevant law.

Answer

[1] This is clearly the first issue, so come to it at once: there is no need for any preliminary remarks.

[2] Extra marks here for two things: a relevant case which is also recent.

[3] This is one of those situations where a really clear knowledge of the facts of a recent case can really boost your marks.

(a) This gift states that the gift of £20,000 to Bernard is 'in full confidence that he will use it'.[1] 'Confidence' may not indicate a trust as in **Re Adams and the Kensington Vestry** [1884] 27 Ch D 394 HC, where a testator left his property to his wife absolutely 'in full confidence that she will do what is right as to the disposal thereof between my children. . . ' It was held that no trust was created but there was only a moral obligation on her to provide for the children. Such a case is often known as a gift with a motive. In the recent case of **Vucicevic v Aleksic** [2017] EWHC 2335 (Ch) HC,[2] the testator made a handwritten will leaving the Serbian Orthodox Church three houses and 'all the money that was left after taxes' for people in need in Kosovo, especially children. He placed a senior bishop of the Church in charge of the gift, expressing 'full confidence' that he would ensure that the benefit went to the right place. It was held that the gift was valid. Although the words 'in full confidence' were problematic, on looking at the gift in context, the testator had no relatives and the confidence was placed in the bishop as a person in a position of authority whom he trusted to make the right decisions. The present situation is comparable.[3] Vincent has no known relatives and one essential element is that the gift is to a person in some position of trust. A vicar may not have the authority of a bishop but he/she is traditionally in a position of trust. The terms of the gift were more formal than in **Day v Harris** [2013] EWCA Civ 191 CA, where the words 'to share and keep or sell if you like' on a note posted at the same time as boxes were handed over, did not show intention; but here it is suggested that there is such

[4] Students sometimes fall into the trap of thinking that there is no certainty of subject matter as we do not know how much each beneficiary is to get. That is not the point. We know the total sum to be held on trust and that is what matters.

[5] We cannot decide if there is certainty of subject matter, so take this point as far as you can and then move on to certainty of objects. You will lose marks (a lot of them!) if you just stop at one point and decide that the gift fails there. Instead, go on to consider the possibility that the gift might just be valid. You can then look at the next point and earn more marks.

[6] Note this important distinction and make sure that you can spot it in an exam. It is likely to arise on the type of facts set out here: if there was a gift of £20,000 to be held on trust to be distributed among my friends this would be a discretionary trust, as there are no individual gifts. Here there are.

[7] An excellent start and a sure way to pick up marks: you can see at once that the terms of this gift need analysis.

intention. The subject matter is certain (£20,000) and although the two objects, Alice and Sarah, are only identified by their first names it ought to be possible to ascertain them.[4]

(b) The next gift is of 'my collection of rare books' and evidence would be needed on whether the actual books can be identified. If not, the gift will fail for lack of certainty of subject matter.[5] If this is certain then we must consider the bequest, which is that they are to be held to enable 'any work colleague of mine or friend who wishes to buy one'. This looks like a gift with a condition precedent attached, as the rare books can only be bought by a work colleague or friend. In *Re Barlow's Will Trusts* [1979] 1 WLR 278 HC, a testatrix directed her executor 'to allow any member of my family and any friends of mine who wish to do so' to purchase paintings belonging to her. The court held that the trust was valid, even though the words 'family' and, more particularly, 'friends' may have been uncertain because this was not a discretionary trust, where trustees had to 'survey the field' but merely a case of conditions being attached to individual gifts.[6] Thus a gift to a person who did come within the meaning of 'family' or 'friend' would not be invalidated by uncertainty as to whether another person does so. Moreover, the court laid down tests to establish if a person is a friend, such as whether they met socially. On this basis it seems that, as the term 'work colleagues' is probably certain and 'friends' can be made so by applying *Re Barlow,* this gift can be upheld.

(c) We first need to clarify the terms of this bequest.[7] There is an initial gift of '£20,000 to my neighbour Helen' and she is told that that she is to use it 'partly for herself' and the rest, which she does not want, is to go to all her children. There is no doubt that there is an initial gift to Helen but the question is whether the second part imposes a trust on her for the benefit of her children or whether this is just a request to Helen which she can comply with, or ignore it and can keep this as a gift.

First, we must decide if there is certainty of intention to create a trust. In *Re Hamilton* [1895] 2 Ch 370 CA, Lindley LJ said that the courts must look at all the words used by the testator or settlor to see if, on their true construction in the context of the particular gift, a trust was intended. So we must look at the wording as a whole.[8] Thus, in **Comiskey v Bowring-Hanbury** [1905] AC 84 HL, a testator left his property to his wife 'in full confidence that she will make such use of it as I would myself'. This might not have been sufficient to create a trust, but later on he instructed her that on his death she was to leave it to one or more of his nieces but if she did not 'I hereby direct' it to be divided equally between them all on her death. The language is clearly intended to create a binding obligation. Here, however, the word is 'wish' which by itself is not as strong as 'direct'.

However, here another significant phrase is 'she is to use it', which is stronger than 'desire', which was not enough in **Re Diggles** (1888) 39 Ch D 253 HC, as this looks like an instruction. It is also stronger than 'in full confidence' in **Comiskey v Bowring-Hanbury**,[9] which in itself is more like a request. In addition, as in **Comiskey**, we need to look at the whole gift and here there is the instruction to Helen to use some of it for herself and then, as in **Comiskey**, a secondary instruction what to do with the property. On this basis it is arguable that there is intention to create a trust.

[9] Note how we have made a very close analysis of the words of this gift and the gift in *Comiskey*. This is a real lawyer's skill and you should practise it.

If there is certainty of intention then is there certainty of subject matter? This is doubtful, as the words used are 'the rest, which she does not want' as in **Sprange v Barnard** [1789] 2 Bro CC 585, where the will gave property to the testatrix's husband 'for his sole use' and then provided that 'the remaining part of what is left, that he does not want . . . to be divided between' members of his family. As the term 'remaining part' was uncertain, the husband took absolutely. It is suggested[10] that the same will apply here and, although the objects (the children)[11] are certain, the lack of certainty of subject matter will cause this trust to fail. Thus, as Helen was intended to take part anyway as a gift and we do not know what part was to be held on trust, she will take all as a gift.

[10] It is better not to be too definite as the matter is not completely certain. These little nuances in the wording of your answer really do help.

[11] Extra marks for picking up this small but relevant point.

Make your answer stand out

- Note that in *Vucicevic* v *Aleksic* the gift was to charity, unlike here. Consider if this could make a difference to the result in this case.
- Analysis and criticism of the decision in *Re Barlow's Will Trusts* [1979] 1 WLR 278 HC: see Emery (1982).
- Clear analysis of each situation, looking at the words of each gift in detail.
- Straightforward conclusion to each part, dealing with what will happen to the property.

! Don't be tempted to . . .

- Plunge straight in without analysing the exact terms of each bequest.
- Fail to mention all three certainties in each question.
- Just mention *Adams and Kensington Vestry* in the first part – contrast it with *Comiskey*.

Question 3

Critically consider the decision in *Hunter* v *Moss* [1994]. Can it be justified on grounds of policy or principle?

Answer plan

→ Issue which *Hunter* v *Moss* dealt with: subject matter of a trust where the goods are unascertained.

→ Consider the decision in *Hunter* v *Moss* itself and look at the question of the legal principle involved.

→ Contrast *Hunter* v *Moss* with *Re London Wine Co.*

→ Analyse the implications of *Hunter* v *Moss* looking across the whole area of trust law.

→ Consider how the Supreme Court of New South Wales dealt with the problem in *White* v *Shortall* and the idea of beneficial co-ownership.

→ Look at the policy issue: if there is a trust then the beneficiary will take precedence over any creditors.

→ Round off the answer by looking again briefly at *Hunter* v *Moss*. Is the legal principle satisfactory?

Diagram plan

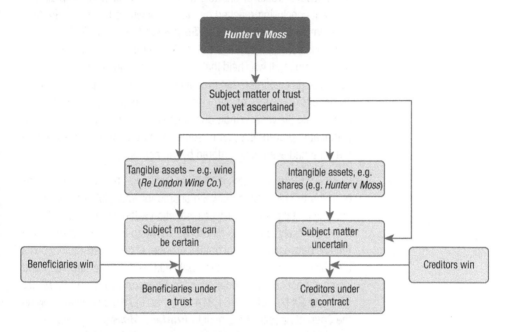

A printable version of this diagram is available from **www.pearsoned.co.uk/lawexpressqa**

Answer

[1] Always try for a clear, succinct start like this, showing the examiner that you know exactly what the issue is.

The decision in **_Hunter v Moss_** [1994] 1 WLR 452 CA concerned the problems which can arise where the subject matter of the trust is not ascertained.[1]

The defendant was the registered owner of 950 shares in a company and executed a declaration that he held 50 of them on trust for the claimant, who was also an employee. The court upheld the trust even though the shares, which were the subject of the trust, could not be identified. The decision has been criticised in terms of legal principle on the ground that the 50 shares were not identifiable from the other 950 shares and so there was no certainty of subject matter of the trust.

Hunter v Moss is usually explained on the basis that the court distinguished between tangible assets such as wine and intangible assets such as shares, although the court simply referred to a distinction between trusts of chattels and shares. This would explain the different conclusion reached by the courts where the goods are tangible. In **Re London Wine Co (Shippers) Ltd** [1986] PCC 121 HC, wine was sold to customers but it often remained at the warehouse of the company. It was held that no trust of the wine had been created even though customers received a certificate of title describing them as beneficial owners of particular wine. Nothing had been done to appropriate the wine to individual customers and the existence of the certificates proved little, as in some cases they were issued before the wine had even been ordered by the company.

[2] This is a straightforward point but missing it will cost you marks: the question specifically asks you to consider legal principle in this area.

However, we need to ask if this is a distinction based on legal principle.[2] Is the distinction between shares (or intangible property) and chattels (or tangible property) a distinction without a difference? Even if there is likely to be less difference between individual shares than there is between individual bottles of wine, is this a satisfactory basis on which to found a distinction between which trusts are valid and which are not? Briggs J pointed out in **Pearson v Lehman Brothers Finance SA** [2010] EWHC 2914 (Ch) that 'the difficulty with applying the Court of Appeal's judgment in **Hunter v Moss** to any case not on almost identical facts lies in the absence of any clearly expressed rationale as to how such a trust works in practice'.[3]

[3] This is a useful quote and you are now starting to build your marks by critically evaluating *Hunter v Moss*.

For example, what if some of the shares have been acquired by a forged gratuitous transfer? What is the position if some of the shares have been gambled away? Are they shares belonging to the trust or not? Had a trust been declared of one-nineteenth of the shares, would this have been valid as there would then be certainty of the subject matter.

[4] An answer such as this needs balance: having criticised the decision, you are now looking at reasons in support of it.

[5] Note how in this paragraph we are using knowledge from other areas; first trustees' duties and now tracing. This shows how only revising certain topics and leaving out others can stop you achieving those really good marks.

In support of the decision,[4] it has been said that the problem of precisely which shares are subject to the trust can be solved by applying the duty to safeguard the trust property, which means that the trustee is under an immediate duty once the trust is declared to separate those shares which are subject to the trust from the rest of them. If a trustee fails to do this, then she has mixed trust property with other assets and would be liable under the tracing rules.[5] It could be argued, however, that this confuses two distinct issues: the rules on establishing a trust, with which we are concerned here; and the rules which apply once a trust has been established, such as the duties of trustees.

The court in **Hunter v Moss** relied on an analogy with gifts of shares in a will. Such a gift is valid even though the shares are part of a larger whole, for example 100 shares out of 1,000 shares of mine in the Hanbury Bank. This analogy is false.[6] Although such a gift is valid, the shares are not held by the executors as trustees but as personal representatives until administration of the estate has been completed (***Commissioner of Stamp Duties (Queensland)* v *Livingston*** [1965] AC 694 PC). The result is that beneficiaries in this situation do not have rights as holders of a proprietary interest in the property.

The Supreme Court of New South Wales did not follow the reasoning in **Hunter v Moss** in **White v Shortall** [2006] NSWSC 1379, where there was a declaration of trust over 1,500,000 shares and the claimant was to acquire an equitable interest in 222,000 of them. Instead of holding that there was a trust of the 222,000 shares, it held that there was a trust of all the shares with the beneficiaries being the settlor and the other party, the claimant. Trustees could elect which of the total 1,500,000 shares would count as the 222,000 to be held on trust. Thus the solution was beneficial co-ownership[7] and this analysis was approved by Briggs J in **Pearson v Lehman Brothers Finance SA.** Is this a better solution than that reached in **Hunter v Moss**?

There is also the issue of policy as contests can arise between a beneficiary under a trust and the creditors.[8] This was the position in **Re London Wine,** whereas in **Hunter v Moss** there was no contest. In **Re Stapylton Fletcher Ltd** [1994] 1 WLR 1181, the judge said that courts should be 'very cautious in devising equitable interests and remedies which erode the statutory scheme for distribution on insolvency'. This may explain **Re Goldcorp Exchange Ltd (in receivership)** [1995] 1 AC 74 PC, where purchasers of bullion for future delivery from Goldcorp received a certificate of ownership, but no bullion was set aside for them, nor was this intended, as the object was to enable the owners to sell it when the price had increased. The court held, as in **Re London Wine,** that title could not pass because the bullion was unidentified and so could not be the subject of a private trust.

In **Goldcorp** the court approved **Mac-Jordan Construction Ltd v Brookmount Erostin Ltd** [1992] BCLC 350 CA, where there was no trust of a sum of money retained by the employer of a builder which

[9] Note how in one paragraph we have brought out the essential differences between these cases: when revising try to practise this technique.

was to be paid over on confirmation that the work done by the builder was satisfactory, as although the employer was called the trustee, no separate fund of this money was set up. This does not necessarily mean that **Hunter v Moss** was, by implication, disapproved as **Mac-Jordan** was a case where there were no identifiable assets, whereas in **Hunter v Moss** the larger asset, the 1,000 shares out of which a trust of 50 was declared, was identified. Moreover **Mac-Jordan** was an insolvency case.[9]

[10] You need in conclusion to draw the issues together, even if only briefly.

The decision in **Hunter v Moss** was approved by Arden LJ in **Lehman Brothers (Europe) (in Administration) v CRC Credit Fund Ltd.** [2010] EWCA Civ 917, as 'the shareholding was in existence, the shares were fungible (interchangeable) and thus the trust property could be identified'. However, whilst the decision may be defensible on its facts, it is clearly not satisfactory in principle due to the failure of the court to explore the implications of declaring a trust in this type of case.[10]

 Make your answer stand out

- Structure the answer so that it focuses directly on the difficult theoretical issues possibly at the expense of the facts of some cases.
- Consider the implications of sections 20A and 20B of the Sale of Goods (Amendment) Act 1995 in this area.
- More detailed consideration, drawn from your knowledge of the material in Chapters 11 and 12, of the impact of the duties of trustees and of the tracing rules on the decision in *Hunter v Moss*.
- Investigate the idea of beneficial co-ownership as proposed in *White v Shortall*. This would lead to a beneficial tenancy in common in the goods. What is the effect of this?

- Discuss the law on certainty of subject matter in trusts in general. Focus on the exact area raised in the question.
- Spend too much time on *Hunter* v *Moss* itself: spend more time on the implications of this case.
- Worse still, begin by listing *all* the certainties.
- Miss the distinction between issues of principle and of policy.

Question 4

'In view of the importance of the discretionary trust today it is vital that the tests for certainty of objects in cases of these trusts are clear and workable.'

Consider why discretionary trusts are important today and whether the present test for certainty is indeed clear and workable.

Answer plan

→ Explain exactly what a discretionary trust is and distinguish it from a fixed trust.

→ Explain with examples why discretionary trusts are used.

→ State and explain the reasons why there needs to be a clear test of certainty of objects in discretionary trusts.

→ Explain the actual decision in *McPhail* v *Doulton* and analyse the judgments.

→ Explain the problem with the words 'is not' as used in the individual ascertainability test in *McPhail* v *Doulton*.

Diagram plan

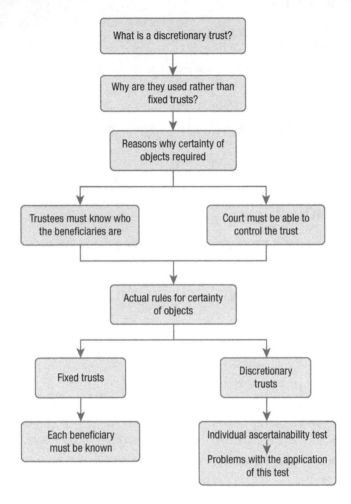

A printable version of this diagram is available from **www.pearsoned.co.uk/lawexpressqa**

Answer

[1] You must begin this answer with a clear account of what a discretionary trust is.

A discretionary trust is where the trustees have a discretion as to which beneficiaries shall benefit from a trust and in what proportion.[1] For instance, the trust may be for 'such of my five children and in such shares as my trustees shall in their absolute discretion decide'. So where the trustees make a particular distribution of money they have a discretion as to which children shall be the recipients and how much they shall receive. They are distinguished from fixed trusts where the trust instrument specifies the share which each beneficiary is to take (the 'list principle').

Discretionary trusts are important today in comparison with fixed trusts for three main reasons. First, they are flexible. If we take the above example of a discretionary trust, then it may be that one of the children is seriously disabled and will not be able to earn their living, whereas the other four will be able to be financially independent. So it may well make sense for the trustees to allocate a larger share of the trust's capital to the disabled child. Second, these trusts have advantages when a beneficiary goes bankrupt. As any money beneficiaries might receive from the trust is entirely at the trustees' discretion, they have no ascertainable interest that their creditors can seize in repayment of their debts.

Third, and probably the most important advantage today, is tax planning.[2] Suppose that James executes his will in 2000 but in 2019 the Government introduces changes to tax laws that mean that as his will stands there is an increased liability to tax. James could make a new will but suppose that he is not interested in doing this or is difficult to contact. However, the trustees, using the discretionary character of the trust, can try to make sure that any distributions of capital are tax efficient.

There are two reasons[3] why some degree of certainty of objects is required:

(a) Unless the trustees know who the beneficiaries are, they cannot distribute the trust property.

(b) The court needs to be able to control the trust so that if the trustees come to the court asking for directions as to who the beneficiaries are, it can give them. In **Morice v Bishop of Durham** [1804] 10 Ves 522 HC, Sir William Grant said, 'There can be no trust over the exercise of which this court will not assume control; for an uncontrollable power of disposition would be ownership, and not trust.' This principle also appears, in the guise of the beneficiary principle, in connection with the linked but not identical principle that a trust must have a beneficiary who can enforce it.[4]

[2] You need to be careful here. This is not a tax examination and the examiner will not expect detailed knowledge of tax law. However, what you do say must be accurate. Here we have contented ourselves with a general example.

[3] In this area the decisions of the courts have been arrived at against a background of fundamental points in trust law about the role of the courts in the administration of trusts. This is why it is vital to begin by stating these clearly and only then go on to look at the cases.

[4] This is a separate, but linked, point and mainly arises in the context of non-charitable purpose trusts. A brief reference to it at this point shows the kind of wider thinking which will bring you extra marks.

The test for certainty of objects in discretionary trusts was laid down in *McPhail v Doulton* [1971] AC 424 HL, where Lord Wilberforce in the House of Lords held that the test was: 'Can it be said with certainty that any given individual is or is not a member of the class?'[5] (This is often known as the individual ascertainability test.)

[5] Make sure for the exam that you can memorise these words and, above all, apply them. It will certainly increase your marks. Students often forget the 'or is not' part.

In *McPhail v Doulton,* the trustees were directed to apply the net income of a fund in making at their absolute discretion grants to the following beneficiaries: the officers and employees or ex-officers or ex-employees of a company or their relatives or dependants. Under the list principle, the trust would have failed as although a list of the officers and employees of the company could doubtless be drawn up, it would not be possible to do so in the case of relatives and dependants. Should this cause the trust to fail?

Following Lord Wilberforce's statement of the individual ascertainability test, the case was remitted to the Chancery Division to decide if the test was satisfied and it was held that it was: *Re Baden's Deed Trusts (No 2)* [1973] Ch 9.

The problem has been to find a way of reconciling the need for a more relaxed test in discretionary trusts than the 'list' test in fixed trusts, as discretionary trusts by their nature are more flexible, with the need for a test which gives the courts a reasonable yardstick with which to exercise control if need be.

[6] Try to think of examples to illustrate theoretical issues – they will make your essay come alive.

Suppose that in the *McPhail* situation a sister of an employee came to the trustees and said that she was a relative.[6] It could doubtless be proved that she was or was not. But suppose that someone came and said that they were a second cousin twice removed? How could it be said with certainty that she was not a relative? She might be able to show that she probably *was* a relative but how could it be proved that she *was not*?

In *Re Baden,* Sachs LJ took a straightforward view: if a person is not proved to be within the class then he is not within it. However, the fact that he cannot be proved to be actually in the class does not mean that he is not, in fact, within it. Proof of a negative does not follow from lack of proof of a positive. Megaw LJ said that the individual ascertainability test was satisfied if 'as regards a substantial number

[7] Note the reference in this paragraph to the views of three judges – it is this kind of detail which makes an answer stand out, as it shows that you have gone beyond the facts of the case and looked at the judgments.

[8] This is the point which most students so often miss in this type of question, whether it is an essay or a problem. Make sure that you are clear about it.

[9] This conclusion seeks to draw the discussion to a close by stating the real difficulty: if we abandon the 'list' test for certainty of objects when we have not yet found a replacement. You could come to a different conclusion and say that the decision in *McPhail* v *Doulton* has stood since 1971 and there does not seem to be evidence from the cases that the 'individual ascertainability' test has not worked.

of objects, it can be said with certainty that they fall within the trust', even though it cannot be proved whether others fall within it or not. This test has merit, but it is not the individual ascertainability test of Lord Wilberforce. Stamp LJ[7] sought the aid of the principle in **Re Benjamin** [1902] 1 Ch 723 HC, in which trustees, having done their best to find the beneficiaries, can apply to the court to be allowed to distribute the estate to those of whom they have knowledge.

The trouble seems to be the words 'is not'.[8] Why not then omit them and the test would then simply be 'can there be certainty that any given individual is a member of the class?' The problem is that if we omit these words we arrive at the one-person test proposed by Denning MR in **Re Gulbenkian's Settlement Trusts (No 1)** [1970] AC 508 HL and rejected by the House of Lords: is it sufficient if it can be said with certainty that any one person is a member of the class? This is considered to be too narrow, as there might only be one certain member of the class.

The difficulty is that the individual ascertainability test if applied strictly is too near to the 'list' test for fixed trusts.[9] To say that it must be said with certainty if a person is or *is not* a member of the class comes near to saying that we need to know who is and who is not within it, and the best way of doing this is by drawing up a list. The truth is that we do not have a satisfactory test for deciding the objects of a discretionary trust and so we are left with the **McPhail** one.

 Make your answer stand out

- Contrast powers of appointment and discretionary trusts.
- Discuss with examples the distinction between evidential and conceptual uncertainty.
- Idea of 'administrative unworkability': is this helpful?
- Read and refer to Harris [1971], which analyses *McPhail* v *Doulton*.

! Don't be tempted to . . .

- Fail to distinguish between fixed and discretionary trusts.
- Fail to consider the practical advantages of discretionary trusts.
- Just state the law on certainty of objects.
- Begin your answer with a long account of the case law.
- Only provide a superficial analysis of *McPhail* v *Doulton*. You must *really* know this case if you attempt this question!

@ Try it yourself

Now take a look at the question below and attempt to answer it. You can check your response against the answer guidance available on the companion website (**www.pearsoned.co.uk/lawexpressqa**).

Is the decision in *Re Barlow's Will Trusts* [1979] 1 All ER 296 based on confusion between conditions attached to gifts and discretionary trusts?

www.pearsoned.co.uk/lawexpressqa

 Go online to access more revision support including additional essay and problem questions with diagram plans, 'You be the marker' questions, and download all diagrams from the book.

Formalities

4

How this topic may come up in exams

This is not a popular topic for students because the facts of the cases tend to be very complex as they often concern convoluted tax avoidance schemes. Remember that the actual facts are unlikely to reoccur in exams simply because this is not a tax law exam. The vital message is to be absolutely clear on the principles established by the cases and then to recognise how they can arise in exam questions.

(Material in this chapter can arise in other areas such as constitution and certainties and you will find a question of this kind in Chapter 13.)

■ Before you begin

It's a good idea to consider the following key themes of formalities before tackling a question on this topic.

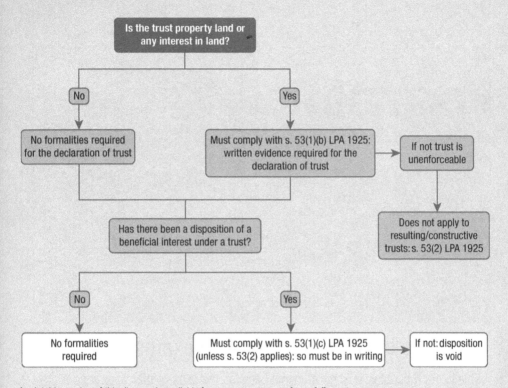

A printable version of this diagram is available from **www.pearsoned.co.uk/lawexpressqa**

❓ Question 1

Nick transferred the freehold house, 'Seaview', which he owned and where he lived with his girlfriend Sally, into her name as he was going to work abroad for five years. There was a properly executed deed of transfer but there was no consideration expressed in the transfer deed nor was it expressed to be by gift.

When he was abroad Nick rang Sally and said, 'As you know I have put my house in your name but any remaining interest which I may have in it is to be held for my friend Freda.'

Nick was visited when abroad by his brother Sam and Nick said to Sam, 'You know those shares in the Hanbury Bank that Aunt Agatha made you a trustee of for me? It would be better if all my interest in them went to your son Tom.'

Sally, Freda, Sam and Tom ask your advice on the legal and beneficial ownership of:

(a) 'Seaview'; and

(b) the shares in the Hanbury Bank.

Answer plan

→ Identify that the transfer of 'Seaview' must comply with section 52(1) of the Law of Property Act 1925 (LPA 1925).

→ Note that the transfer of 'Seaview' by Nick to Sally may create either an express trust or a resulting trust.

→ Set out the formal requirements for an express trust of land in section 53(1)(b) of the LPA 1925 and apply them to the question.

→ Explain how a resulting trust could arise on these facts and explain that there are no formal requirements for this type of trust.

→ Identify where section 53(1)(c) applies as there is a transfer of an equitable interest.

→ Apply the relevant law.

→ Consider the consequences where either of the above requirements are not complied with.

→ Examine whether Nick's beneficial interest in the shares has been disposed of applying section 53(1)(c) and cases.

Diagram plan

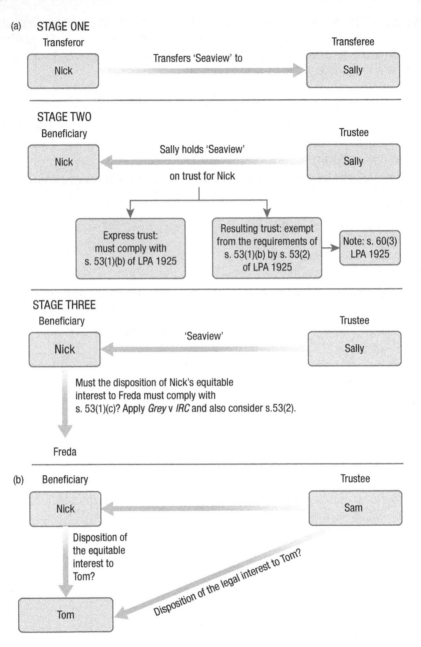

(a) STAGE ONE

Transferor — Nick — Transfers 'Seaview' to → Transferee — Sally

STAGE TWO

Beneficiary — Nick ← Sally holds 'Seaview' on trust for Nick — Trustee — Sally

- Express trust: must comply with s. 53(1)(b) of LPA 1925
- Resulting trust: exempt from the requirements of s. 53(1)(b) by s. 53(2) of LPA 1925 → Note: s. 60(3) LPA 1925

STAGE THREE

Beneficiary — Nick ← 'Seaview' — Trustee — Sally

Must the disposition of Nick's equitable interest to Freda must comply with s. 53(1)(c)? Apply *Grey* v *IRC* and also consider s.53(2).

Freda

(b) Beneficiary — Nick ← Trustee — Sam

Disposition of the equitable interest to Tom?

Disposition of the legal interest to Tom?

Tom

A printable version of this diagram is available from **www.pearsoned.co.uk/lawexpressqa**

Answer

(a) The first point is that Nick transferred Seaview to Sally by a properly executed deed of transfer. We are told that it is validly executed and so will satisfy section 52(1) of the LPA 1925.[1] However, the transfer was for no consideration and no words of gift were expressed.

There are two possibilities here.[2] One is that there was an express trust of 'Seaview'. Although Nick did not actually say to Sally when he transferred the house that it was to be held on trust, he later rang her and said, 'As you know I have put my house in your name but any remaining interest which I may have in it is to be held for my friend Freda.' The reference to 'any remaining interest' and the need to tell Freda of this at all may indicate that the transfer by Nick to Sally was expressly on trust for Freda. If so then the requirements of section 53(1)(b) of the LPA 1925 must be complied with. This provides that 'a declaration of trust concerning land or any interest therein must be manifested and proved by some writing signed by some person who is able to declare the same or by his will' and it is clear that there was no written declaration of trust here.

Section 53(1)(b) is silent on the position when these requirements are not complied with [3] but it is accepted that this will not make the trust void but only unenforceable, in line with what was the position under section 40(1) of the LPA 1925 (**Gardner v Rowe** [1826] 5 Russ 828 HC). Therefore Nick could not enforce the trust against Sally who could thus take 'Seaview' beneficially.

The other possibility is that there is a presumed resulting trust.[4] These arise on the basis that the presumed intention of the transferor, Nick in this case, was not to make an outright transfer but to transfer the legal title to the transferee, Sally here, with the intention that Sally should hold on a resulting trust for Nick. Thus in **Re Vinogradoff** [1935] WN 68 HC, the testatrix had transferred an £800 War Loan which was in her own name into the joint names of herself and her four-year-old daughter. It was held that the daughter held it on a resulting trust for the testatrix. In this case Nick's later conversation with Sally in which he states that 'any remaining interest which I may have in it is to be held

---

[1] There is no need to set out the requirements of section 52(1) for a valid deed as you are told that the transfer is validly executed, but you will gain credit for picking this issue up at the start.

[2] This is a nice confident start – clearly you know where you are going!

[3] Students generally miss this point entirely – so a mention of it is bound to increase your marks.

[4] This shows the importance, when revising for an exam, of making sure that you have a basic understanding of all the main areas as they constantly relate to each other. As you can see here, the provisions of section 53(2) of the LPA 1925 provide a link between formalities and resulting and constructive trusts.

[5] Note how we have analysed these facts to show how there are two possible results: an express or a resulting trust. This is the type of reasoning that really does add to your marks. The trick is very simple: study the exact words used in a question and remember that there might be more than one possible answer!

[6] This is a useful point to mention in order to clarify the position.

[7] Do remember this – it is one of those vital points which, if you get it wrong, could send your answer off in a completely wrong direction.

[8] This point of detail is worth recalling – it is almost universally omitted by students.

[9] Note how the essential point of the case has been emphasised first, as this is what you need to recall in formalities questions.

for my friend Freda' does not provide evidence of an express trust but instead supports the presumption of a resulting trust on the basis that Nick may well have regarded himself as having retained some interest in 'Seaview'.[5]

Section 60(3) of the LPA 1925 provides that in a voluntary conveyance, as was the case here, 'a resulting trust for the grantor shall not be implied merely by reason that the property is not expressed to be conveyed for the use or benefit of the grantee'.[6] However, this merely means that just because the transfer to Sally did not expressly state that she was to hold 'Seaview' for her own benefit does not by itself mean that she holds it on a resulting trust. It is submitted, however, that there is sufficient evidence of a resulting trust for Nick by the omission of any words of gift in the transfer and Nick's later reference to Freda.

If there is a resulting trust then the requirements of section 53(1)(b) of the LPA 1925 do not apply[7] and section 53(2) of the LPA 1925 provides that section 53(1)(b) 'does not affect the creation or operation of resulting, implied or constructive trusts'. Therefore there is no need for any written evidence of this trust and the result is that Sally holds the legal title of 'Seaview' but, as she does so on a resulting trust for Nick, Nick has the equitable interest.

However, this analysis means that Nick originally retained the beneficial interest in 'Seaview' under a resulting trust and so when he later said to Sally that he wanted Freda to have 'any remaining interest' that he has in 'Seaview' he was making a disposition of his equitable interest under the trust. Must it comply with section 53(1)(c) of the LPA 1925, which provides that a disposition of an equitable interest or trust must be in writing signed either by the settlor or by his authorised agent? Failure to comply with section 53(1)(c) makes the disposition void. This has always been accepted as the correct view and this is supported by the word 'must' in the subsection although, as with section 53(1)(b), the subsection is silent on this point.[8] In this case Nick does not make a direct disposition but directs Sally as trustee to hold on trust for another person, Freda.

In *Grey v IRC* [1960] AC 1 HL, it was held that such a transaction was caught by section 53(1)(c) and so required writing.[9]

However, by s.53(2) of the LPA the formalities requirements do not apply to the creation or operation of resulting trusts and it is the word 'operation' which is important here as this means that s.53((l)(c) does not apply to dispositions of equitable interests under resulting trusts. As a result the oral disposition by Nick to Freda is valid.

(b) Nick was visited when abroad by his brother Sam and Nick said to Sam, 'You know those shares in the Hanbury Bank that Aunt Agatha made you a trustee for me? It would be better if all the rights in them went to your son Tom.'

[10] There is no need to set out section 53(1)(c) again.

[11] This phrase – or something similar – in a question often indicates the possible application of *Vandervell* v *IRC*.

Is this a disposition of Nick's beneficial interest in the shares? If so, it will be caught by section 53(1)(c) of the LPA 1925[10] and, as it is not in writing, it will be void so that Nick will still be the beneficiary. The vital point is that Nick directs 'all the rights' in the shares[11] to be transferred and so it can be argued that he is not transferring a beneficial interest, as there will no longer be any beneficial interest as Tom will own the shares absolutely.

[12] It is Sam as he is the legal owner.

Thus in ***Vandervell v IRC*** [1967] 2 AC 291 HL, a bank which held shares on trust for Vandervell as a bare trustee then transferred them, on Vandervell's instructions, to the Royal College of Surgeons. It was held that as the bank's legal title to the shares and Vandervell's equitable interest were both transferred, section 53(1)(c) did not apply as there was no equitable interest to dispose of as it had merged with the legal interest. If this applies here then all that Sam needs to do is transfer the shares to Tom.[12]

 Make your answer stand out

- Look very closely at the exact words used in the question and make a clear distinction between an express and a resulting trust.
- Be prepared to look beyond the formalities issue and apply the relevant law on certainty of objects to the question.
- Avoid too much detail on the cases involving formalities and concentrate on the principles which they establish.
- Read Green (1984) especially at pp. 396–8. It is a really useful and clear explanation of the law on formalities.

! **Don't be tempted to . . .**

- Set out the sections of the LPA 1925 in great detail at the expense of application of the facts.
- Set out facts of cases and not see the underlying point.
- Fail to point out the consequences of failing to comply with the formalities requirements.
- Fail to find a home for the property if the intended trust fails.

⬛ Question 2

Critically examine the decision in *Oughtred* v *IRC* [1960] on the application of section 53(1)(c) of the LPA 1925 to dispositions of equitable interests or trusts.

Answer plan

→ Explain the background: the formal requirements in section 53(1)(c) of the LPA 1925 and the taxation implications.

→ Set out the facts of *Oughtred* v *IRC* [1960] AC 206.

→ Explain in detail the impact of the three equitable principles involved: remedy of specific performance; maxim that equity looks on that as done which ought to be done; and the constructive trust.

→ Now explain the decision in *Oughtred* v *IRC*, making sure that you analyse the dissenting speech of Lord Radcliffe.

→ Look at other cases in this area to see how they have dealt with the tension between legal formalism and equitable principles.

Diagram plan

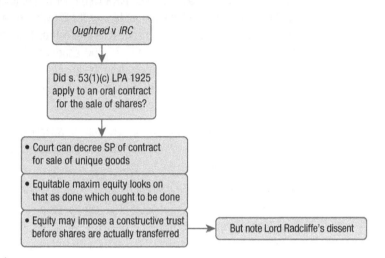

Oughtred v IRC

↓

Did s. 53(1)(c) LPA 1925 apply to an oral contract for the sale of shares?

↓

- Court can decree SP of contract for sale of unique goods

- Equitable maxim equity looks on that as done which ought to be done

- Equity may impose a constructive trust before shares are actually transferred → But note Lord Radcliffe's dissent

A printable version of this diagram is available from **www.pearsoned.co.uk/lawexpressqa**

Answer

[1] A useful extra point setting your answer apart from average ones.

Section 53(1)(c) 1925 provides that a disposition of an equitable interest or trust must be in writing signed either by the settlor or by his authorised agent. It is generally accepted that failure to comply with section 53(1)(c) makes the disposition void although in fact the subsection is silent on this point.[1] ***Oughtred v IRC*** [1960] AC 206 concerned the application of section 53(1)(c) to cases where there is a contract to dispose of such an interest.

[2] Mention this point now and then refer to it more detail in your answer as you go on.

The problem is that tax in the form of stamp duty is payable on some written instruments. The result is that there is a clear motive for settlors to seek to make dispositions orally. The question then becomes whether section 53(1)(c) applies. ***Oughtred v IRC*** is such a case.

[3] Note that instead of plunging at once into the facts of *Oughtred*, we have first set the decision in context and are only now considering the facts. This should add to your marks as we are showing the examiner that we are aware of the underlying issues.

The issue in ***Oughtred v IRC*** was whether an oral contract to dispose of an equitable interest operates as a transfer of that interest so that section 53(1)(c) is avoided. It will be seen that there are issues of legal principle here as well as the policy consideration of the extent to which the courts ought to uphold what are simply tax avoidance schemes.[2]

In ***Oughtred v IRC*** [1960], Mrs Oughtred and her son Peter both had interests in shares in a private company.[3] Mrs Oughtred owned

72,000 shares absolutely on which estate duty (a predecessor of the present Inheritance Tax) would be payable on her death. In addition, 200,000 shares were held in trust for her for life with remainder to Peter. They orally agreed to exchange their interests so that she transferred her absolute interest in the 72,000 shares to Peter and he transferred his share in remainder under the trust to her, and this was confirmed by two documents of transfer. The IRC claimed stamp duty on these actual written transfers of the shares.

Was the transfer effected by the oral contract, in which case no stamp duty would be payable, or was it payable on the documents of transfer, in which case it would be payable?

[4] This paragraph, and the next two, set out the equitable principles forming the background to this case. It is important to do this before you deal with the actual decision in *Oughtred,* as you will then be able to show how the equitable principles are applied here. A mediocre answer would go straight from the facts to the decision and miss discussion of the principles.

There is a principle of equity[4] that where there is a contract to sell unique goods then the court has a discretion to decree the remedy of specific performance precisely because the goods are unique and so it would be impossible to buy them elsewhere and thus the common law remedy of damages would be inadequate. This applies to contracts for the sale of land and, as here, contracts for the sale of shares in a private company as these cannot be traded on the open market.

The equitable maxim 'equity looks on that as done which ought to be done' applies, so where a contract has been made of which specific performance can be decreed by equity then equity regards the contract as having been performed as soon as it is made on the principle that although the formalities have yet to be completed they ought now actually to be completed.

However, there is a gap. Take the situation where X agrees to sell shares in a private company to Y. Equity regards this as a completely performed agreement but as yet the shares have not been transferred from X to Y. Here the last weapon in equity's arsenal comes in, for equity imposes a constructive trust on X to hold the shares for Y until the formal transfer. This was the reasoning of, for instance, Megarry J in *Re Holt's Settlement* [1969], who accepted that where a contract is specifically enforceable, the purchaser's right to specific performance passes to him as an equitable interest under a constructive trust as soon as the contract is made. Moreover section 53(2) of the LPA exempts constructive trusts from the formalities required by section 53(1)(c) and thus no writing is needed.[5]

[5] Note how we have carefully traced the application of different equitable principles in this section. This shows how important it is to have a secure grasp of these.

[6] This is unusual but effective here: as Lord Radcliffe's dissent was arguably more influential than the reasoning of the majority, we are looking at it first.

In **Oughtred**, Lord Radcliffe adopted this reasoning[6] and held that as the contract was for the transfer of shares in a private company this was specifically enforceable and so, pending the formal transfer, Mrs Oughtred was in the position of Y in the example above and as she had a beneficial interest in the shares she was entitled to call for a transfer of them to her. Thus the transfer occurred without writing and so there was no stamp duty to pay. The formal documents simply recognised an existing fact.

[7] Now we come to the majority decision. This is one of the very few cases where a dissenting judgment has proved more influential than the majority one and therefore it is best considered first.

However, he was in the minority and all the other law lords held that even if Mrs Oughtred did acquire a beneficial interest in the shares, the buyer does not acquire a full beneficial interest until the formal written transfer.[7] In effect the later formal documents had been intended to be part of the transaction and section 53(1)(c) applied. Thus stamp duty was payable and the equitable principles, although relevant, did not apply to the whole transaction. In effect the same principles were applied as in **Grey v IRC** [1960] AC 1 HL. It is worth mentioning that policy considerations may have played a part in the decision as if the argument had succeeded, avoidance would be extremely simple where a contract is specifically enforceable. The contract would displace the need for a written instrument so that no duty would be payable.

However, *Oughtred* is not a satisfactory decision. The majority in the Lords did not decide what interest Mrs Oughtred held before the formal transfer and the argument of Lord Radcliffe seems more compelling.

[8] Rather than end our answer with *Oughtred* itself, we are earning extra marks by looking at how the issue raised by that case has fared subsequently.

Neville v Wilson [1996] Ch 144 supports Lord Radcliffe's argument.[8] Here nominees held shares in one company (X) on trust for another (Y). The shareholders of Y agreed to put it into liquidation and to divide the company's equitable interest in these shares amongst themselves. This agreement was not in writing. If the agreement was not effective the interest in the shares would pass to the Crown but the Court of Appeal held that the agreement was effective to transfer the equitable interest to the shareholders by applying the analysis of Lord Radcliffe in *Oughtred*. It is significant that in this case there was no issue of avoiding tax but only the question of whether the shareholders or the Crown obtained the equitable interest.

The debate is not over. In **United Bank of Kuwait plc v Sahib** [1997] Ch 107, Chadwick J could not see why, on the basis of **Neville v Wilson**, an oral contract could transfer an equitable right but a disposition could not. In ***Chinn v Collins*** (1981) AC 533 HL, Lord Wilberforce had recognised that where in a scheme legal title to shares was held by a nominee then an agreement to sell those shares would pass the equitable interest in them once the purchase price had been paid, regardless of whether any formalities, such as section 53(1)(c), had been complied with.

[9] We are coming back to the question and also showing that the debate is not closed: this is important because poor answers are often too definite. This would be wrong here.

The debate on whether section 53(1)(c) applies in these situations is not over. Although the decision of the majority in ***Oughtred v IRC*** was based on legal formalism and not equitable principles, the dissenting speech of Lord Radcliffe, which was based on equitable principles, may have proved more influential.[9]

Make your answer stand out

- Look at the decision of the Australian High Court in *Halloran* v *Minister Administering National Parks and Wildlife Act 1974* [2006] 80 AJLR 519. This case is helpfully considered by Turner (2006). Do make diagrams of the cases as you go along – it will help here a great deal.

- Note that in *Oughtred,* if Lord Radcliffe's analysis is correct, then the constructive trust under which Peter would hold the shares for his mother would be a subtrust of Peter's reversionary interest under the main trust. What would be the implications of this?

- Discussion of *Neville* v *Wilson* in the context of the relationship between section 53(1)(b) and section 53(2) of the LPA 1925 and the article by Nolan (1996). Nolan refers to the 'extreme technicality and artificiality of the case law' in this area, a view with which it is impossible to disagree!

- Discussion of views in academic literature, e.g. Green (1984). Although this is now slightly outdated, it is a useful starting point.

! Don't be tempted to . . .

- Simply discuss *Oughtred* v *IRC* and leave out an analysis of the surrounding equitable principles.

- Forget to distinguish clearly between section 53(1)(b) and section 53(2) of the LPA 1925.

- Leave out mentioning the policy issue of whether the court should approve tax avoidance schemes.

- End your answer with *Oughtred* – still leave time to look at other cases.

Try it yourself

Now take a look at the question below and attempt to answer it. You can check your response against the answer guidance available on the companion website (**www.pearsoned.co.uk/lawexpressqa**).

Critically consider the litigation involving the trusts of Mr Vandervell and assess its impact on the law governing formalities for the disposition of equitable interests.

www.pearsoned.co.uk/lawexpressqa

 Go online to access more revision support including additional essay and problem questions with diagram plans, 'You be the marker' questions, and download all diagrams from the book.

Constitution of trusts

5

How this topic may come up in exams

This is a frequent topic for problem questions where you may also find that the question includes material on certainties and/or formalities and so you need to make sure that you are confident in these areas as well before you tackle a constitution question. You need to adopt an extremely structured approach to problems as there are many marks to be picked up by a detailed, thorough approach. There is also material for essay questions, especially as there have been fairly recent cases on the application of the principles in *Milroy* v *Lord* and on *donationes mortis causa*.

Before you begin

It's a good idea to consider the following key themes of constitution of trusts before tackling a question on this topic.

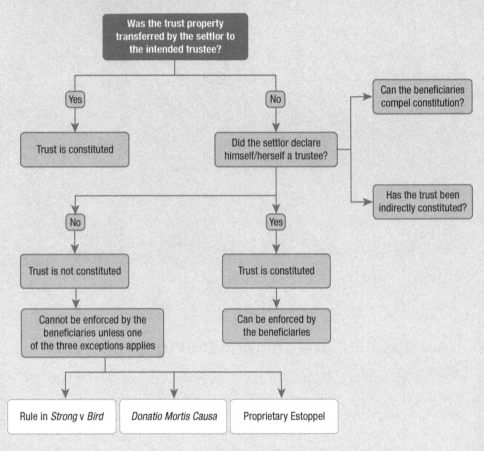

A printable version of this diagram is available from **www.pearsoned.co.uk/lawexpressqa**

❓ Question 1

John lived in a nursing home but still owned a cottage, 'Rosemount'. In April 2018, he thought that he had not long to live and so he wrote to his favourite granddaughter, Amanda: 'I would like you to have Rosemount when I die. You have been so kind to me and you have done so much work in helping me to renovate the cottage.' John then took the title deeds of 'Rosemount' and wrote: 'These deeds and all that they refer to I give to Amanda Jones from this time forth.' He then put the deeds back in their box which he kept.

In August 2018, John recovered sufficiently to leave the nursing home and returned to live at 'Rosemount' with live-in carers. In January 2019, still at 'Rosemount', John died from a stroke. John's will appoints Anita, Amanda's mother, as his executor and leaves Anita all his property.

Advise Amanda whether she has any claim to 'Rosemount'.

Answer plan

→ Examine why the actual transfer by John was invalid.

→ Explain methods one and two of constitution of a trust/gift.

→ Apply these to the question to see if the gift by John of 'Rosemount' can be upheld.

→ Look at possible ways in which equity may intervene even though the methods of constitution were not complied with: *donatio mortis causa* and estoppel.

Diagram plan

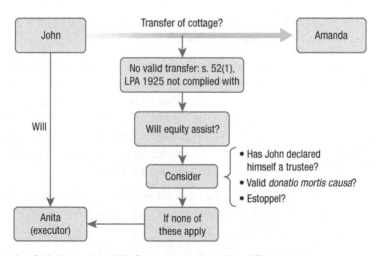

A printable version of this diagram is available from **www.pearsoned.co.uk/lawexpressqa**

Answer

¹ Always start a problem question on constitution in this way. It is likely that the correct formalities will not have been followed, which is precisely why you are being asked the question, but this is the logical way to start.

² A good, extra, relevant point for an extra mark. Note that we have picked up the point that we do not know if title is registered or not.

³ Look for this point: there is no contract and so no question of Amanda seeking contractual remedies.

⁴ This classification of the methods of constitution really does help to clarify your thoughts, so do remember it.

⁵ It is worth mentioning that this is what appears to lie behind many of the cases in this area.

The first question is whether there has been a valid transfer, using the correct formalities, of 'Rosemount' from John to Amanda.¹ Legal estates in land must be transferred by deed (section 52(1), LPA 1925) and, if title is registrable, then the requirements of the Land Registration Act 2002 must be observed.² It is clear that this has not happened and so we must ask if equity will assist.

John appears to have made an attempted gift³ of the cottage to Amanda and, as Lord Eldon put it in ***Ellison v Ellison*** [1802] 31 ER 1243 HC, 'Equity will not assist a volunteer.' Thus in principle Amanda cannot compel John, by the equitable remedy of specific performance, to transfer the cottage to her nor can she seek damages at common law as she has not provided consideration.

However, Amanda may try to argue that John has, by his words and actions, made himself a trustee of the cottage for her. A trust of land requires written evidence (section 53(1)(b), LPA 1925) and John has written that he would like Amanda to have the house when he dies although he has kept the keys to the deed box. Thus there is written evidence of what John has done but, and this is the crucial question, is it written evidence of a trust?

In ***Milroy v Lord*** [1862] 4 De GF & J 264 HC, Turner LJ indicated that a trust will be completely constituted when either:

(a) the settlor has vested the legal title to the trust property in the trustee(s) (Method One); or

(b) the settlor has declared that he now holds the property as trustee (Method Two).⁴ Clearly, John did not transfer the cottage to a trustee to hold on trust for Amanda but Amanda may argue that John has made himself a trustee of the cottage for her and so constituted a trust. In effect, a transfer which has failed to comply with the statutory formalities will be rescued by a finding that there is a trust.⁵ But is there a trust?

In fact the courts have not been willing to impose the duties of a trustee on a person such as John without clear evidence that a trust was intended.

A decision which is very similar on its facts to this one is ***Richards v Delbridge*** [1874] LR 18 Eq 11 HC: Delbridge was tenant of premises and, shortly before his death, he wrote and signed the following memorandum on the lease: 'This deed and all thereto belonging I give to Edward Bennetto Richards, from this time forth, with all the stock-in-trade.' Edward was his grandson. Delbridge then gave the document to Edward's mother to hold for him. On Delbridge's death there was no mention of the property.

[6] This is an example of a useful quote which will add to your marks.

The court held that there was no effective transfer of the lease because there was no declaration of trust. Jessell MR observed that 'for a man to make himself trustee there must be an expression of intention to become a trustee'.[6] This was not so as an outright gift was intended and here it is suggested that the same will apply. John put the deeds in a box, whereas in ***Richards v Delbridge*** they were given to the intended donee's mother, and John's actions seem even stronger evidence that no trust was intended.[7]

[7] Note the close comparison between the facts of the case and those of the problem: always the sign of a good answer.

There are two other possibilities. One is whether there is a valid *donatio mortis causa* of the cottage. In ***Sen v Headley*** [1991] 2 WLR 1308 CA, it was held that there can be a valid *donatio* of land but are the conditions for one fulfilled?[8]

[8] As a general rule, you should go through all three conditions for a valid *donatio* as it is likely that the answer as to whether there is a valid *donatio* will not be certain.

The first is that the donor must have contemplated death in the near future. In ***Vallee v Birchwood*** [2013] EWHC 1449 (Ch), it was held: 'the gift must be made in contemplation, although not necessarily in expectation, of impending death'. When he made the gift John thought that he had not long to live and, although he does not seem to have been terminally ill at this point, it is suggested that he clearly contemplated death and this is sufficient.

The second is that the subject matter of the gift must be delivered to the donee in the lifetime of the donor with the intention of parting with dominion over it. In ***Sen v Hedley*** dominion of land was parted with when the donor handed the donee the keys to the house and a key to a box containing the title deeds. Here John did not hand over the deeds to Amanda but kept them himself in a box. It is doubtful if this would suffice. Moreover there was a gap of nine months between the statement by John that he would leave Amanda the house and his death and in that time he had moved back to the house. In ***Vallee v Birchwood*** the fact that the donor continued to live in the house for

[9] Make it a habit to check for this point in questions on *donationes* of land. If you are in doubt about whether title is registered or not then do not worry – this is not a land law exam – but answer on the basis of both.

[10] Estoppel is of course a topic on its own, so in this type of question concentrate on the essential conditions for estoppel to apply.

[11] The reference to a decision of the House of Lords will boost your marks rather than the alternative of a bald mention of the need for a representation.

[12] Notice that this conclusion sums up the process by which we arrived at the answer: first the lack of a valid transfer; then an examination of how equity might assist; and finally, on the basis that equity could not assist, the identification of a destination for the property.

four months after the *donatio* was not, surprisingly, held to affect the fact that he had parted with dominion over it, but here John actually moves back into the cottage after the purported gift to Amanda. It seems that title to 'Rosemount' was unregistered as John has the title deeds.[9] As title appears to be unregistered, then as in *Sen v Hedley* and *Vallee v Birchwood* a *donatio* is possible although as dominion of the land was not parted with then it is suggested that there is in fact no *donatio*.

The final condition is that the gift must be conditional on death but John may have intended Amanda to have the cottage as an outright gift, as it is not clear whether at the time of the gift John intended to return there. In any event, as there was no parting with dominion there is no valid *donatio*.

The other possibility is estoppel.[10] John says to Amanda that he would like to give her the cottage for two reasons: she has been kind to him; and she has helped him to renovate it. Helping to renovate the cottage may amount to detrimental reliance by Amanda on a representation by John that he would leave her the cottage but, although in *Thorner v Major* [2009] UKHL 18[11] the House of Lords was prepared to accept various hints and remarks made by one party to the other over the years as amounting to an estoppel, there is no evidence of even these here. Nor do we know the extent to which Amanda did help John: trivial acts will not be enough.

In conclusion, as there was no valid transfer of the cottage by John to Amanda and as none of the ways in which equity might assist Amanda apply, when John died the cottage formed part of his estate and so will pass to Anita.[12]

 Make your answer stand out

- Make reference to academic discussion, e.g. Baker (1993) on *donationes* where the decision in *Sen v Headley* is considered.
- Refer to the article on *Vallee v Birchwood*: Panesar (2013) and mention the apparent relaxation of the 'contemplation of death' rule in this case and in *King v Dubrey* [2014] EWHC 2083 (Ch).
- Include further discussion of *Thorner v Major* – see e.g. Dixon (2009).

- Consider other cases on constitution, e.g. *Jones* v *Lock* [1865] 1 Ch App 25 HC, which you can compare with *Richards* v *Delbridge*.
- Mention that if title to land is registered, then the Singapore High Court held in *Koh Cheong Heng* v *Ho Yee Fong* [2011] SGHC 48 that a *donatio* is possible.

! Don't be tempted to . . .

- Start the answer without checking first whether there has been an invalid transfer. It is very likely that there will have been, but you will lose marks if you miss this out.
- Forget to distinguish between the two methods of constitution.
- Mention *donationes* or estoppel unless you have first satisfied yourself that the trust/gift has not been constituted.
- Go into great detail on estoppel.

? Question 2

Luke died intestate last month. He was not married and had no children. His niece and nephew, Babs and Norman, are his administrators and, together with 26 other nieces and nephews, are entitled to all the estate. You are asked to advise on the following claims against the estate:

(a) Babs tells you that Luke allowed her to borrow his car while she was a student at Newtown University. At the time, he said that he would transfer the car into her name but later, after Babs went to study for a year abroad, Luke started using the car again himself. Babs now finds that, whilst Luke filled out the vehicle registration documents, he did not send them off to the Vehicle Licensing Authority.

(b) Dan tells you that the day before Luke's death, he visited him and Luke said, 'I'm done for and will never leave this room again. Take this key to my strong box and you will have a nice surprise.' Dan took the key and, on opening the strong box, he found a jewellery box containing a diamond ring, Luke's car keys and a cheque for £1,000 made out to Dan.

Answer plan

→ Consider the possible application of *Strong* v *Bird* to the intended gift of the car.

→ If *Strong* v *Bird* is inapplicable then move on to consider the *Re Rose* principle and how the law stands now in view of *Pennington* v *Waine* to see if this can validate the transfer.

→ Next consider whether there is a valid *donatio mortis causa* by Luke to Dan of the diamond ring, car keys and cheque.

→ Remember to decide what will happen to the property in each case if the intended gifts cannot be upheld.

Diagram plan

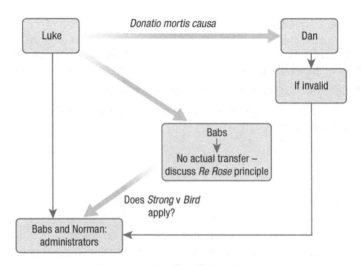

A printable version of this diagram is available from **www.pearsoned.co.uk/lawexpressqa**

Answer

[1] As it is always vital to find a home for the property, you can usefully make this point here.

The question is whether in any of these cases there is a valid transfer of the property from Luke to the intended transferees. If not, the property will form part of Luke's estate on his death and will pass to those entitled on his intestacy.[1]

(a) Luke allowed Babs to borrow his car while she was a student at Newtown University. At the time, he said that he would transfer the car into her name but did not do so. Later, after Babs went to study for a year abroad, Luke started using the car again himself. As Babs is one of the administrators under Luke's will, she may try to use the rule in **Strong v Bird** [1874] LR 18 Eq 315 HC to claim the car.[2] The rule states that if an incomplete gift is made during the donor's lifetime and the donor has appointed the donee his executor, then the vesting of the property in the donee completes the gift.

[2] If an intended transferee is also an executor/administrator then almost certainly you should mention and apply *Strong* v *Bird*.

[3] Watch for this point in exams but note that there is some doubt as to whether the rule in *Strong* v *Bird* can apply where there is an administrator rather than an executor.

[4] This is a very common exam point – watch for it as it means that the rule in *Strong* v *Bird* will not apply and you will have to look elsewhere to see if the gift can be saved.

[5] This is a good example of how to earn extra marks: the question obviously involved *Strong* v *Bird* and most students will probably spot this. However, the extra information concerning Luke's failure to send the documents off to the Vehicle Licensing Authority does not seem to affect the application of *Strong* v *Bird* as we have *already* decided that it will not apply. Therefore, this information must relate to something else.

[6] In cases involving the *Re Rose* principle you must now always follow *Re Rose* with this case and explain how the reasoning in it differs from that in *Re Rose*.

[7] We have given fairly full details of the facts of this case. This is because it involves the question of whether conduct was unconscionable and this often turns on the details of each case.

[8] This is the kind of detail which impresses examiners as it shows that you have read the judgments in the case. It was the reasoning of Clarke LJ which differed although he concurred with the result.

The rule may be said to rest upon the donor's intention but Babs was not appointed executor but administrator[3] and this is an important difference, as an executor is appointed by the testator but an administrator is appointed by the court. Thus there can be no question of Luke appointing Babs as administrator in order to perfect the gift to her. In *Re James* [1935] Ch 449 HC, the rule was extended to administrators. In *Strong* v *Bird* [1874] itself the rule was said to apply only to an executor and in *Re Gonin* [1979] Ch 16, Walton J would only have followed *Re James* with the greatest reluctance. If the rule does apply to administrators then the fact that Norman was also appointed administrator will not affect Babs's claim as the whole estate vests in each administrator (*Re Stewart* [1908] 2 Ch 251 HC). However, what will be fatal to Babs's claim under *Strong* v *Bird* is that after Babs went to study for a year abroad, Luke started using the car again.[4] This is because the rule only applies where the donor has a continuing intention to make an immediate gift (*Re Gonin*) and here the fact that he starts to use the car again shows that he does not.

The other point is that Babs now finds that whilst Luke filled out the vehicle registration documents, he did not send them off to the Vehicle Licensing Authority.[5] In *Re Rose* [1952] Ch 499 CA, Evershed MR added a kind of gloss on the principle in *Milroy* v *Lord* that, in order to constitute a trust, the settlor must have done all in his power to vest the legal interest in the property in the donee. Obviously, Luke did not as he did not send the documents off. However, in *Pennington* v *Waine* [2002] EWCA Civ 227, this rule seemed to be relaxed.[6] Mrs Crampton, a shareholder in a private company, told Pennington, a partner in a firm who acted for the company, that she wished to transfer some of her shares to her nephew, and she later signed a share transfer form to this effect and gave it to Pennington. He took no further action and the question was whether, on her death, the shares had been transferred to the nephew.[7]

The Court of Appeal held that they had, although the reasonings in the two main judgments differ.[8] Arden LJ upheld *Re Rose* but also held that the fact that there was clear evidence that Mrs Crampton intended an immediate gift of the shares amounted to an assignment of them to the nephew anyway. She held that, on the facts, it would be unconscionable to allow Mrs Crampton, in view of all that she had done to transfer the shares to the nephew, to then turn round and change her mind and say that they were not his. Thus, it may be that in this case the court could hold that it would be unconscionable for Luke to have said that the car still belonged to him but this is very doubtful as he started using it again, showing that he may well have changed his mind about giving it to Babs, and there really does not seem to be any evidence that it would actually be unconscionable if the car went to Babs and not to the estate.

(b) The question is whether there is a valid *donatio mortis causa* by Luke to Dan of the diamond ring, car keys and cheque. The cheque can be eliminated now, as it cannot pass by a *donatio*.[9] The reason for the exclusion of cheques is that the donor's death terminates the bank's authority to pay on it (***Re Beaumont*** [1902] 1 Ch 889 HC). A holder for value may sue, but in this case there will, by definition, have been a contract and the rules on *donatio* will be inapplicable. A possible exception to this rule is where a cheque is paid immediately after death before the banker has been told of the death and closed the account (***Tate v Hilbert*** [1793] 30 ER 548 HC). In this case there would be a *donatio* of the money represented by the cheque and not of the cheque itself. So Dan should be quick![10] The ring and car can pass by *donatio* provided that the conditions are satisfied.

The first is that the donor must have contemplated death in the near future.[11] In ***Vallee v Birchwood*** [2013] EWHC 1449 (Ch), it was held that the test is not whether the donor expected death but whether he or she contemplated it. This seems to be the case as Dan visited Luke the day before his death and Luke said, 'I am done for and will never leave this room again.'

Second, the subject matter of the gift must be delivered to the donee in the lifetime of the donor with the intention of parting with dominion over it. In ***Woodard v Woodard*** [1995] 3 All ER 580 CA, a donor gave his son the keys to his car and said to him, 'You can keep the keys. I won't be driving it anymore.' Even though he retained another set of keys, it was held that these words indicated that he intended to part with dominion over the

[9] In a problem question on *donatio* watch for a cheque appearing. If so, you can eliminate *donatio* at once.

[10] This extra discussion should bring a bonus in marks as it shows the examiner that you know exactly why there cannot normally be a *donatio* of a cheque.

[11] When you get a problem question involving a *donatio mortis causa* you should apply each point in turn to the question as marks will be allocated to knowledge of each.

car. Here the keys are in a strong box to which Dan is given the keys and this should be sufficient delivery of both the car and the ring.

[12] This point often arises: the donor does not say that the gift is conditional but in these circumstances this can be inferred. Be confident in your advice here.

Finally, the gift must be conditional on death in that the donor intends to keep the gift if he recovers. The courts may infer an intention where there are no words indicating a gift and the gift is made when the donor is *in extremis* (**Re Lillingston** [1952] 2 All ER 184) and it is suggested that this would be the case here.[12] Thus it is submitted that there is a valid *donatio* of the ring and of the car but the money represented by the cheque remains in Luke's estate and will pass to those entitled on his intestacy.[13]

[13] Note that we always need to decide where the property will go.

 ## Make your answer stand out

- Reference to Kodilinye (1982). There is little published on *Strong* v *Bird* and you will find this research should add to your marks.
- Look in more detail at *Re Gonin* – this decision deals with a number of areas.
- Read and refer to Doggett (2003), who examines the decision in *Re Rose* in the light of *Pennington* v *Waine.*
- Look at the discussion on parting with dominion of land in cases of *donationes mortis causa* in *Vallee* v *Birchwood.* Although the case concerned land it also considers what *dominon* means in general.
- Articles on cases on *donatio* – there were a number on *Sen* v *Headley,* e.g. Baker (1993).

Don't be tempted to . . .

- *Assume* that the rule in *Strong* v *Bird* can apply to administrators.
- Apply *Re Rose* without also discussing *Pennington* v *Waine.*
- Neglect to go through all the conditions for a valid *donatio.*
- Say that a cheque can pass by *donatio.*

Question 3

Critically examine the situations when equity will and will not perfect an apparently imperfect gift and assess whether there is any clear rationale behind them.

Answer plan

→ Explain clearly what is meant by an 'imperfect gift', showing how equity 'follows the law'.

→ Explain what 'gift' and 'imperfect' mean.

→ Set out the rules in *Milroy* v *Lord* and show their relevance to this situation.

→ Distinguish between gifts and trusts.

→ Look at the three situations identified by Arden LJ in *Pennington* v *Waine* where equity will perfect an imperfect gift.

→ Conclusion: is there any clear rationale behind these cases?

Diagram plan

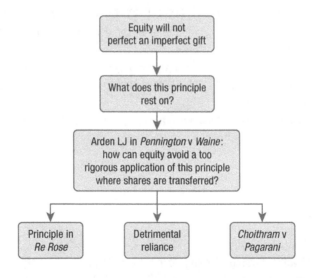

A printable version of this diagram is available from **www.pearsoned.co.uk/lawexpressqa**

Answer

[1] In this opening sentence you have set the scene by explaining what an imperfect gift is. A poor answer would have gone straight to the cases where equity has exceptions to this rule and actually perfects imperfect gifts, but start with the basic point.

[2] A discussion of this case scores marks in two ways: it gives an example of the fundamental rule; and shows knowledge of a recent application of the rule.

[3] Go back to basic principles and show the examiner that you are clear on them.

[4] A failure to appreciate this distinction often confuses students.

[5] Keep the focus on this area and do not stray into a general discussion of constitution of trusts. We have used the classification of Arden LJ as a basis for our answer but you could use other formulations of the cases where equity may perfect an imperfect gift.

The fundamental principle is that where there is a gift but the formalities have not been complied with, and which is therefore imperfect, equity will not aid in its enforcement as to do so would assist a volunteer.[1] This is an illustration of the maxim 'equity follows the law'. Equity, as with the common law, places great importance on consideration for the enforcement of contracts which is why equity follows the law, although its definition of consideration is wider as it includes marriage consideration. Where a person has not provided consideration for a promise they are volunteers and, as Lord Eldon said in **Ellison v Ellison** [1802] 31 ER 1243, 'Equity will not assist a volunteer.'

A modern illustration of this old rule is **Curtis v Pulbrook** [2011] EWHC 167 (Ch).[2] Pulbrook made two deeds of gift of shares in a company that he controlled which were effected by the execution of new share certificates and an entry in the company's share register. However, neither his daughter nor his wife, the intended transferees, received a stock transfer form. Pulbrook had misappropriated money from the bank account of T, his financial adviser, in payment of personal legal fees and T sought a charging order over the shares. However, Pulbrook contended that they were no longer his, legal title having passed to his wife and daughter. However, the court held that the shares were still his as the formalities for the transfers had not been complied with. As the intended transferees were volunteers equity would not compel the completion of what was an imperfect gift.

There are two vital terms: gift and imperfect.[3] In this context our focus is on outright gifts rather than declarations of trust[4] although we shall also deal with trusts.

Arden LJ in **Pennington v Waine** [2002] EWCA Civ 227 noted that 'the principle that equity will not assist a volunteer at first sight looks like a hard-edged rule of law not permitting much argument or exception'. Moreover, she observed that, 'The principle against imperfectly constituted gifts led to harsh and seemingly paradoxical results'. As a result, Arden LJ identified three ways where equity might, as she put it, 'temper the wind to the shorn lamb'.[5]

[6] It is important to make the connection between the basic rule in *Milroy* v *Lord* and what the court said in *Re Rose*.

The first derives from **Re Rose** [1952] Ch 499 CA, where Evershed MR added a kind of gloss on the principle in **Milroy v Lord** [1862] 4 De GF & J 264 CA.[6] In **Milroy v Lord** itself, Turner LJ indicated that a trust will be completely constituted when either:

(a) the settlor has vested the legal title to the trust property in the trustee(s); *or*

(b) the settlor has declared that he now holds the property as trustee.

[7] Note that we have once again made the distinction between gifts and trusts.

On the basis that neither of these has occurred, the principle in **Re Rose** is that in order to constitute a trust, or to perfect a gift in this context,[7] the settlor must have done all in his power to vest the legal interest in the property in the donee. The word donee reminds us that this principle can apply to trusts, where the intended trustee will be a donee, or to outright gifts. This case concerned possible liability to estate duty at the time when a transfer of shares was complete and it was held that the transfer was complete when the transferor executed the transfer as there was no more that the transferor could do. The principle was applied to land registration in **Mascall v Mascall** [1984] 50 P&CR 119 HC, and in **Zeital v Kaye** [2010] EWCA Civ 159 it was applied to an attempted transfer of a beneficial interest in shares where on the facts the transferor had not done all in his power.[8]

[8] There was a choice here of which case to mention in more detail. *Zeital* v *Kaye* won as it is more recent and also as it illustrates a different point of law: transfers of the beneficial interests rather than the legal one as in *Mascall*.

The second is where, as Arden LJ put it, 'some detrimental reliance by the donee upon an apparent although ineffective gift may so bind the conscience of the donor to justify the imposition of a constructive trust'. This applied in **Re Rose**[9] so that the beneficial interest in the shares passed when the share transfers were delivered to the transferee, and thus the transferor was a trustee of the legal estate in the shares from that date.

[9] We could have used another case to illustrate this point but why? The facts of *Re Rose* have already been given and so it saves time to mention this one. You can then use this time to mention an extra point and earn those valuable extra marks!

[10] You do need to set the facts of this case out in some detail as there were two issues in this case and so you need to give sufficient detail of the facts to make the decision on each point understandable.

The third is where in Arden LJ's phrase by 'a benevolent construction an effective gift or implied declaration of trust may be teased out of the words used'. In **Choithram (T) International SA v Pagarani** [2001] 2 All ER 492, Mr Pagarani, in his last illness, executed a trust deed establishing a foundation which would act as an umbrella for four charities which he had established.[10] Immediately after he had signed, he stated that all his wealth, including shares in a number of companies, would now belong to the trust. He himself was one of the trustees. He told his accountant to transfer all his money to the trust but he failed to sign the necessary forms and the companies in which he held shares duly registered the trustees of the foundation as shareholders. After Pagarani died, his family claimed that he had not effectively transferred his wealth to the foundation, which accordingly belonged to them. The Privy Council's decision that the trust was constituted rested on two points:

(a) Pagarani had made a declaration of trust. He did not use the word 'trust' and his actual words appeared to indicate a gift but the context of the words clearly indicated a trust: he intended to give to the foundation and this body was a trust.

(b) It did not matter that the trust property was not vested in the other trustees as Pagarani had executed a solemn declaration of trust and it would be unconscionable to allow him to go back from this promise.

[11] Come back to the issue raised in the question at the end: what, if any, is the rationale for this area of the law?

One can see a tension in these cases[11] between trying to give effect to the wishes of testators and settlors, which clearly influenced the court in Pagarani, and trying to adhere to the principle that 'equity does not assist a volunteer' which itself seems to derive merely from a desire by equity to follow the law. Beyond this, as Arden LJ observed in **Pennington v Waine,** 'the cases to which counsel have referred us do not reveal any, or any consistent single policy consideration behind the rule that the court will not perfect an imperfect gift'. We can conclude that there is no clear rationale behind these cases and that they are just responses by equity to needs arising from different situations.

✓ Make your answer stand out

- Ensure that your answer is grounded on basic principles: what is meant by an imperfect gift? How is a trust constituted?
- Consider paragraph 62 of Arden LJ's judgment in *Pennington* v *Waine* [2002] EWCA Civ 227, which goes into more detail on the possible rationales for the rule that equity will not perfect an imperfect gift.
- Read and refer to the recent article on the *Re Rose* situation by Ollikainen-Read (2018).
- Doggett (2003), Halliwell (2003) and Garton (2003) discuss the two cases which are the main subject of this question. Make sure that you read and refer to at least one of them.

> **!** **Don't be tempted to . . .**
>
> ■ Just set out the facts of the cases without any discussion of the principles.
> ■ Discuss the cases without first setting out the basic law on constitution in *Milroy* v *Lord*.
> ■ Discuss *Pennington* v *Waine* without first setting out the *ratio* of *Re Rose*.

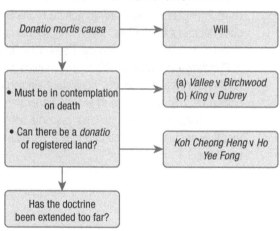 Question 4

'Recent cases have extended the doctrine of *donatio mortis causa* to such an extent that it is moving towards validating simple gifts.'

Critically evaluate this statement.

Diagram plan

Means of disposing of property on death

```
┌──────────────────────────┐        ┌──────────────────────────┐
│   Donatio mortis causa    │ ─────▶ │          Will            │
└──────────────────────────┘        └──────────────────────────┘
             │
             ▼
┌──────────────────────────┐        ┌──────────────────────────┐
│ • Must be in contemplation│ ─────▶ │ (a) Vallee v Birchwood    │
│        on death           │        │ (b) King v Dubrey         │
│                           │        └──────────────────────────┘
│ • Can there be a donatio  │
│   of registered land?     │ ─────▶ ┌──────────────────────────┐
└──────────────────────────┘        │ Koh Cheong Heng v Ho      │
             │                       │       Yee Fong            │
             ▼                       └──────────────────────────┘
┌──────────────────────────┐
│     Has the doctrine      │
│   been extended too far?  │
└──────────────────────────┘
```

A printable version of this diagram is available from **www.pearsoned.co.uk/lawexpressqa**

Answer plan

→ Describe the origin of the *donatio mortis causa* principle.

→ Explain how a *donatio* can override a gift in a will and note the wider issue of rules of equity setting aside rules of common law and statute.

→ Identify that the main issue is the requirement that a gift must be in contemplation of death and explain the existing case law.

→ Evaluate the cases of *Vallee* v *Birchwood* and then *King* v *Dubrey* and assess whether they have changed the law and whether this is justified.

→ Note the decision in *Koh Cheong Heng* v *Ho Yee Fong* on a *donatio* of registered land and ask why the doctrine was used here at all.

→ Conclude with some thoughts on how this area of the law might develop in future.

Answer

[1] We could have begun with the three requirements for a valid *donatio* but this would have led to a descriptive answer when what is needed for high marks is an analytical answer.

[2] It is quite acceptable to say '*donatio*' rather than '*donatio mortis causa*' in full. Another abbreviation is 'DMC'. Take your choice.

[3] This shows that you are thinking beyond just this particular area and looking more widely and setting your discussion in the context of equity as a whole.

[4] A poor answer would plunge straight into the details of the recent cases mentioned in the question but we have chosen to set the discussion in the context of the question as a whole. This makes sure that we bring out the principles involved rather than just focusing on the cases.

A *donatio mortis causa* has traditionally been used as a means of allowing a person to dispose of property informally when they contemplated death.[1] They were recognised by Roman law, and in English law the principle that such a gift could validly dispose of property was recognised soon after the passage of the Statute of Frauds 1677, which introduced strict rules for the validity of oral wills and effectively ended them. However, they are an anomaly as they enable property to be transferred without formalities and in effect to override gifts in a will.

Such gifts by *donatio*[2] need justification and the question whether they should be allowed has been given added importance by three cases which seem to have extended the operation of the doctrine. Moreover, this issue is of wider significance as it concerns the extent to which equitable principles should in effect nullify the operation of statutory requirements.[3]

The first two recent cases deal with the requirement that the donor must have contemplated death in the near future.[4]

Earlier cases such as **Hedges v Hedges** [1708] Prec. Ch. 269 held that the donor had to be dying (*in extremis*) but this restrictive view soon changed. Thus in **Walter v Hodge** [1818] 2 Swans 92, it was held that it was not 'necessary that the donation should be in the last illness; it is sufficient that it is made in contemplation of death'. So the donor must be expecting a near possibility of death, even though he or she may be healthy at the moment, rather than a general expectation that death will eventually come as it does to us all. In fact the interval between the gift and death is often short: in **Re Craven's Estate** [1937] Ch 423 HC it was five days; in **Sen v Headley** [1991] 2 WLR 1308 CA it was three days; and in **Woodard v Woodard** [1995] 3 All ER 580 CA it was three days.

5 This paragraph does two things: it raises a crucial issue in the context of this question and it supports it by a simple example. It also relates directly to the question. This is good examination technique.

This is important, as if gifts were allowed when there was no real contemplation of death then the law would simply be allowing informal gifts. Suppose that a person reached the age of 90 in excellent health, he could then dispose of his estate by informal gifts on the basis that anyone over 90 must contemplate death.[5]

The question is whether the High Court in **Vallee v Birchwood** [2013] EWHC 1449 (Ch) HC extended the circumstances when a person could be said to be in contemplation of death too far. The donor was visited in August by his daughter, who lived in France. She had been adopted by others and so had no rights of intestate succession to his estate. She found him 'quite unwell' and 'coughing' but no diagnosis was discussed. He referred to her next visit at Christmas and said that 'he did not expect to live very much longer and may not be alive then' and then told his daughter that he wanted her to have his house when he died. He then handed over to her the title deeds and a key to the house. He died four months later and the *donatio* was upheld.

The obvious question is why equity should enforce such a promise given that the donor had plenty of time to make a will. Moreover, the court emphasised that 'the case law requires only that the gift be made in the *contemplation* and not necessarily the *expectation* of death'. Thus it held that 'the question is not whether the donor had good grounds to anticipate his imminent demise . . . but whether the motive for the gift was that he subjectively contemplated the possibility of death in the near future'.

6 It is difficult to see many clear principles in the law on *donatio*, which is why we have said 'there seemed' and not 'there was'. What may appear to be small points are in fact vital in building up an overall impression that you have fully mastered the topic.

This seemed to push the doctrine beyond previous cases where there seemed to be an understanding that although the criterion was a subjective belief that death is likely, this must have some factual basis.[6] In **Thompson v Mechan** [1958] OR 357 HC, it was held that contemplation of death from the ordinary risks of air travel was not enough as this was a cause that 'exists only in his [the donor's] fancy'.

7 This is an important point and shows lateral thinking: should estoppel be the right avenue for claims that occur when the donor is not terminally ill?

Moreover, the court in **Vallee v Birchwood** seemed to rest the doctrine on some general principles of unconscionability: 'I do not consider that Equity intervenes in such cases only out of sympathy for those caught out in extremis but rather to give effect to the intentions of donors sufficiently evidenced by their acts such that the conscience of the donor's personal representative is affected.' This is wider than estoppel as detrimental reliance is not required.[7]

This wide interpretation of what counts as contemplation of death was, however, rejected by the Court of Appeal in **King v Dubrey** [2015] EWCA Civ. 581 CA which held that In order for a *donatio mortis causa* to be established, the requirement that the donor should be in contemplation of death was not satisfied in a situation where an elderly donor was approaching the end of his natural life span, but had no reason to anticipate death in the near future from a known cause. **Vallee v Birchwood** was wrongly decided.

[8] This issue has less discussion as it is not the main theme but needs to be mentioned as the question asked about recent cases.

The last case deals with a different issue: can there be a *donatio* of registered land?[8] The above two cases concerned unregistered land but in **Koh Cheong Heng v Ho Yee Fong** [2011] SGHC 48, the Singapore High Court indicated that a *donatio* of registered land was possible. However, with the disappearance of Land Certificates it is not clear what could be handed over to represent delivery of the subject matter of the gift. Moreover, this case raised a fundamental issue: why was the question of *donatio* in issue at all? The parties were married and the flat where they lived was in the donor's name. The donor's health deteriorated and so he transferred his interest in the property to himself and his wife as joint tenants to provide for her in case he predeceased her. This seemed perfectly valid and there appeared no need for the doctrine of *donatio* to be invoked at all.

[9] Short, memorable quotes such as these always add marks to your answer provided that you integrate them into it as we have done here.

[10] It is a good idea to end an answer such as this one with a practical suggestion about how the law might be taken forward.

Thus in two recent cases the idea of what is in 'contemplation of death' has been considerably extended and in the third the doctrine has been used when it need not have been. Baker (2002) has observed that the rules on *donatio* have 'characteristically developed slowly and haphazardly'.[9] Is there a need for a complete restatement of them so that they are not extended to become almost an automatic means of elderly people leaving property without a will?[10] Such a restatement could ask if the rules on *donatio* should be restricted to cases where the donor is terminally ill and explore whether alternative means of rewarding donors such as by the use of proprietary estoppel would be more effective.

Make your answer stand out

- Ask if there are policy elements in these recent decisions. In *Vallee* v *Birchwood* the alternative claimants were distant relatives. Research the case to see the way in which the relatives were found. With the increasing use of the Internet to search for potential claimants, are 'heir hunters' becoming more prevalent?

- Look at alternative claims such as estoppel and one based on the Inheritance (Provision for Families and Dependants) Act 1975. Look at the facts of the cases mentioned in the answer and ask if these would have been more appropriate.

- Locate your answer within fundamental equitable principles such as the maxim that 'equity does not allow a statute to be used as an instrument of fraud'. Could this be applicable here?

- Do some research in the cases on *donatio*: they are usefully collected in Borkowski (1999). You could then either add them to this answer or, preferably, substitute those which you consider more appropriate for those mentioned here.

- Look at articles on important cases – e.g. Brook (2014) on *King* v *Dubrey* and Cumber (2016).

 Don't be tempted to . . .

- Just go through the requirements for a valid *donatio*.

- Spend too long on individual cases without drawing out the actual point which was decided. It is easy to get immersed in the facts of cases in this area, as many of them are memorable.

- Neglect to explain the idea behind allowing *donationes* in the first place.

- End without putting forward some ideas for the future.

@ Try it yourself

Now take a look at the question below and attempt to answer it. You can check your response against the answer guidance available on the companion website (**www.pearsoned.co.uk/lawexpressqa**).

> Do the decisions in *Choithram* v *Pagarini* [2001] 2 All ER 492 and *Pennington* v *Waine* [2002] EWCA Civ 227 taken together represent a liberalisation in the requirements for constitution of a trust? Do you consider that this is a welcome development?

www.pearsoned.co.uk/lawexpressqa

Go online to access more revision support including additional essay and problem questions with diagram plans, 'You be the marker' questions, and download all diagrams from the book.

Secret and half-secret trusts; mutual wills

6

How this topic may come up in exams

This is often a problem question topic where there is a mix of fundamental points which all students should get and less obvious ones which give you an opportunity to spot them and gain those vital extra marks. There can also be an essay question on why secret trusts exist at all. In addition, as secret trusts can be considered constructive, a question on constructive trusts will also require you to mention secret trusts. Finally, you may get a question on mutual wills which has generated a number of recent cases and which also provides material for a discussion of constructive trusts.

Before you begin

It's a good idea to consider the following key themes of secret and half-secret trusts before tackling a question on this topic.

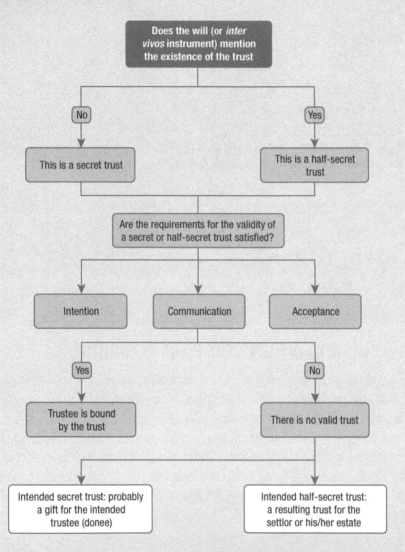

A printable version of this diagram is available from **www.pearsoned.co.uk/lawexpressqa**

❓ Question 1

Colin, a married man, was due to enter hospital for an operation and asked his friends, Ted and Sam, if they could help him over a 'private matter'. He told them that he had been married before, to Alice, but had never disclosed this to his present wife, Margaret, as he felt that she would disapprove. He wanted Alice to have something to remember him by and asked them if they would help. Ted said, 'Of course', but Sam just smiled.

The next day Colin executed his will which left £20,000 to Ted and Sam 'for the purpose which we have discussed' and £5,000 to Janet, a long-standing friend, absolutely. Sam witnessed the will.

Colin then wrote to Ted and Sam 'confirming what we have agreed – all to Alice'.

Colin then wrote to Janet asking her to hold the £5,000 'for the benefit of such people as shall be specified in a letter to be found in the top drawer of my desk'. He added, 'If you do not reply within a week I shall assume that you agree to this'.

Colin has now died. Janet has found a letter in his desk specifying that the £5,000 is to be divided, at Janet's discretion, among Colin's 'immediate family'.

Advise Steve, Colin's executor, on who is entitled to the gifts in Colin's will.

Diagram plan

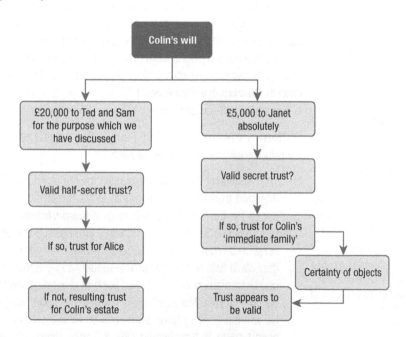

A printable version of this diagram is available from **www.pearsoned.co.uk/lawexpressqa**

Answer plan

→ Identify that the bequest to Ted and Sam is a half-secret trust.

→ State and apply the requirements for the validity of a half-secret trust.

→ Explain the significance, if any, of the fact that Sam witnessed the will.

→ Identify that the bequest to Janet is a secret trust.

→ State and apply the requirements for the validity of a secret trust.

→ Consider the certainty of objects point as applied to the bequest to Janet.

Answer

[1] Unless you are given any information to indicate otherwise, you should assume that the will is valid. Do not waste marks which you could get elsewhere by ploughing through the rules on formalities for making a will and capacity to make a will.

[2] The applicable law for each situation in a secret trusts question will be different, so it is best to deal separately with each.

[3] Always go to the words of the will first in a secret trusts question, as this will tell you if the trust is secret or half-secret.

[4] You will gain marks in a question on half-secret trusts if you spend time asking what the actual words used by the testator mean: trust or not?

[5] Note how information in the first paragraph has been used and analysed: often students ignore this first paragraph and so lose marks.

We can assume that Colin's will is valid[1] and so the question is whether the gifts to those actually mentioned in it will take effect or whether a trust will be imposed on Ted, Sam and Janet.

Taking the bequest to Ted and Sam first,[2] Colin's will[3] states that he has left £20,000 to Ted and Sam 'for the purpose which we have discussed'. This looks like a half-secret trust, which arises where property is left by will to a beneficiary but although the will states that the beneficiary is to hold on trust, the terms of the trust are not declared in the will but are agreed between the testator and beneficiary. Therefore, the will mentions the existence of a trust but not the terms of the trust. Here the word 'trust' is not actually mentioned but the words 'purpose which we have discussed' are similar to those used in ***Blackwell v Blackwell*** [1929] AC 318 HL.[4] So here there is a potential half-secret trust.

In ***Ottaway v Norman*** [1972] Ch 698 HC, Brightman J held that the following requirements must be proved:

(i) The intention of the testator to subject the primary donee (i.e. the intended trustee) to an obligation in favour of the secondary donee (i.e. the intended beneficiary). In ***Kasperbauer v Griffith*** [2000] WTLR 333 HC, Peter Gibson J emphasised that all three certainties must be satisfied. Here Colin asked Ted and Sam if they could help him over a 'private matter' and told them that he had been married before to Alice but had never disclosed this to his present wife, Margaret, as he felt that she would disapprove. He wanted Alice to have something to remember him by and asked them if they would help.[5] These words do not by themselves indicate any certainty of intention to create a trust, but Colin's will states that the £20,000 is left to them for 'the purpose which we have discussed' and so their conversation might have been more specific. Later, Colin wrote to Ted and Sam 'confirming what we have agreed – all to Alice'. This looks more like certainty of intention. There is certainty of subject matter (the £20,000) and objects (Alice).

(ii) The second requirement is communication of that intention to the primary donee. Where the trust is half-secret then the probable rule is that communication must occur before or at the time of the making of the will (**Re Keen** [1937] Ch 236 CA) and this was confirmed in the recent case of **Re Freud** [2014] EWHC 2577 (Ch).

In the conversation between Colin and Ted and Sam, communication seems tentative, and only after the execution of the will did Colin become explicit and say 'all to Alice'. However, he also uses the word 'confirming', indicating that at an earlier stage this intention had been communicated. Another explanation of the decision in **Re Keen**[6] is that communication must be in accordance with the terms of the will. Colin's will says 'for the purpose which we have discussed', so this means that any communication must be before the will, but here it is not clear if this is so.

(iii) The final requirement is acceptance[7] of the obligation by the primary donee either expressly or by acquiescence. We are told that Ted said 'of course' but Sam just smiled, and so Ted has accepted expressly and Sam probably by acquiescence.

If we assume that all three requirements were satisfied, the other issue is that Sam witnessed the will.[8] Attestation of a will by a trustee of a half-secret trust should not affect the validity of the legacy, and therefore of the trust, because he is not a beneficiary on the face of the will (**Cresswell v Cresswell** [1868] LR 6 Eq 69 HC) and so the trust in favour of Alice will be valid.

If the trust fails then the trustee cannot take beneficially.[9] Unlike secret trusts (see **Wallgrave v Tebbs** [1855] 20 JP 84 HC), the trustee of a half-secret trust cannot take beneficially if the trust fails. As Ted and Sam have been named as trustees, they will hold on a resulting trust for the testator's estate. An interesting but as yet

[6] You will gain extra marks if you also mention this alternative means of communication.

[7] Do not forget to mention acceptance – it is easily overlooked.

[8] There is clearly some doubt as to whether the trust is valid or not but it *could* be. This means that it is time to move on and gain more marks from another point, in this case the question of the witnessing of the will.

[9] Do remember to find a home for the property to round off your answer.

[10] This mention of an unresolved point of law shows your confidence in handling the subject matter.

[11] It makes for a much more logical answer if you deal with each bequest separately.

[12] It is important to stress this, as it saves you having to set out the rules again. But remember where they do differ!

[13] Here is an excellent chance to earn extra marks, as there is a certainty of objects point. You do not need to answer it in the same detail as you would if this was a certainties question but you must deal with it.

[14] Again, do not ignore acceptance.

unresolved issue is the position where the trustee is himself the residuary legatee.[10]

The second possible trust results from the bequest of £5,000 to Janet absolutely.[11] This will be a secret trust as this arises where a will states that property is left to a beneficiary as an absolute gift, but the testator has agreed with the beneficiary that the beneficiary is to hold the property as trustee. There is therefore no mention in the will of any trust.

There are the same basic requirements for the validity of a secret trust as for a half-secret trust.[12] Colin asked Janet to hold the £5,000 'for the benefit of such people as shall be specified in a letter to be found in the top drawer of my desk' and after Colin died, Janet found a letter in his desk specifying that the £5,000 is to be divided at Janet's discretion, among Colin's 'immediate family'.[13] Although there seems to be certainty of intention with the words 'hold for the benefit of' and the subject matter of £5,000 is certain, there is a problem with certainty of objects: who are Colin's 'immediate family'? This is a discretionary trust as indicated by the word 'discretion' in the gift and so the test for certainty of objects is that laid down in *McPhail v Doulton* [1971] AC 424 HL: can it be said with certainty if a person is or is not a beneficiary? It is submitted that evidence could be brought to show who Colin's immediate family are.

If so, the question is then whether there has been communication. Where the trust is secret, communication must take place and the details of the trust must be communicated to the legatee before the testator's death (*Wallgrave v Tebbs*). It does not matter whether communication is before or after the will.

However, it also appears that the secret trust can be enforced if the legatee is not actually told its details *before* the testator's death but is told where to find them after his death (*Re Keen*) and this is what seems to have happened here, as Colin then wrote to Janet asking her to hold the £5,000 'for the benefit of such people as shall be specified in a letter to be found in the top drawer of my desk' and this is where she found the letter with details of the trust.

Finally, although Janet did not expressly accept the trust, she did so by implication[14] in that she complied with his statement that 'if you do not reply within a week I shall assume that you agree to this'. It is suggested that this trust is valid.

Make your answer stand out

■ Discussion of the standard of proof required for the existence of a secret trust: see Megarry VC in **Re Snowden** [1979] Ch 528 HC. This is only a short point but it is a practical one and can easily be integrated into your answer.

■ A brief mention of whether the law should actually enforce half-secret trusts at all. The reason is that if they were *not* enforced then there would still be no question of the trustees committing a fraud as they could not take beneficially because a trust had been declared in the will.

! Don't be tempted to . . .

■ Just set out the rules on the validity of secret and half-secret trusts and not apply them.
■ Ignore the certainties points.
■ Only mention one rule on communication of a half-secret trust.
■ Fail to mention what happens to the property if the trust fails.

❓ Question 2

On 13 March 2019, Eileen met her friend Vincent and his wife Anne at a party. Vincent had acted as her solicitor for many years but was also a personal friend. She said to them, 'Here is an envelope containing instructions for my will. I know that this is an odd time to give this to you but of course you are my friends as well as Vincent being my solicitor.' Vincent nodded but Anne, who is very deaf, did not hear. When Vincent arrived home and opened the envelope he found that he and Anne were left £30,000. The letter then said, 'Half is for you and Anne and I wish you both to hold the other half on trust for my two grandsons, James and Philip. I also want you both to hold my house "The Larches" on trust for my niece Teresa.' Vincent was named as sole executor.

John, a solicitor in another firm, then saw Eileen who confirmed that these were her wishes.

Eileen executed the will on 15 March. It left £30,000 and 'The Larches' to Vincent and Anne absolutely. The will was witnessed by James and also by Robert and Aidan, two residents of the care home where Eileen lived.

Philip died on 2 April 2019. Eileen died on 1 July 2019.

Vincent asks you, as a professional colleague, to advise him on who is entitled to the gifts in Eileen's will.

Answer plan

→ Identify that the bequest to Vincent and Anne is a secret trust.

→ State and explain the requirements for the validity of a secret trust.

→ Identify the certainty of intention point in this part of the question and explain how it could affect the outcome.

→ Consider the relevance of the fact that Vincent is a solicitor.

→ Apply the rule in *Re Stead*.

→ Note that the will was witnessed by a beneficiary.

→ Note that a beneficiary predeceased the testator.

→ Note that it is a trust of land and explain how this could affect its validity.

Diagram plan

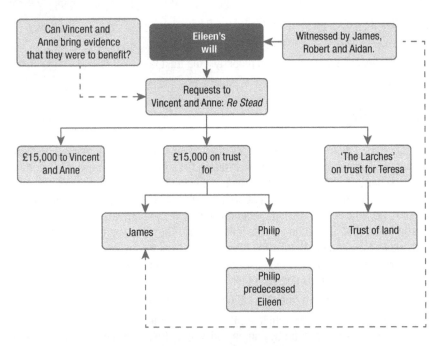

A printable version of this diagram is available from **www.pearsoned.co.uk/lawexpressqa**

Answer

We can assume that Eileen's will is valid[1] and so the question is whether the gifts to those actually mentioned in it will take effect or whether a trust will be imposed on Vincent and Anne.

Eileen's will states that she has left £30,000 and 'The Larches' to Vincent and Anne absolutely.[2] This will be a secret trust as this arises where a will states that property is left to a beneficiary as an absolute gift, but the testator has agreed with the beneficiary that the beneficiary is to hold the property as trustee. Here there is no mention in the will of any trust.

In **Ottaway v Norman** [1972] Ch 698 HC, Brightman J held that the following requirements must be proved:

(i)   The intention of the testator to subject the primary donee (i.e. the intended trustee) to an obligation in favour of the secondary donee (i.e. the intended beneficiary). Here Eileen said to Vincent and Anne, 'In [my will] you are left £30,000. Half is for you and Anne and I wish you to hold the other half on trust for my two grandsons, James and Philip. I also want you to hold my house "The Larches" on trust for my niece Teresa.'

The problem is where Eileen uses the words 'I wish you to hold' in the gift to James and Philip.[3] The word 'wish' may not indicate a trust as in **Suggitt v Suggitt** [2011] EWHC 903 (Ch), where the words were: 'And I express the wish (without imposing a trust)'. However, it is important to look at the gift as a whole (**Comiskey v Bowring-Hanbury** [1905] AC 84) and here the word 'trust' is used later and so it is clear that there is an intention to create a trust of £15,000. The intended trust of 'The Larches' is clear as the words are: I want you to hold on trust. There is certainty of subject matter: £15,000 and 'The Larches'.[4] The objects are James and Philip. Teresa is the object of the trust of the house.

Can Vincent and Anne bring evidence that they were intended to be beneficiaries as any evidence will be extrinsic to the will?[5] This is important as Vincent is a solicitor although it was another solicitor, John, who drew up the will. In **Re Rees' Will Trusts** [1950] Ch 204 HC, Evershed MR said, 'In the general public

---

[1] There is no evidence that the will is *not* valid and it would be unusual to have to deal with the validity of wills in a trusts exam as this is part of the law of succession.

[2] The word 'absolutely' in a question like this indicates a secret trust as there is no evidence of who the intended beneficiaries are and so it appears on the face of the will that there is a secret trust.

[3] This is a good example of how a certainties point can appear in a secret trusts question. Make sure that you address it. Note how a recent decision has been used as an authority. This always impresses an examiner.

[4] This point is quite straightforward but you do need to mention it.

[5] Always check if the gifts under the secret or half-secret trust include ones to the trustees – if so, you will need to mention these cases and here you can show knowledge of a recent one which has clearly inspired this question.

interest it seems to me desirable that if a testator wishes his property to go to his solicitor and the solicitor prepares the will, that intention on the part of the testator should appear plainly on the will and should not be arrived at by the more oblique method of what is sometimes called a secret trust.' Thus the court refused to allow extrinsic evidence to be admitted that the trustees, who included a solicitor, were intended, after certain payments had been made, to hold any surplus for themselves, but here there is a straightforward gift to Vincent and Anne. In **Re Tyler's Fund Trusts** [1967] 1 WLR 269 HC, Pennycuick J found difficulty with **Re Rees** and it was considered in **Re Freud** [2014] EWHC 257. Here the will contained a bequest to the testator's solicitor and it was recognised that 'one reasonable explanation for a clause which confers a beneficial gift on a solicitor is that the testator intended to impose a fully secret trust', which may have been so here. Whilst the court accepted that Evershed MR's words in **Re Rees** required it to be vigilant, it did not see this as an obstacle to admitting evidence that the solicitor was intended to benefit and it is suggested that there is no reason why Vincent and Anne cannot bring evidence that they were intended to be beneficiaries. It should also be noted here that as John, and not Vincent, prepared the will, this not only distinguishes this case from **Re Rees** but also will operate as a defence to any claim that Vincent was guilty of undue influence.[6]

[6] Where a problem contains many separate issues, as here, we need to deal with them succinctly: here we have dealt with two in one sentence. Practise this skill.

[7] Note how in this answer we have only mentioned the relevant part of the decision in Re Stead: resist the temptation to set it out in great detail regardless of whether all of the decision is relevant to the question!

[8] It is likely that in a trusts exam this point will not be a difficult one: the existence or lack of existence of words of severance will be made fairly clear and marks will not be gained by a detailed discussion of this point. This is not a land law exam!

(ii) Communication of that intention to the primary donee. Where the trust is secret, as here, the details of the trust must be communicated to the legatee before the testator's death (**Wallgrave v Tebbs** [1855] 20 JP 84 HC). Vincent heard the details of the trust but Anne is deaf and did not hear. Whether Anne is bound depends on the application of **Re Stead.** This provides that[7] communication to one joint tenant before the execution of the will binds the other. Vincent and Anne are joint tenants as there are no words of severance[8] in the gift in the will to them and communication appears to have been made to Vincent before the execution of the will. It is submitted that Anne is bound as well as Vincent.

(iii) Acceptance of the obligation by the primary donee either expressly or by acquiescence. Vincent said, 'Whatever you wish dear, we'll do what we can', and so he seems to have agreed to act as a trustee and Anne is bound on the basis of *Re Stead.*

[9] Leave these points until you have established that the trust satisfies the requirements for its validity.

There are three other points.[9] Firstly James, as a beneficiary under the secret trust, witnessed the will although there were two other witnesses, Robert and Aidan. In *Re Young* [1951] Ch 344 HC, the beneficiary under a half-secret trust had witnessed the will which declared the existence of the trust. The rule that a witness to a will cannot normally take a legacy (Wills Act 1837, section 15) was held not to apply here because the beneficiary did not take by virtue of the gift in the will but by virtue of the half-secret trust. The result would of course have been the same had the trust been secret, and so James can take a benefit. In addition, as there were two other witnesses, it would be possible to disregard the signature of James.[10] This is because section 15 of the Wills Act, which provides that a witness cannot take a benefit under a will which either the witness or his/her spouse or civil partner attested, as amended provides that where there are more than two witnesses then the signature of the witness who is a beneficiary is ignored.

[10] Always check how many witnesses there are – if there are three then you will know why!

Secondly Philip has predeceased Eileen, the testator. In *Re Gardner (No 2)* [1923] 2 Ch 230 HC, one of the beneficiaries under a secret trust predeceased the testatrix but it was held that the share of the deceased beneficiary did not lapse but passed to her personal representative. This decision has been doubted in most of the leading textbooks and thus it is doubtful if *Re Gardner* would be followed. If it is not, then Philip's share would pass to Eileen's estate.[11]

[11] It is extremely unusual to have to say this in an answer but here the decision in *Re Gardner* is so generally disapproved that you need to mention this otherwise you will lose marks.

[12] Make it a habit to check at the start of any question on secret or half-secret trusts if land is involved. If so, you will have to mention this point.

Finally, as this is a trust of land, the question is whether the trust of 'The Larches' is required to be in writing to satisfy section 53(1)(b) of the LPA 1925,[12] which requires a declaration of trust of land to be evidenced by writing. However, constructive trusts are exempted from this requirement by section 53(2) and secret trusts are generally regarded as constructive. Thus writing is not required for this trust to be valid.

Make your answer stand out

■ Discussion of whether the rule in *Re Stead* should represent the law and what should be the rule instead: see Perrins (1972).

■ In *Re Freud* the court, having held that the solicitor could take beneficially, then admitted evidence that the solicitor was intended to benefit under a secret trust. Consider if this is relevant to this problem.

■ Discussion of why the questionable decision in *Re Gardner* was actually reached.

■ Discussion of whether secret and half-secret trusts are express or constructive. For one view see Perrins (1985) at p. 253.

■ Mention that *Re Young* may illustrate the point that secret trusts operate *dehors* the will – or do they?

 Don't be tempted to . . .

■ Spend time discussing whether the will is valid when there is nothing in the facts to suggest that it is not.

■ Set out the rules for the validity of these types of trusts in a lengthy fashion without applying the law.

■ Miss the certainty of intention point.

■ Miss the point that one trust concerns land.

Question 3

'Secret and half-secret trusts should be abolished.'
Critically examine this proposition.

Answer plan

→ Account for the origin of secret and half-secret trusts to assess the case for their validity.

→ Consider each type separately.

→ Explain one possible basis of secret trusts: prevention of fraud.

→ Then go on to look at another basis: valid declaration of an *inter vivos* trust.

→ How can half-secret trusts be justified?

→ Consider their practical use – is this a sufficient justification by itself?

→ Do they fulfil a social need?

→ Possible alternative: letters of wishes?

Diagram plan

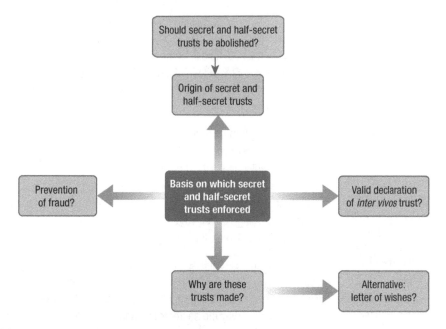

A printable version of this diagram is available from **www.pearsoned.co.uk/lawexpressqa**

Answer

[1] This is an excellent opening as it shows the examiner that you have a clear structure for your answer, based on looking at secret and half-secret trusts separately.

[2] You do need to state clearly what a secret trust is, but do this concisely and do not fall into the temptation of writing a general essay on them!

To assess whether secret and half-secret trusts should be abolished, we must begin by looking at their origin. Secret trusts can be traced to immediately after the passage of the Statute of Frauds in 1677, but the recognition of half-secret trusts came much later and their complete recognition can be said to date from **Blackwell v Blackwell** [1929] AC 318 HL. This is important as it means that the justification for both types need to be considered separately.[1]

A secret trust arises[2] where a will states that property is left to a beneficiary as an absolute gift, but the testator has agreed with the beneficiary that the beneficiary is to hold the property as trustee. There is therefore no mention in the will of any trust. The original justification for them was to avoid fraud which could occur where statutory provisions were not complied with, and so they are an example of the maxim that equity 'will not allow a statute to be an engine of fraud'. The Statute of Frauds 1677 imposed formal requirements even on oral wills of more than £3 in value and also on declarations of trust of land, and very soon after testators began to avoid these provisions by leaving property to a particular person but imposing a trust on them to hold it for the benefit of others. The first reported case is **Thynn v Thynn** [1684] 1 Vern 296.[3] The present law on the formal requirements for a will is contained in the Wills Act 1837 and specifically in section 9.[4]

[3] The reason for mentioning this case is its date, as it shows that in 1684, not long after the passage of the Statute of Frauds, the courts of equity were enforcing secret trusts.

[4] It is important to make this clear now, as you will be discussing the Wills Act later.

The clearest statement of the principle is found in the speech of Lord Westbury in **McCormick v Grogan** [1869] 4 App Cas 82 HL: 'the jurisdiction which is involved here is founded altogether on personal fraud'. Thus, if John, the testator, says to Susan,[5] 'I will leave you £1,000 absolutely in my will but you are to hold this sum on trust for my daughter Mary', then it would be a fraud on John if Susan were to disregard this and keep the money for herself.

[5] An example here does really help to clarify this point so do not be afraid to use it!

The principle that secret trusts are imposed to prevent fraud is indeed a strong reason for retaining and not abolishing them because otherwise the intended trustee would take beneficially.[6] However, it is not by itself a reason why the secret trust should be enforced in favour of the beneficiaries. A resulting trust in favour of the testator's estate would achieve the desired result by making sure that the intended trustee did not take.[7] A possible way round the difficulty is to give the word fraud a wider meaning as fraud on the beneficiaries through their not receiving their entitlement under the trust. The point seems to have been recognised by Lord Buckmaster in **Blackwell v Blackwell** [1929] AC 318 HL: 'the trustee is not at liberty to suppress the evidence of the trust . . . in fraud of the beneficiaries'.

[6] This is where you start to climb out of the average zone and earn those extra marks: an average student would stop at the end of the previous paragraph!

[7] More marks gained: you have not only criticised the law but suggested a solution.

The modern view is that secret trusts are enforced simply because the testator validly declared an *inter vivos* trust[8] and on the testator's death this trust became completely constituted by the property vesting in the trustee. Their essence is therefore the acceptance by the legatee of a personal obligation. Thus, Lord Warrington in **Blackwell v Blackwell** said, 'what is enforced is not a trust imposed by the will

[8] Do remember what this means: a declaration of trust between the living (*inter vivos*) as distinct from a declaration of trust in a will.

but one arising from the acceptance by the legatee of a trust communicated to him by the testator on the faith of which acceptance the
will was made or left unrevoked'. This principle is often expressed by
saying that secret trusts operate '*dehors* [outside] the will'. However,
the theory does not account for not imposing a resulting trust [9]
because the effect of this would usually be that the testator's family
received the property which, if the testator had intended to benefit a
mistress or an illegitimate child, would run counter to the obligations
imposed on the legatee. Critchley (1999) argues that the '*dehors* the
will' theory is wrong and points out that section 1 of the Wills Act
1837 provides that its provisions apply to 'any testamentary disposition' and she argues that this can include a secret trust.[10]

Critchley concludes that the fraud theory is still a possible justification
for the enforcement of fully secret trusts if certain conditions are met
but cannot explain the enforcement of half-secret trusts. Why is this
so? [11]

A half-secret trust arises where property is left by will to a beneficiary
but, although the will states that the beneficiary is to hold on trust, the
terms of the trust are not declared in the will but are agreed between
the testator and beneficiary. The result is that because their existence
is declared in the will, there is no possibility of the intended trustee
taking beneficially. The will states that he is a trustee. By the time that
the validity of half-secret trusts was accepted in **Blackwell v Blackwell** in 1929, the fraud theory had long been established and so
clearly this could not be their rationale. Thus the only possible justification for half-secret trusts can be that the testator has declared a
valid *inter vivos* trust. On this basis one could argue that whilst there
is a case for retaining secret trusts, half-secret trusts should indeed
be abolished.

Another way to assess if secret and half-secret trusts should be abolished is to ask if they fulfil a social need.[12] Both types of trusts have
traditionally been used where a testator does not wish his family to
know who is to benefit from his will, a familiar example being where
a man wished to leave property to a mistress of whom his wife was
unaware, as in **Re Keen** [1937] Ch 236 CA. There are other considerations too, as illustrated by Meager (2003) in an article based on a
postal survey in 2001 of solicitors specialising in wills and probate.
This shows that 35% of respondents had clients who had asked them

[9] The phrase '*dehors* the will'
is a well-known explanation of
secret trusts and you need to
mention it. Note also that you
have followed your statement
of the theory by also
criticising it – this is a sure
way to increase your marks.

[10] Although you will not, of
course, be able to quote
academic authorities at length
in an answer, it will help your
marks a great deal if you can
incorporate ideas from them,
as here.

[11] Here is where you look at
half-secret trusts separately.
Note again that we have
briefly said what they are but
without unnecessary detail.

[12] Here we break away from
technical legal arguments to
practical issues. This point,
and the research which
accompanies it, will certainly
gain marks.

about 'a secret testamentary bequest'. The article lists a number of reasons why these trusts are made, one being where a gentleman wished to make a gift to 'a lady friend' without causing her any embarrassment as she was in 'reduced circumstances'. This may be acceptable but what of another instance where a secret trust was suggested 'to make a gift for the benefit of a handicapped child on state-funded support so as not to break the personal asset threshold'. This brings us back to the fundamental question: should secret trusts be allowed, as the element of secrecy can allow a beneficiary to profit in a way which would not be possible were the gift made publicly. Is this right?

The issue of the possible abolition of secret and half-secret trusts ultimately rests on whether or not we see the importance of the wishes of the testator being carried out as paramount, even if it means disregarding statutory formalities. However, we should remember that there were good reasons for requiring formalities in the first place. However, now that the courts are upholding letters of wishes[13] one could ask if these could replace secret and half-secret trusts as vehicles for wishes that testators wish to be kept out of the will. The disadvantage of this is that the courts may, as in **_Breakspear_ v _Ackland_** [2008] EWHC 220 (Ch), order that the letters should be disclosed. In the end, why should testators have anything to hide anyway? There is certainly an arguable case for abolishing half-secret trusts and possibly secret trusts also.

[13] In this conclusion we are going to another area of trusts law and making a comparison. Try to think like this as in practice different areas are not pigeonholed and it certainly adds to your marks.

 Make your answer stand out

- Make more use of statistics from Meager (2003) to show the continued usefulness of secret trusts.

- Greater use of Critchley (1999) and her views of the theoretical basis of secret trusts.

- Explain another possible reason why secret and half-secret trusts should be retained: that they are a species of remedial constructive trust (see Chapter 8). This will help you to add depth to your answer by explaining exactly why the idea of a remedial constructive trust could be a possible basis for secret trusts.

- Look further into letters of wishes as a possible alternative to secret and half-secret trusts. These are considered in Chapter 11.

- Consider the issue from another angle: what if it is the testator who seeks to change the will and so disappoint the (secret) beneficiary? This is considered by Pawlowski and Brown (2004).

> ! **Don't be tempted to . . .**
>
> ■ Fail to set these trusts in their historical context.
> ■ Just state the law on what secret trusts are – this question is about the underlying principles behind them.
> ■ Fail to subject the theories which you mention to critical examination.
> ■ Forget to distinguish between secret and half-secret trusts – the trusts are different and so the reasons for enforcing them will also differ.
> ■ State theories and not test them against the evidence.

? Question 4

Mike and his wife Mary are happily discussing the future. They have two children, Bob and Sue. Mary says to Mike, 'I wonder which of us will die first?' Mike says, 'I don't know but now that you mention it I would like to make a will leaving all of my property to you for life and then after your death it will go to Bob and Sue. Then I think that you should do the same so that if you die first then all will go to Bob and Sue in the end.' Mary says, 'That is a good idea – let's do it soon. You never know what is round the corner.' Their house is in Mike's name and they have savings in a number of accounts, some held jointly. In addition, Mary has a large sum invested in shares which formed part of the estate of her late Aunt Maud and which she has inherited.

Mike and Mary come to you for advice on what the legal effect will be if they put into effect what they have agreed to. Advise them.

Diagram plan

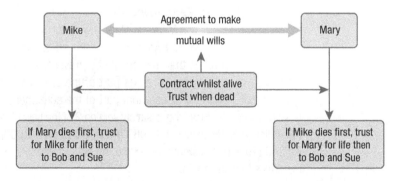

A printable version of this diagram is available from **www.pearsoned.co.uk/lawexpressqa**

Answer plan

→ Explanation of exactly what a mutual will is.

→ Explain the position where one party, Mike or Mary in this case, breaks the agreement to have mutual wills by revoking the will they have made, and consider the remedies and when they are available.

→ Mention that any will made can be revoked.

→ Then consider the position where the first spouse dies. Look at the part played by equity in holding that a constructive trust comes into existence and the problems which this causes.

→ End by advising Mike and Mary of alternative ways of putting their wishes into effect.

Answer

[1] Try for a clear and confident start like this. In these two opening sentences we have first answered the question directly by explaining that Mike and Mary should make mutual wills and then defined exactly what a mutual will is. In the process, we have gained a lot of marks for relatively few words.

The best way for Mike and Mary to put their wishes into effect would be for them to make mutual wills. These are where two people, having mutually agreed that the same person(s) should have their property after they are both dead, make separate wills, usually in which they leave property to each other, but which have the essential characteristic that there is a gift to the same agreed beneficiary and it is mutually agreed that the trust which arises cannot be revoked by the survivor.[1] Although each party's will is often in similar terms, as is intended to be the case here, there seems no reason why this should always be so in order for the doctrine of mutual wills to apply. In this case they both wish each other to benefit during their lives and the property to go to their children, Bob and Sue, after they have died.

[2] This is a vital point, which you must stress: if the parties have not agreed to make mutual wills then there cannot be mutual wills.

What is essential is that the agreement must make it clear that the wills are to be mutually binding and both are clear as to what making mutual wills involves (**Re Oldham** [1925] Ch 75 HC). It seems that the conversation between Mike and Mary may satisfy this requirement but this is not clear.[2] In **Re Oldham** the parties made wills in similar form but did not agree that they should be irrevocable and so they were not mutual wills. However, as part of the property concerns land[3] as Mike owns the house, that part of the agreement at least must be evidenced in writing to satisfy section 2 of the Law of Property (Miscellaneous) Provisions Act 1989 (**Healey v Brown** [2002] All ER (D) 249 (April) HC). It would, of course, be better if the whole agreement was then in writing.

[3] This point often arises in mutual wills questions.

The first question is what will happen if, while Mike and Mary are still alive, one of them revokes this agreement and makes a will in different

[4] Note how this question
requires knowledge of the law
of wills and then the law of
contract. Equity comes later.

terms? No action can be brought to restrain the actual revocation of
the mutual will because wills are always revocable (**Re Hey's Estate**
[1914] P 192 HC). However, under the law of contract the revocation
by either of them without notice to the other of a mutual will made in
pursuance of the agreement will be a breach of contract, and damages will be payable by the party in breach.[4] An action could probably
also be brought by Bob and Sue as beneficiaries under the Contracts
(Rights of Third Parties) Act 1999. This Act can apply as the agreement was entered into after 11 May 2000 but it will only apply if the
agreement can be construed as conferring a benefit on them as third
parties.[5] The oral agreement mentioned in the question certainly
shows an intention that they should benefit and it is suggested that
any written agreement should be made in the same terms so that they
can sue for breach.

[5] Do not *assume* that any third party can sue using this Act.

[6] This is a good practical point and worth making.

However, until the party in breach has died it is likely that any damages for breach of contract would not be substantial as at this stage
it is impossible to quantify the loss.[6] For example, if Mike made
another will leaving all his property to Sarah then if Mary sued him at
this stage it would be impossible to tell what the value of Mike's
property would be at the date of his death and thus what loss Mary
has suffered. The only case where there would be no right of action
would be if Mike's will was revoked by operation of law (**Robinson v
Ommanney** [1883] 23 Ch D 285 HC), as where he and Mary divorced
and he then remarried.

[7] This is a separate point and must be considered separately.

The same applies if the breach consists of a refusal by a party to
make a will.[7] If, for example, it was only found after Mike's death that
he has not left a will in accordance with the agreement, then damages
can be recovered from his estate as in **Robinson v Ommanney**
(above). Here also it is not clear how damages would be calculated in
these cases. In **Re Parkin** [1892] 3 Ch 510 HC, Stirling J referred to
the possibility also of an action for specific performance to complete
the transfer of the property.

[8] Note the point where equity intervenes and make this clear in an answer.

Suppose, though, that Mike dies and Mary inherits his property under
the terms of his will but then breaks the agreement for mutual wills
by revoking her will so that Bob and Sue are no longer beneficiaries.
Here equity intervenes,[8] as on the death of Mike, Mary holds the
property on a constructive trust for Bob and Sue. However, as under
the law of wills Mary is entitled to make another will then, if that will

[9] Do keep this point in mind: although the making of a will may be in breach of the agreement, the will itself can still be valid. What you have to do is then explain how equity resolves this. Note also that we have said 'if that will is valid', as if for some other reason it is not then the agreement is not broken as there is no will. This type of small but possibly significant point impresses examiners.

[10] This is an important and difficult issue. The law is by no means certain and you will gain marks by recognising this and setting out the possibilities.

[11] Although you may not have time to say much on this point, you will gain marks by showing that you are aware that it is a potential problem.

[12] This is a good way to end: it brings you back to the actual question and it is a practical point.

is valid,[9] any property will be held by the executors under a constructive trust for Bob and Sue.

What property is the subject matter of this trust?[10] This will primarily be determined by the agreement and obviously includes the property of Mike, which means that the house held in his name and any property in an account in his own name will be held on trust by Mary. The question is the extent to which Mary's own property will be held on trust. In **Re Hagger** [1930] 2 Ch 190 HC, it was held that the trust attaches to all the property which was held by the survivor, Mary, at her death. This means that any disposition by Mary would be in breach of trust. What then of property acquired by Mary after the agreement to make mutual wills? If the trust applies to this also then Mary is a life tenant of all the property standing in her name and is entitled to enjoy the income but the capital must be preserved for the beneficiaries. However, in **Re Cleaver** [1981] 1 WLR 939 HC, it was held by Nourse J that the survivor can enjoy the property as an absolute owner in her lifetime subject to a fiduciary duty which 'crystallised' on death. He held that a person in Mary's position was only disabled from making dispositions which were calculated to defeat the whole agreement, which in this case could mean selling the house, and that she could make gifts of small value. The problem then is that the actual subject matter of the trust is not certain.[11]

The final point is that, in view of the complications involved with making mutual wills, Mike and Mary might well be better advised not to make one and instead make joint wills which take effect as separate wills which can be revoked by either of them at any time.[12]

 Make your answer stand out

- Mention that in *Healey* v *Brown* it was suggested that if an agreement to make mutual wills involving land was not in writing then it would be unconscionable for the party in breach to rely on this.

- Note that by section 7(1) of the Contracts (Rights of Third Parties) Act 1999 the operation of this Act does not affect any other rights or remedies. This means that it is possible to use the trust basis as a means of enforcement also.

- Mention the theoretical basis of the enforcement of mutual wills: the prevention of fraud because any revocation of the mutual will after the death of the first to die would be a fraud by the survivor.

- Consider possible alternative ways of enforcing these obligations. One would be to use the reasoning in *Beswick* v *Beswick* [1968] AC 58 HL but this was not accepted in *Re Dale* [1994] Ch 31 HC.

- Mention that the constructive trust may not be the best solution: Hodkinson (1982) suggested that a floating charge could be imposed over the assets of the first to die.

! Don't be tempted to . . .

- Mix up the contractual, succession and equity issues. Make sure that you are clear where each arises.

- Begin before you have clearly explained what a mutual will is.

- Use this question as an excuse to write all that you know about mutual wills. Link your answer to the facts of the question.

- Omit any discussion of the problems in deciding what the subject matter of the trust is.

@ Try it yourself

Now take a look at the question below and attempt to answer it. You can check your response against the answer guidance available on the companion website (**www.pearsoned.co.uk/lawexpressqa**).

> Kate wished to make provision for her daughter Mollie in her will but did not want her husband Chris to know this as he strongly disliked Mollie. She asked her friends Sue and Mel if they could help over what she called a 'delicate matter' and they both said that they would.
>
> Kate then wrote to them both telling them that in her will they were left £20,000 on trust and that they were to hold this for Mollie.
>
> Sue received the letter but Mel did not.
>
> Kate executed her will on 8 March but on 9 March Mollie died. Kate herself died on 15 March.
>
> Advise Sue and Mel on whether they are bound by the trusts.

www.pearsoned.co.uk/lawexpressqa

 Go online to access more revision support including additional essay and problem questions with diagram plans, 'You be the marker' questions, and download all diagrams from the book.

Resulting trusts

7

How this topic may come up in exams

One area which is a favourite of examiners is the actual basis on which the courts impose a resulting trust. This requires you to be familiar with a number of theories and is a good opportunity for students who have done their homework on this to really shine. Another favourite is the extent to which presumptions play a part in deciding if there is a resulting trust or not and another is the Quistclose trust. In addition, a clear understanding of when resulting trusts can arise and of how they operate is essential in many other areas, as the case of *Prest* v *Petrodel Resources Ltd.* illustrates, and an area where there has been some recent activity is the precise effect of section 60(3) of the Law of Property Act 1925 (LPA 1925). Another important area where resulting trusts operate is when an unincorporated association is dissolved (which is considered in Chapter 10).

▍Before you begin

It's a good idea to consider the following key themes of resulting trusts before tackling a question on this topic.

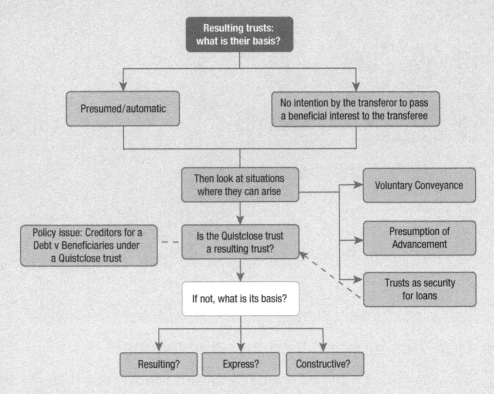

A printable version of this diagram is available from **www.pearsoned.co.uk/lawexpressqa**

Question 1

'The most difficult question one can ask about resulting trusts is why they arise.' (Swadling, 2008.)

Critically comment on this view.

Diagram plan

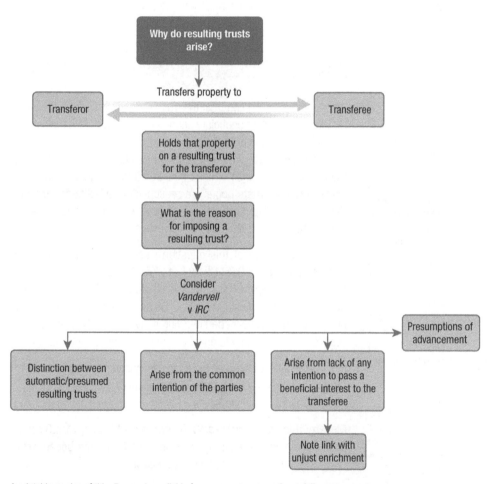

A printable version of this diagram is available from **www.pearsoned.co.uk/lawexpressqa**

Answer plan

→ Identify the main issue: what is the basis on which resulting trusts are imposed, when are they imposed and why?

→ Critically consider the classification of Megarry J in *Re Vandervell's Trusts* [1974] Ch 269 HC and the views of Lord Browne-Wilkinson in *Westdeutsche Landesbank Girozentrale* v *Islington BC* [1996] AC 669 HL.

→ Look at the theory of Chambers (1997) that resulting trusts arise from the absence of an intention by the transferor to pass any beneficial interest to the transferee.

→ Refer to the possible link between resulting trusts and unjust enrichment.

Answer

When there is a resulting trust the trust 'springs back' (from the Latin *resilare*), so that the beneficiary under the resulting trust is the person who made the transfer of rights in the property. The quotation in the question 'The most difficult question one can ask about resulting trusts is why they arise' means that although the circumstances in which resulting trusts occur are reasonably well settled, although there are some disputed areas, what has never been settled is exactly *why* a resulting trust should arise in these cases.[1]

[1] This is an excellent start as it directly engages with the precise issue raised by the question. You may not always choose to set out the exact words of the quotation in your answer but here it does help, especially as the quotation is short.

A clear explanation of this question was given by Plowman J in ***Vandervell v IRC*** [1966] Ch 261 at 275, 'A man does not cease to own property simply by saying "I don't want it". If he tries to give it away the question must always be, has he succeeded in doing so or not? If he has not succeeded in giving it away, it still belongs to him, even if he does not want it; and that, I think, is really the position here.'

It is this question of whether a person has indeed succeeded in transferring the beneficial interest that requires an examination of the theoretical basis of resulting trusts.[2]

[2] This is an important paragraph: it takes us from a discussion of the quotation in the question to a wider look at the basis on which resulting trusts arise.

Megarry J in ***Re Vandervell's Trusts (No 2)*** [1974] Ch 269 proposed two types of resulting trust and this for a time became the prevailing orthodoxy.[3] These were as follows:

[3] This classification of resulting trusts is not the end of the story but it is a good place to start. It is also useful as you are able to give some actual examples of resulting trusts to illustrate these categories, and this helps to anchor your answer to factual situations rather than becoming too theoretical.

(a) Automatic resulting trusts, where there was a resulting trust independent of the intentions of the settlor, as where the settlor has failed to specify the beneficial interests and so there is either a lack of certainty of objects or no objects at all, as in ***Vandervell***

v IRC. Vandervell had given Vandervell Trustees Ltd an option to purchase shares which he had transferred to the Royal College of Surgeons, but had failed to specify the trusts on which the shares were then to be held. There was thus a resulting, or what Lord Wilberforce in the House of Lords called an automatic trust for Vandervell. The beneficial interest, he said, could not 'remain in the air', therefore 'it remains in the settlor'.

(b) Presumed resulting trusts, as where a person transferred property to another without consideration but where no words of gift were used. These were considered to arise from the presumed intention of the transferor. Thus in **Re Vinogradoff** [1935] WN 68 HC[4] the testatrix had transferred an £800 War Loan which was in her own name into the joint names of herself and her four-year-old daughter. It was held that the daughter held it on a resulting trust for the testatrix.

[4] This particular case is easy to recall and is an excellent illustration of a resulting trust.

This view clearly distinguishes between two situations to which the law gives different answers. In the case of the automatic resulting trust there is an intention by the settlor, such as Vandervell, to create an express trust, but a failure to specify who shall receive the benefit. The second situation rests on presumptions: the initial presumption of a resulting trust, as in **Re Vinogradoff**,[5] which can then be rebutted by showing that there is a presumption of advancement, often known as a presumption of gift. One example is the presumption of advancement between parent and child.

[5] This summing up on the two possible types of resulting trusts will add to your marks: an average answer would have just set them out as above.

The classification of Megarry J was disapproved of by Lord Browne-Wilkinson in **Westdeutsche Landesbank Girozentrale** v **Islington BC** [1996] AC 669 HL,[6] who suggested *obiter* that resulting trusts were 'traditionally regarded as arising from the common intention of the parties'. Yet this cannot explain all cases of resulting trusts. For example, in **Re Vinogradoff** the transferor could not have intended that the granddaughter should be the trustee. Moreover, it risks resulting trusts being swallowed up by the notion of the common intention constructive trust, put forward by Lord Diplock in **Gissing** v **Gissing** (1971) AC 886 HL and used thereafter as a tool to resolve disputes about beneficial entitlement of the family home.

[6] Having mentioned Megarry J's two theories above, you need to follow it with this counter view.

However, the common intention constrictive trust was used as a vehicle for finding if there was a resulting trust in **National Crime**

Agency v Dong [2017] EWHC 3116 (Ch).[7] This concerned the application of section 60(3) of the LPA 1925, but for our purposes the court held that it is the common intention of the parties which is crucial in determining whether a resulting trust arises in the context of a voluntary transfer as opposed to the unilateral intention of the person making the transfer.

[8] What is essential in an essay in this area is to recognise that the law is not settled and to test a number of theories against each other. Here is another.

A different test suggested by Chambers in *Resulting Trusts* (1997)[8] is that all resulting trusts should be considered as arising from the presumption of the *lack of* any intention by the transferor to pass any beneficial interest to the transferee when the transferee has not provided the entire consideration for the property. Thus, as Chambers points out, the resulting trust operates to return specific property to the transferor because he/she did *not* intend to benefit the transferee. One example would be in a case where the objects of the trust were not sufficiently certain and so the trustee holds the trust property on a resulting trust for the settlor *precisely because* the settlor cannot have intended the trustee to benefit, as in **Vandervell v IRC.**[9] The advantage of this theory is that it fits all the cases where a resulting trust has been imposed because the one certain fact is that in none of them was the transferee intended to benefit. Its effect is to give presumptions a greater role than in Megarry J's classification as on the basis of this theory they operate in all cases of resulting trusts whereas Megarry J's classification saw no place for them where the trust was automatic.

[9] You will see that we have used this case before in this essay: it is often a good idea to do this: it saves time and impresses the examiner, showing that you can look at a case from more than one angle.

[10] This possible link between resulting trusts and unjust enrichment is worth stressing as it takes your answer slightly outside the average answer and is a very relevant point.

The theory of Chambers that resulting trusts respond to the lack of any intention to pass a beneficial interest to the transferee has been linked to the use of the resulting trust where one person has been unjustly enriched at the expense of another.[10] For instance if X pays £10,000 to Y under a mistake of fact, then Y has been unjustly enriched at X's expense and Y will then hold the money on a resulting trust to return it to X. This could potentially result in a great expansion of the use of the resulting trust but is open to the obvious objection that, if X is insolvent, then Y will, by virtue of her proprietary interest, take priority over X's creditors. Is this just?

In short, the quotation is correct: it is easy to recognise the situations when resulting trusts arise but so far we lack any generally accepted theory to explain the imposition of such a trust.

Make your answer stand out

- A clear recognition of exactly what a resulting trust is and what it does.
- Engage with the different theories of the basis of resulting trusts and recognise that there is no certain answer.
- Look at the suggestion of Lord Browne-Wilkinson in *Westdeutsche Landesbank Girozentrale* v *Islington BC* that a resulting trust should not arise until the conscience of the trustee is affected. Note the criticism of Chambers (1997) that this makes the imposition of a resulting trust depend on notice. What, he asks, is the position until the trustee has notice of the trust?
- Look carefully at Swadling (2008) who has a number of criticisms of the use of the term 'presumption' by Chambers, and who remarks: 'Before any progress can be made in the search for an explanation of resulting trusts, a secure understanding of presumptions is required.'
- Discussion of the extent to which presumptions of advancement are relevant today and a mention of the not yet in force section 199 of the Equality Act 2010. See Andrews and Parsons (2018).

Don't be tempted to . . .

- Just set out cases. Instead you must explain the theoretical basis for resulting trusts.
- Come to a very definite conclusion about the basis of resulting trusts. There is no theory which is very generally accepted and you will lose marks if you give the impression that there is.
- Spend all of your time discussing the theories behind resulting trusts and none on how they operate. Give your essay balance.

? Question 2

Daphne is the sole director and majority shareholder in Bluebells Ltd, which runs garden centres. Her husband, David, is bringing divorce proceedings against her. Daphne has transferred the legal title to their holiday home, Seacrest, from her name into the name of Bluebells Ltd for only nominal consideration.

Bluebells Ltd receives an order from Mega Ltd a large company, for flower displays to decorate its offices. Mark, the Managing Director of Mega Ltd, tells Daphne that he can only pay her when he receives a payment for a large order but that it will be made within a week of delivery of the flowers. Daphne is reluctant but she desperately needs the money because of her impending divorce and because her own business has been going through financial difficulties and so she agrees, provided that Mark's father, John, agrees to lend Mega Ltd £100,000 'for the sole purpose of paying Bluebells Ltd for flower displays supplied and for no other purpose'.

Daphne delivers the flowers but, despite John's loan, Mega Ltd goes into liquidation. The liquidator has taken over all its assets. Meanwhile David has commenced proceedings, arguing that Seacrest forms part of Daphne's assets.

(a) Advise Daphne on David's chances of success in her claim against him.

(b) Advise John on his chances of success in an action to recover the £100,000, explaining the relevant law fully.

Diagram plan

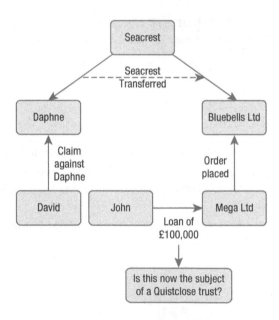

A printable version of this diagram is available from **www.pearsoned.co.uk/lawexpressqa**

Answer plan

→ Consider David's claim referring to the possibility that Daphne still has a beneficial interest in Seacrest on the basis that it is held on a resulting trust for him.

→ Note that this concerns land and consider the effect of section 60(3) of the LPA 1925.

→ Analyse the decision in *Prest* v *Petrodel Resources Ltd*.

→ Then move on to look at a possible action by John based on the principle in *Barclays Bank* v *Quistclose Investments Ltd.* and consider also *Bailey* v *Angove's Pty Ltd.*

→ Look carefully at the facts of this problem and compare them to those in *Re EVTR.*

→ Conclude by applying both your analysis of the facts and of the nature of the trust to the question.

Answer

(a) When Daphne transferred the legal title to the holiday home, 'Seacrest', from her name into the name of Bluebells Ltd for only nominal consideration it is arguable that this created a resulting trust in her favour. So although the legal title to 'Seacrest' is held by Bluebells Ltd, she has a beneficial interest under a resulting trust. There are no words of gift nor, of course, is there any presumption of advancement in favour of Bluebells Ltd.[1] and so a resulting trust will arise from the presumed intention of Daphne, the transferor as in *Re Vinogradoff* [1935] WN 68 HC.

There are, however, two other issues. One is that, unlike in *Re Vinogradoff,* this was a transfer of land and section 60(3) of the LPA 1925 provides that where, as here, there is a voluntary conveyance of land (i.e. the actual transfer is by gift or nominal consideration), a resulting trust for the grantor (i.e. the transferor) is not to be implied merely because the land is not expressed to be conveyed on trust for him.[2] One interpretation of section 60(3) is that, where, as here, there is no mention that the grantee (Bluebells Ltd) is to take 'Seacrest' beneficially then this does not *automatically* lead to a presumption of a resulting trust in the grantor's (Daphne's) favour as was held at first instance in *Lohia* v *Lohia* [2001] WTLR 101 HC. However, a resulting trust could still be found on the facts if Daphne establishes that no gift by her to Bluebells Ltd was intended. In fact, given that Daphne's motive may well have been to put her assets out of David's reach pending a divorce settlement, she will wish to show the reverse, that a gift *was* intended.

Another view of section 60(3) is that it is just a reminder to transferors of land that a resulting trust will not be implied *purely* because the transfer does not expressly state that the transfer is for the benefit of the grantee. On this basis there is still a

[1] In any problem question of this kind on resulting trusts watch for either of these as they may well prevent a resulting trust from arising.

[2] Watch in questions on resulting trusts to see if it is a trust of land. If so you will be expected to mention section 60(3) of the LPA and you will also need to assess the debates on what it means. Not easy but this is the approach for high marks.

presumption of a resulting trust on a voluntary transfer of land (**National Crime Agency v Dong** [2017] EWHC 3116 (Ch)).

Before we take this further we must note **Prest v Petrodel Resources Ltd** [2013] UKSC 34 SC.[3] This involved ancillary relief proceedings following a divorce where the wife (W) alleged that her then husband (H) had a beneficial interest in eight homes. He had transferred the ownership of these to companies which he controlled in return for nominal sums. If W's claim succeeded then H could be ordered to transfer the homes to her. No explanation had been given for why the homes had been transferred to the companies with only nominal consideration and so the presumption that the companies held them on a resulting trust for H would apply and W could claim them.

Much of the reasoning was on company and family law[4] but the court relied on the express allegation by W that H had used the companies to hold the legal title to properties which actually belonged beneficially to him and H did not rebut this evidence. Lord Sumption remarked, 'Whether assets legally vested in a company are beneficially owned by its controller is a highly fact-specific issue. But, in the case of the matrimonial home, the facts are quite likely to justify the inference that the property was held on trust for a spouse who owned and controlled the company.' Incidentally section 60(3) of the LPA was, surprisingly, not mentioned.

In this case David can allege that Daphne placed 'Seacrest' into the name of Bluebell Ltd so that it no longer counted as her assets in any divorce proceedings but she still had a beneficial interest in it. However, unlike in **Prest v Petrodel,** this was not the matrimonial home but a holiday home jointly used. Why, however, should a holiday home be placed in the name of a garden centre company? There is surely a presumption that Bluebells Ltd held this on a resulting trust for Daphne and so it will form part of her assets. Daphne will have to rebut this by evidence that she intended a gift of the home to Bluebells Ltd.[5] If section 60(3) is raised then if anything this would work in Daphne's favour, as it would make it more difficult to establish a resulting trust of the land forming 'Seacrest', but given the circumstances and the authority of the Supreme Court in **Prest v**

[3] This is the most recent Supreme Court decision in this area and you must be aware of it in questions on resulting trusts.

[4] Do not get sidetracked into areas that are outside trusts law, especially as in this case the result was eventually arrived at on trust principles.

[5] Some students will go off the point here by speculating what Daphne might say, but there is no point in this as we simply do not know. Also if we look ahead we will see that we still have to tackle another part of the question and so we must move on.

Petrodel Resources Ltd. it is unlikely that this would be an obstacle to establishing a resulting trust.

(b) John agreed to lend Mega Ltd £100,000 'for the sole purpose of paying Bluebells Ltd for flower displays supplied and for no other purpose'. As Mega Ltd has gone into liquidation, John is at risk of being an unsecured creditor and almost certainly being unable to reclaim his money. However, he may be able to claim[6] the return of the £100,000 under the principle in ***Barclays Bank Ltd v Quistclose Investments Ltd*** [1970] AC 567 HL.[7] Rolls Razor was in financial difficulties and declared a dividend on its shares but did not have the money to pay it and so Quistclose made a contract to make it a loan for the express purpose of enabling it to pay this dividend. The money was paid into a separate account at Barclays Bank and it was agreed with the bank that the account would 'only be used to meet the dividend due on July 24th 1964'. Before this was paid, Rolls Razor went into liquidation and the question was whether Barclays Bank could set the sum in the account off against Rolls Razor's overdraft or whether they held it on trust for Quistclose.

The House of Lords held that there was a trust for Quistclose, as the letter clearly indicated that the money was to be used to pay the dividend and for no other purpose. It followed that if, for any reason, the money could not be used for this purpose, then it had to be returned to Quistclose. Accordingly, it was held by Rolls Razor on trust for Quistclose.

The lending of money to purchase equipment, bearing in mind that in this context flowers count as equipment, can create a Quistclose trust[8] as in ***Re EVTR*** [1987] BCLC 646 CA the appellant lent £60,000 to a company to assist it in purchasing new equipment and the court held that the Quistclose principle applied and that the £60,000, less agreed deductions, should be held on a resulting trust for the appellant.

As Lord Millett put it in ***Twinsectra v Yardley*** [2002] UKHL 12: 'The question in every case is whether the parties intended the money to be at the free disposal of the recipient.' In this case it is clear that this was not so, as John lent the £100,000 so that

[6] It would be a mistake at this point to commit yourself and say that John 'will' be able to recover the money.

[7] You need to set out the facts of this case in sufficient detail to make any discussion which follows understandable.

[8] This is a crucial link in your answer. You need to make the connection between payments of money so that dividends can be paid, as in *Quistclose* itself, and payments of money to purchase goods as here and then go on to quote the relevant authority.

[9] Note how this conclusion achieves two objects: it provides a conclusion on the facts and it uses the reasoning on the nature of the Quistclose trust, as explained by Lord Millett, to explain how this happens.

Mega Ltd could obtain the flowers from Daphne 'and for no other purpose'.

It is suggested that, on the analysis of Lord Millett in ***Twinsectra v Yardley,*** the £100,000 advanced by John to Mega Ltd was held on an express trust for him as soon as he transferred it and that as the purposes for which it was lent were not carried out in full, this trust for John now takes effect.[9]

 Make your answer stand out

- Consider *Prest* v *Petrodel* in more detail and consider whether the SC analysed the resulting trust issue fully given that much of the judgments concerned company and family law. Assess whether the presumption of a resulting trust applied or not.
- Note that on Lord Millett's analysis quoted in this answer, the end result is an express trust yet *Quistclose* is often analysed as a resulting trust for the lender, John in this case, if the purpose fails, as it did here. Which view is correct? Does how the trust is categorised matter in practice?
- Consider in more detail where the beneficial interest lies in a Quistclose trust: does, as suggested by Chambers (1997), the borrower retain a beneficial interest in the money throughout the transaction? Note that this is at variance with the views of Lord Millett in *Twinsectra* v *Yardley* mentioned in the answer.

! Don't be tempted to . . .

- Just say that in part (a) there is a resulting trust: the mention of impending divorce proceedings should give you a clue that there is more than this.
- Go off at a tangent in part (a) and discuss company and family law.
- Just quote the *Quistclose* case and fail to analyse it in connection with the facts of the problem.
- Just say that a trust arises in these types of cases without considering what type of trust it may be.

Try it yourself

Now take a look at the question below and attempt to answer it. You can check your response against the answer guidance available on the companion website (**www.pearsoned.co.uk/lawexpressqa**).

'The common feature of resulting and constructive trusts is that, unlike express trusts, they are not created by the express agreement of the parties.'

Do you consider that this statement represents an accurate view of the law? In your answer, consider the distinctions between resulting and constructive trusts.

www.pearsoned.co.uk/lawexpressqa

Go online to access more revision support including additional essay and problem questions with diagram plans, 'You be the marker' questions, and download all diagrams from the book.

Constructive trusts and estoppel

8

How this topic may come up in exams

This topic is an absolute must for your revision as it comes up right across an equity exam. You may get essay questions on constructive trusts, the nature of a fiduciary, estoppel and on the particular area of the remedial constructive trust. Problem questions can deal with unauthorised profits made by a fiduciary, trusts of the home, estoppel and other topics. Moreover, knowledge of this area may be relevant in questions on the nature of equity, trustees, secret trusts, resulting trusts, breach of trust and really any area of equity.

■ Before you begin

It's a good idea to consider the following key themes of constructive trusts and estoppel before tackling a question on this topic.

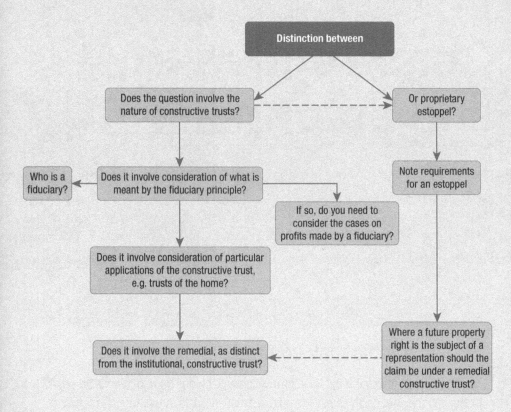

A printable version of this diagram is available from **www.pearsoned.co.uk/lawexpressqa**

◤◢ Question 1

'Under an institutional constructive trust, the trust arises by operation of law as from the date of the circumstances which give rise to it: the function of the court is merely to declare that such trust has arisen in the past . . . a remedial constructive trust, as I understand it, is different. It is a judicial remedy giving rise to an enforceable equitable obligation: the extent to which it operates retrospectively to the prejudice of third parties lies in the discretion of the court.'(Lord Browne-Wilkinson in *Westdeutsche Landesbank Girozentrale* v *Islington BC* [1996] AC 669 at 714–15.)

Comment critically on this view of the nature of both institutional and remedial constructive trusts.

Diagram plan

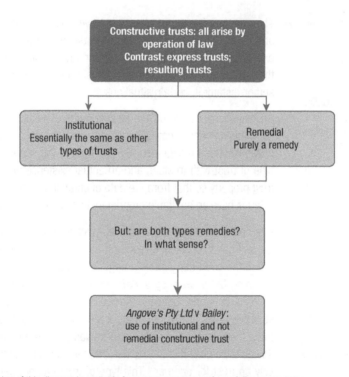

A printable version of this diagram is available from **www.pearsoned.co.uk/lawexpressqa**

Answer plan

→ Clear explanation of what a constructive trust is.

→ Distinguish between institutional and remedial constructive trusts.

→ Explore the notion of a remedy in the case of both types of trust.

→ Institutional constructive trusts are imposed to give effect to an equitable principle; remedial ones are not.

→ Look at the similarities between the two types of trust.

→ Note the Supreme Court decision in *Angove's Pty Ltd* v *Bailey*.

→ End by emphasising that the remedial constructive trust is not recognised in English law.

Answer

[1] Essays on general issues like this one can easily lose their thread. Make sure that you anchor them with clear statements like this.

[2] Note the careful wording regarding resulting trusts: there are various theories about how they arise and there is no time here to be more specific.

The common feature of all constructive trusts is that they arise by operation of law, unlike express trusts,[1] which arise through the express creation of the settlor/testator, and resulting trusts where, through the intervention of equity, trust property results back to the settlor/testator in certain situations.[2]

An institutional constructive trust arises where the facts of the dispute fall within an existing category of cases where a constructive trust has previously been recognised. Such a trust is the same as any other type of trust with trustees and an actual existence with identifiable trust property so that from the date of creation of the trust the beneficiaries have an equitable proprietary interest in the trust property.

A remedial constructive trust is one which is imposed 'whenever justice and good conscience require it . . . it is an equitable remedy by which the court can enable an aggrieved party to obtain restitution' (Denning MR in **Hussey v Palmer** [1972] 3 All ER 744). Thus the essential difference between the two is that whereas institutional constructive trusts are actual trusts a remedial constructive trust is no more than a remedy which a court awards when, in the exercise of its equitable discretion, it decides that the defendant is to hold property on trust for another.[3] This type of trust has not generally been recognised in English law, due to the uncertainty of its application.

[3] Emphasise the idea that remedial constructive trusts are remedies here and then follow through this idea of remedy in this essay.

[4] So far we have dealt with theoretical issues but we also need to locate our answer firmly in the case law. This is a good case to start with.

Does the idea that remedial constructive trusts are remedies really distinguish them from institutional constructive trusts? A familiar example of the latter category is **Keech v Sandford** [1726] Eq Cas Abr 741 HC,[4] where a trustee (X) of a lease of a market was granted a renewal of the lease in his own name because the landlord did not wish to renew it on trust as the beneficiary (Y) was a minor who could not be bound by the usual covenants. It was held that X held the renewed lease on trust for Y. In one way the trust was certainly being used as a remedy to enable Y to continue to be a beneficiary under the trust. However, the trust was not used as a remedy on the basis of judicial discretion: instead it was imposed because of an equitable principle.[5] In **Bray v Ford** [1896] AC 44 HL, Lord Herschell stated: 'It is an inflexible rule of a Court of Equity that a person in a fiduciary position . . . is not, unless expressly authorised, entitled to make a profit; he is not allowed to put himself in a position where duty and interest conflict' and this is the basis of **Keech v Sandford.**

[5] Note these two points: the extent to which these trusts are remedies and the extent to which they rest on principle.

A contrasting case on the remedial constructive trust is **Binions v Evans** [1972] 2 All ER 70 CA,[6] where Lord Denning imposed a constructive trust to prevent a licensee from being evicted by purchasers of a cottage despite a promise made when they bought it that she could remain. There was no written evidence of a trust as required by section 53(1)(b) of the Law of Property Act 1925 (LPA 1925) but the effect was that the licence was held on trust for the licensee and this gave her an equitable interest in the property which bound the purchasers as they had notice of it when they bought the cottage.

[6] *Binions* v *Evans* is not the only case on this point but it is clear and easily recalled.

The essential difference is that whilst in **Keech v Sandford** the trust was imposed to give effect to a fundamental equitable principle, the fiduciary duties of trustees, in **Binions v Evans** the trust was imposed to evade a fundamental principle of land law:[7] that a licence by itself does not create an interest in land and so cannot bind a purchaser. Moreover, whereas in **Keech v Sandford** there was identifiable trust property, the lease, in which the beneficiary had an equitable proprietary interest, here there was none: the court simply held that the licence was held on trust.

[7] The examiner will be looking for you to stress this fundamental distinction.

However, we must not push the distinction between the two types of trust too far. In both cases the trust is indeed being used as a remedy and this has led Swadling (2011) to argue[8] that the term 'constructive trust' simply hides its real purpose in all cases: to either return money or transfer property to the claimant. Moreover, when we talk of an institutional constructive trust these are not institutional in the sense that an express trust set up under, for instance, a will for family

[8] This is where you start to earn those extra marks with pushing the argument forward beyond obvious points and including some research detail.

members is. Here there are trustees who have consented to act, whereas in **Keech v Sandford** X was made a trustee of the market for Y against his will.

Nor is it true to say that institutional constructive trusts are always imposed to give effect to a settled equitable principle. For instance, the courts have swayed between two different principles on the question of whether an agent who receives a bribe does so as a fiduciary.[9] In **FHR European Ventures LLP v Cedar Capital Partners LLC** [2014] UKSC 45 SC, the Supreme Court held that benefits obtained from a third party in breach of fiduciary obligation, such as bribes, belong in equity to the principal from the moment of receipt and confirmed that the approach in **Attorney General for Hong Kong v Reid** [1994] 1 AC 324 PC was the correct one, not that in **Lister & Co v Stubbs** [1890] 45 Ch D 1 CA, where it was held that a bribe received by a fiduciary from a third party was not held on trust for the principal. However, this misses the point: in these cases, the courts were searching for the correct principle, whereas in cases of possible remedial constructive trusts there is no fundamental principle involved at all.

[9] It would be possible to go into great detail on the cases in this area but do resist this temptation: it is the extent to which equitable principles apply that matters here.

An institutional constructive trust is a real trust, a point emphasised by Lord Sumption in **Angove's Pty Ltd v Bailey** [2016] UKSC 47,[10] which arose from the insolvency of a wine importer who had acted as agent for the appellant, a winemaker. When the importer went into liquidation, the liquidators sought to collect the sums due under two invoices, deduct the importer's commission and leave the remainder available for distribution to the creditors. The winemakers argued that these sums were instead held on constructive trust for them, the significance of this being that their equitable proprietary interest in the wine would give them priority over other claimants. The court rejected this and held that purely because an agent becomes insolvent before accounting to his principal for monies received on his behalf did not mean that a trust would be imposed on the agent. It disapproved of the reasoning of Bingham J in **Neste Oy v Lloyd's Bank** [1983] 2 Lloyd's Rep 658, that where a reasonable and honest person would have returned money or other property in these circumstances then a trust would be imposed.

[10] This has the advantage of being a recent as well as a very relevant one.

This reasoning, with its accompanying references to 'good conscience', looked too much like the reasoning of remedial constructive

[11] The part played by the institutional constructive trust in insolvency matters does need to be mentioned, as it is so important.

[12] This last paragraph ties up the question and also explains the subsequent fate of *Binions v Evans,* which you need to mention.

trusts and Lord Sumption said, 'English law is generally averse to the discretionary adjustment of property rights, and has not recognised the remedial constructive trust favoured in some other jurisdictions, notably the United States and Canada.' In the adjustment of rights arising on an insolvency, for instance, the certainty of the institutional constructive trust is needed.[11]

Whilst the institutional constructive trust is a valuable tool in the adjustment of rights, the remedial type has not found favour, mainly on the ground of the unpredictability of when it might operate. The reasoning in **Binions v Evans,** for instance, was rejected in **Ashburn Anstalt v Arnold** [1989] 1 Ch 1 CA as a 'heresy'.[12]

✓ Make your answer stand out

- Look at other cases on the remedial constructive trust: how do they fit into the pattern described in this essay?
- Read and refer in more detail to the arguments of Swadling (2011) on the nature of constructive trusts.
- Consider arguments about the true basis of the constructive trust and refer to them in your answer, such as the argument that certain types of constructive trusts can be analysed as correcting a loss suffered in reliance on the undertaking of another. See Gardner (2010).
- Look in detail at *Angove's Pty Ltd v Bailey* and evaluate both why the winemakers sought an institutional constructive trust and why the idea of a remedial constructive trust was rejected.
- Look at other cases, for instance at the Court of Appeal decision in *Halifax Building Society v Thomas* [1996] Ch 217.

! Don't be tempted to . . .

- Simply write all that you know about constructive trusts with masses of cases and no connecting theme.
- Discuss facts of cases without relating them to the theoretical debate.
- Go into too much detail on facts of cases which tell us nothing on the fundamental nature of these two types of constructive trust.

Question 2

Frankie is trustee of a small trust which provides short breaks for ten named people with disabilities aged 18 and over. There are three other trustees, Dave, Jack and Fiona.

The trust owns a house which provides residential accommodation and some farm buildings. Frankie's daughter, Liz, needs a home quickly and Frankie asks at a trustees' meeting if the other trustees will agree to him buying one of the farm buildings so that he can convert it into accommodation for Liz. Frankie leaves the meeting whilst they are considering this. The other trustees unanimously agree.

The trust has a partnership with the local college and through this connection Frankie learns of an opportunity to buy another building from the college which is already equipped as a sensory room and to run it himself as a separate venture. He told the trustees after he had acquired it and they agreed that they would not have wished to buy it even had they had the chance.

Anne has just been appointed as a trustee and she is concerned about these events. She asks you for advice on whether either of the transactions were in accord with Frankie's duties as a trustee.

Answer plan

→ Explain the responsibilities of trustees and how this relates to the question.

→ State and explain the 'self-dealing' rule and how it can apply to the purchase of trust property by Frankie.

→ Then move on to consider the remedies available to the beneficiaries if the purchase by Frankie was in breach of trust.

→ Consider the 'no conflict of interest rule' in relation to the purchase of the building by Frankie.

Diagram plan

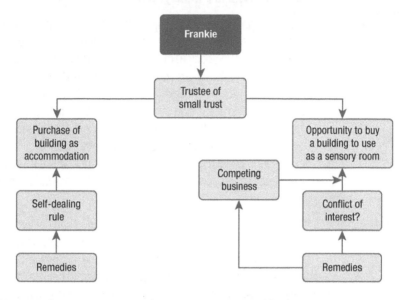

A printable version of this diagram is available from **www.pearsoned.co.uk/lawexpressqa**

Answer

There are two issues in this question. The first is the purchase by Frankie personally of a farm building which is trust property.

[1] You should set out this fundamental principle first in any discussion about trustees' duties and then look at particular aspects of this duty.

Trustees are fiduciaries and are subject to the 'distinguishing obligation of a fiduciary' which is 'the obligation of loyalty' [1] (Millett LJ in ***Bristol and West Building Society v Mothew*** [1998] Ch 1). Thus, fiduciaries must not act in situations where there is a conflict between their duty as fiduciaries and their personal interest.

[2] You are now relating the general principle set out in the first paragraph to the particular application of this principle to the facts of this case. In this way you are giving your answer a clear structure.

As a result of this principle there is a general rule that a trustee must not purchase trust property because to do so can conflict with his duty as a trustee. [2] This is known as the 'self-dealing rule' and in ***Tito v Waddell (No 2)*** [1977] Ch 106 CA, Megarry V-C said that in such a case the sale is voidable at the instance of any beneficiary 'however fair the transaction'. The honesty of the trustee is irrelevant and the rule is based on the trustee's status as a trustee. The rule applies even where the price is fixed by a third party, as in ***Wright v Morgan***

[1926] AC 788 CA, where the price was fixed by a valuer. A modern illustration is **Kane v Radley-Kane** [1999] Ch 274 HC.[3]

A trustee can, however, purchase if the court allows it, or the beneficiaries, all being of full age and capacity, agree, or the trust instrument permits it. In addition, the trustee must have made full disclosure of all material facts (**Newgate Stud Co v Penfold** [2008] 1 BCLC 46 HC). In this case the beneficiaries of the trust will probably be all those who are likely to use it, and even though we are told that they are ten adults, it might be difficult to obtain the consent of all of them and in addition there might be questions of capacity. Although Frankie left the meeting whilst the decision was being made, this does not affect the matter as the point is simply that the sale is voidable however it was arrived at.

Any action should be taken by the beneficiaries and not by the trustees such as Anne, who has brought this to our notice.[4] As the property has not been resold as it is intended as a home for Frankie's daughter, Liz, they can insist that the property is transferred back to the trust or they can insist that the property is offered for sale again and if this results in a higher price being offered than that paid by the trustee, Frankie, then the property must be sold at that price. It is very unlikely that the property will be sold, as any buyer would be advised that the title of Frankie was defective, but if a resale did take place, the beneficiaries could insist on any profit being paid to them or they could take steps to avoid the sale, as it could be argued that the purchaser had knowingly received trust property. In **BCCI (Overseas) Ltd v Akindele** [2001] Ch 437 CA, Nourse LJ held that the test was if 'the recipient's state of knowledge . . . make it unconscionable for him to retain the benefit of the receipt'[5] and it is suggested that on this test a purchaser would be liable.

Finally, this does not look like a charitable trust, as it exists for the benefit of ten named people and so there is a lack of public benefit. However, if it does happen to have charitable status then the matter of the sale should be reported by Anne to the Charity Commission who can take action.[6]

The other issue is the purchase by Frankie of another building from the local college in order to run it as a sensory centre. It is not quite clear whether Frankie came by the information about the building which is equipped as a sensory room in his capacity as a trustee.[7]

[3] The facts of this case do not really help in your answer but it does no harm to show the examiner that you are aware of it.

[4] It is in this paragraph that you can earn those extra marks. Most students will probably spot that the purchase of trust property by a trustee is in breach of the trustee's fiduciary duties but many students will stop at that.

[5] You should not spend long on this point as otherwise you will get right away from the question, but it is worth a mention.

[6] This is a really excellent extra point to include in your answer. It shows that you are looking at all the possibilities, as a good lawyer should.

[7] This apparent vagueness on the part of the examiner is of course deliberate, as you are expected to discuss this point. The effect is that you will lose marks if you just say that Frankie will be liable.

[8] You could give the facts of
this case but those of
Boardman v *Phipps* are more
relevant to this situation.
However, you should mention
that the principle seems to
originate from *Keech* v
Sandford.

The question merely says that he learnt of the opportunity to buy it as the trust has a partnership with the local college and he learnt of it through this connection. This is a crucial point, as persons in a fiduciary position such as Frankie must not use that position to make an unauthorised profit for themselves. If they do so, they will be a constructive trustee of those profits (**Keech v Sandford** [1726] 2 Eq Cas Abr HC).[8]

[9] This is not an easy case to summarise and the facts are very relevant to those in the problem and this is why it has been set out in some detail.

A parallel case to this one is **Boardman v Phipps** [1967] AC 46 HL. The trust owned a substantial holding of shares in a company and the appellant, a solicitor to the trust, and one of the beneficiaries were dissatisfied with its performance.[9] They obtained information, through this connection with the trust, about the company's affairs and so they decided to obtain control of it by purchasing the remainder of its shares. They reorganised it and made considerable profits for themselves. The appellants were held liable to account to the trust for the profits made because they were constructive trustees, as they had used the trust shareholding to acquire the necessary information about the company and in addition the respondent beneficiary had not been kept fully informed of the situation.

Lord Cohen held that the liability of the appellants rested on the fact that they came by the information which led to them purchasing the shares when acting for the trust, and it could be argued that Frankie is in the same position if he came by the information about the centre in his capacity as a trustee. The fact that the trustees decided that they would not have bought it does not affect Frankie's liability, as in **Boardman v Phipps** the trust had decided that it did not wish to acquire the shares. Thus, Frankie can be liable to hold the sensory centre on a constructive trust for the trust which he chairs and account for any profits made.

[10] If you mention the decision in *Boardman* v *Phipps* then you should try to include a reference to the dissenting speeches, as whether this decision was correct is still debated.

It is worth mentioning that Lord Upjohn dissented in **Boardman v Phipps**[10] and observed that 'the appellants have bought for themselves and with their own money shares which the trustees never contemplated buying and they did so in circumstances fully known and approved of by the trustees'. This could be said to be the case here too.

[11] Here is another example of where you can pick up extra marks by thinking clearly about the question.

The other point is that if the sensory centre competes for the business of the trust then Frankie will be in breach of the rule which states that a trustee must not carry on a business in competition with the trust.[11]

In **Re Thompson** [1934] Ch 342 HC, the executors of a will carried on the testator's business of a yacht broker and one executor wished to set up a competing business. He was restrained by injunction from doing so.

 Make your answer stand out

■ Consider the argument that the decision in *Boardman* v *Phipps* was wrong as information cannot be trust property and so cannot be made the subject of a trust.

■ Look at the remarks in *Murad* v *Al-Saraj* [2005] WTLR 1573, where the Court of Appeal suggested *obiter* that the rule as applied in *Keech* v *Sandford* and *Boardman* v *Phipps* might be looked at again where the fiduciary has acted in good faith with no concealment. Was this the case here?

■ Ask what remedy was used in *Boardman* v *Phipps*. Was it liability to account or was it a personal remedy? It is arguable that the courts did not make this clear.

! **Don't be tempted to . . .**

■ Forget to stress that this question is primarily about the duties of fiduciaries and that you need to be clear on what the duties of fiduciaries are.

■ Deal with liability but not consider the remedies.

■ Set out the facts of *Boardman* v *Phipps* in great detail but not apply them clearly to the question.

 Question 3

In *Boardman* v *Phipps* [1967] Lord Upjohn referred to the 'fundamental rule of equity that a person in a fiduciary capacity must not make a profit out of his trust which is part of the wider rule that a trustee must not place himself in a position where his duty and interest may conflict'.

Critically consider in relation to this statement what a fiduciary relationship is and the extent of its core obligations.

Diagram plan

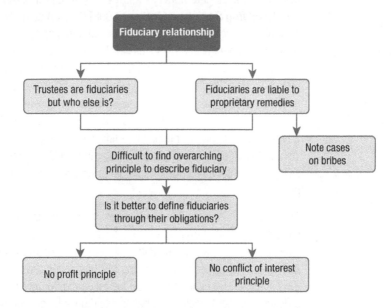

A printable version of this diagram is available from **www.pearsoned.co.uk/lawexpressqa**

Answer plan

→ Explain and evaluate the core meaning of the term 'fiduciary'.

→ Outline the well-recognised categories of fiduciary relationships and then give instances of where the courts have held relationships to be fiduciary in more controversial cases.

→ Identify and analyse the core fiduciary obligations: the 'no profit' rule and 'no conflict of interest rule'.

→ Are they two rules or one? Does this matter?

Answer

[1] This is the type of start to aim for: you have clearly identified that there is not one but two issues in this question.

There are two issues in this question: the nature of a fiduciary[1] and, given that a person is a fiduciary, the extent of their core obligations not to make a profit and not to allow a conflict of interest between their duty as a fiduciary and their other interests.

[2] Although you will probably decide that there is no satisfactory all-embracing definition of a fiduciary, you still do need to look at the attempts which have been made.

[3] This is the first of a number of references to the views of academic authors in this essay. If you tackle an area such as this where there has been so much academic debate then you must show familiarity with it to gain a really good mark.

[4] You need to make this clear at the start. If the only example of a fiduciary was a trustee, we would know who a fiduciary was!

[5] The examiner will be looking for you to mention this as there is no point in identifying a person as a fiduciary for the sake of it – they are identified as fiduciaries to make them liable as fiduciaries.

[6] The reason for this example is not to describe the law on receipt of bribes by fiduciaries but to show how the courts veer from one view to another, possibly because of their reluctance to label a relationship as fiduciary and so unleash equitable remedies.

The origin of the word fiduciary is the Latin *fides* meaning trust. Thus, obviously, trustees are fiduciaries but who else is?[2] In **Bristol and West Building Society v Mothew** [1998] Ch 1 CA at 18, Millett LJ said that a 'fiduciary is someone who has undertaken to act for or on behalf of another in circumstances which give rise to a relationship of trust and confidence'. Finn (1992, p. 8)[3] says that all that one can do is to describe a fiduciary but adds that when the fiduciary does act for another he does so 'to the exclusion of his own several interest'. Correct though these statements may be, as Birks points out (1996), attempts at general descriptions of a fiduciary 'have a low predictive value'. That is, they do not get us very far. Indeed Mason (1985) has said, 'The fiduciary relationship is a concept in search of a principle.'

The problem is that there are a number of well-recognised relationships outside that of trustee and beneficiary which can be classed as fiduciary but how far they extend is unclear.[4] In **Lloyds Bank Ltd v Bundy** [1975] QB 326 CA, Denning MR mentioned the following in the context of a presumption of undue influence, 'parent over child, solicitor over client, doctor over patient, spiritual adviser over follower', and there have been a number of cases where the courts have extended the term fiduciary to apply in new situations. In **Norbert v Wynrib** [1992] 92 DLR (4th) 449, the Canadian courts held a doctor to be a fiduciary so that a patient could claim equitable compensation for a failure to act in her best interests.

One reason for what might be called the timidity of the courts in defining who is a fiduciary was given by Mason (1985), 'realisation that breach of the fiduciary duty unleashes equitable remedies, particularly the constructive trust'. Thus if it is found that a particular category of person counts as a fiduciary, this will mean that they will be liable in particular to proprietary remedies.[5]

The result is that where a relationship lies at the margins of fiduciary relationships, the courts may be uncertain whether to brand it as fiduciary, which can then lead to conflicting case law. An example of this is the situation where persons receive bribes in breach of their fiduciary duty.[6] Do they become a constructive trustee of them? In **A-G for Hong Kong v Reid** [1994] 1 AC 324 PC, it was held, overruling previous authority (**Lister v Stubbs** [1890] 45 Ch D 1 CA) that they did but this was itself overruled by **Sinclair Investments (UK)**

Ltd **v** *Versailles Trade Finance (In Administration)* [2011] EWCA Civ 347. However, in the latest case, *FHR European Ventures LLP* **v** *Cedar Capital Partners LLC* [2014] UKSC 45 SC, the Supreme Court held that the approach in *Attorney General for Hong Kong* **v** *Reid* was the correct one, not that in *Lister & Co* **v** *Stubbs.* The result is that once again a fiduciary who receives a bribe becomes a constructive trustee of it.

[7] This is the second part of your answer and the transition needs to be clearly indicated.

Given the difficulty of finding an overarching principle based on the term 'fiduciary', we can look at the matter from the angle of the obligations which are imposed on a fiduciary.[7]

[8] Once you have mentioned this point do not spend too long on it as, although relevant, it is something of a side issue.

Resulting trusts can be left apart,[8] because, as Chambers (1997) points out (at p. 196), in most cases of resulting trusts all that is sought is the 'second measure of the surviving trust property'. In other cases it is accepted that the 'distinguishing obligation of a fiduciary is the obligation of loyalty' (Millett LJ in *Bristol and West Building Society* **v** *Mothew*). Precisely what that duty means can be seen by examining the two duties of fiduciaries which seem to be accepted as fundamental:

(a) Fiduciaries must not act in situations where there is a conflict between their duty as fiduciaries and their personal interest.

(b) Fiduciaries must not make an unauthorised profit out of their fiduciary position.

[9] You will earn extra marks for an awareness of this. It is a common error to assume that there can be only one principle here.

[10] You will need to decide at this point whether you have time to give all the facts of *Boardman* v *Phipps,* which cannot be easily stated, bearing in mind that you must bring out this principle.

Sometimes these are treated as one principle.[9] In *Boardman* **v** *Phipps* [1967] AC 46 HL, Lord Upjohn's statement that the 'no profit' rule is part of the 'wider rule that a trustee must not place himself in a position where his duty and his interest may conflict' is not universally accepted. The appellants were in a fiduciary relationship towards the trust, out of which they obtained the opportunity to make a profit. Thus we could say that they broke the 'no profit' rule.[10] However, the 'no profit' rule does not stand on its own: there is no law against a person making a profit. The 'no profit' rule applies where a person is, as a result of their fiduciary position, in a position where his duty and interest conflict. Was this so? Lord Upjohn, who dissented, said that it was not and observed that 'the appellants have bought for themselves and with their own money shares which the trustees never contemplated buying and they did so in circumstances fully known and approved of by the trustees'. Moreover, their actions benefited the trust as the trust's own shares increased in value. In **Queensland Mines v Hudson** [1978] 52 AJLR 399 PC they were treated as two distinct rules but, as Conaglen (2007) remarks (at p. 115), the facts of any one case can generally be explained on the basis that either the 'no profit' rule or the 'no conflict of interest' one was broken. It is suggested that it is preferable to treat them as one for the reason given by Lord Upjohn.[11]

[11] At the end of a discussion such as this show the examiner that you have thought about the issues yourself.

[12] This essay could have been quite different. Instead of ending with specific cases it could have consisted entirely of cases. However, our mark would have been reduced because a really good answer here demands a knowledge of principle.

Once a relationship has been identified as fiduciary then the 'no profit' and 'no conflict' rules can apply.[12] Thus, in **Boston Deep Sea Fishing and Ice Co v Ansell** [1888] 39 Ch D 339 HC, a director bought ice for the company from another company in which he held shares and from which he received bonuses. The identification of the director as owing fiduciary duties to it enabled an action to be brought for an account of commissions and bonuses received by him. In **Boardman v Phipps** [1967] AC 46 HL, the identification of Boardman, who was a solicitor to a trust, as owing fiduciary duties to it enabled the court to award an account of profits made by him when he had bought shares in a company using information available only to the trust.

So in the end it is impossible to arrive at a neat definition of a fiduciary. Thus, Denning MR, having mentioned that a trustee is a fiduciary, simply remarked, 'The cases show that the categories where the fiduciary relationship imposes the duty are open', without taking the matter any further. We could say that, using Mason's phraseology, the concept of a fiduciary has found principles and these are not the identification of fiduciaries themselves but the identification of fiduciary duties.

✓ Make your answer stand out

- Asking if, in fact, there is only one fiduciary duty: look at Conaglen (2005) at p. 466.
- Read Conaglen (2007) especially pp. 114–125 on the 'no profit' and 'no conflict' principles.
- Look at the view of Smith (2003), who suggests that the distinguishing characteristic of a breach of fiduciary obligations is disloyalty by the fiduciary.
- Pointing out that other duties, for example that of good faith, are not fiduciary as they can arise in situations which are not fiduciary, for example in employment contracts.
- Referring to the thesis of Conaglen (2005) that the concept of fiduciary loyalty is not an end in itself but a means of ensuring that non-fiduciary duties are carried out.

! **Don't be tempted to . . .**

- Think that the only fiduciaries are trustees.
- Just go through cases involving fiduciaries without attempting to address the issue of exactly who is a fiduciary.
- Neglect to deal with the idea of a 'concept' and a 'principle' at the start.
- Fail to ask if there are two rules: 'no profit' and 'no conflict of interest'.
- State various definitions of a fiduciary without attempting to consider whether they are satisfactory.

Question 4

'Equity will not allow a statute to be used as an instrument of fraud.'

Critically examine this maxim of equity and consider whether it has any continued usefulness today.

Answer plan

→ Explain what the maxim means.

→ Explain the maxim in operation, for example *Rochefoucauld* v *Boustead*.

→ Contrast this with cases where the maxim was not applied, for example *Midland Bank* v *Green*.

→ Critically consider the attitudes of different judges.

→ Provide other examples, for instance secret trusts.

→ Conclude by evaluating whether it is true that equity does generally apply this maxim.

Diagram plan

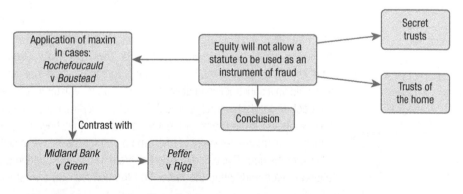

A printable version of this diagram is available from **www.pearsoned.co.uk/lawexpressqa**

Answer

This is a well-known maxim of equity which means that to shelter behind the requirements of a statute may be to allow a fraud to be committed and thus the statute becomes an instrument of fraud. Therefore, the question is asking whether equity will not allow a statute to be a means of achieving fraud.[1]

[1] This is a vital sentence, as it actually explains what the maxim means.

Is this true? In **Rochefoucauld v Boustead** [1897] 1 Ch 196 CA, land was transferred to the defendant and it was alleged that he took it on trust for the claimant. She was having difficulty in repaying the mortgage and therefore she wanted him to take the land off her hands and repay the mortgage but the land would still be held on trust for her. The problem was that there was no written evidence of the trust as required by what was then section 4 of the Statute of Frauds 1677 (now section 53(1)(b) of the Law of Property Act 1925 (LPA 1925)).[2] If the lack of written evidence was fatal to her claim, then the defendant would commit the fraud of keeping the land absolutely and beneficially when he was not intended to. So equity imposed the trust despite the lack of written evidence. The effect was that oral evidence was admitted of the trust despite the statute providing that evidence of the trust must be in writing. The trust in this case appeared to be express but now section 53(2) of the LPA 1925 exempts resulting, implied and constructive trusts from the requirement of writing imposed by section 53(1)(b) and the tendency today is to categorise trusts imposed on the basis of this maxim as constructive.[3] An example of this is **Lyus v Prowsa Developments Ltd** [1982] 1 WLR 1044 CA.[4]

[2] Note how we have made it clear exactly what the problem in the case was and also how we have added the detail that the relevant statute has now been replaced by another statute – this last point will gain you marks for extra precision in your answer.

[3] This is where you can gain extra marks by pointing out that there is doubt as to exactly what type of trust was involved here.

[4] If you have time give the details of this case but at least mention this case or another fairly recent one, as *Rochefoucauld,* although an excellent authority, is over 100 years old!

[5] Having mentioned one case (*Rochefoucauld*), now mention a case which seems to go the other way. You would be wasting your time by mentioning a similar case to *Rochefoucauld,* which just makes the same point.

Although the above case is an example of the maxim in operation, equity operates on the basis of discretion and so we cannot expect to find that there is a rigid rule that equity will always act in the way it did in the above case.[5] In **Midland Bank Trust Co Ltd v Green (No 1)** [1981] AC 513, the House of Lords refused to hold that land was held on a constructive trust so that the failure to register an estate contract meant that a purchaser took free of the contract. This might have seemed a strong case for the intervention of equity because the contract was made between a father and a son for the father to sell a farm to the son. The contract was not protected by registration as a land charge and, when the father and the son fell out, the father took advantage of the lack of registration to make a sham sale of the farm to his wife with the sole object of defeating the son's contract. Yet the House of Lords was not persuaded and Lord Wilberforce said that 'it is not fraud to rely on the requirements of a statute'. In effect, the requirements of the Land Registration Acts were given precedence over the need to prevent a fraud, although Lord Denning in the Court of Appeal had held in favour of the son and would have imposed a trust.[6] Thus, we must often look at the policy behind decisions and not see the maxim as an all-embracing mantra which can be uttered to solve disputes.

Much also depends on the attitudes of different judges. For example, a constructive trust was imposed in the much-criticised case[7] of **Peffer v Rigg** [1977] 1 WLR 285 HC, where a party sought to rely on the lack of compliance with the Land Registration Act 1925. This point is also seen by contrasting **Binions v Evans** [1972] 2 All ER 70 CA with **Ashburn Anstalt v Arnold** [1989] 1 Ch 1 CA. In **Binions,** Lord Denning in the Court of Appeal had imposed a constructive trust to prevent a licensee from being evicted by purchasers of a cottage despite a promise made when they bought it that she could remain. There was no written evidence of a trust (see section 53(1)(b)) but the effect was that the licence was held on trust for her and this gave her an equitable interest in the property which bound the purchasers as they had notice of it when they bought the cottage.[8] Yet in **Ashburn** Browne-Wilkinson V-C condemned as a heresy the notion that a constructive trust could give a licensee a right which was binding on purchasers.

A classic illustration of the maxim is found in the doctrine of secret trusts.[9] If I promise to leave X by will £1,000 on the strength of an oral promise by him that he will hold it on trust for Y then X can argue that the promise is not binding on him as it does not comply with the requirements of the Wills Act.[10] So equity holds that X is bound by a secret trust in favour of Y which it will enforce despite the failure to comply with the formalities. The alternative would be that X, despite his promise, keeps the money, which would be using the failure to comply with the statutory requirements as a means of committing fraud. This doctrine, unlike the cases mentioned above, does not depend on equitable discretion to any great extent and can be regarded as a rule. It has also applied to half-secret trusts, with less

[6] Boost your marks by bringing in the views of another judge in the same case.

[7] Where a case is of very doubtful authority, make sure that you say so!

[8] This is not an easy case to sum up briefly but the facts are useful, as they were the basis of a controversial decision and you need to show exactly why it was controversial.

[9] You will waste time – and so lose marks – if you just set out details of cases on secret trusts. Instead, concentrate on the principle behind them and show how it relates to the question. This is not a problem question on secret trusts!

[10] It helps to make this point clearer if you use an example of the general principle rather than a case, as we are not looking at the detailed application of the law.

justification. Here I actually declare in my will that the property is left to X on trust but I do not say what the trusts are. Again, X will be bound if he has agreed with me that he will hold the £1,000 on trust for Y. The difference is that here there is no possibility of X committing fraud by keeping the property himself, as the will declares that there is a trust. Yet in **Blackwell v Blackwell** [1929] AC 318 HL, it was held that half-secret trusts would be enforced.

Another example of the intervention of equity to prevent fraud is in the area of trusts of the family home, where an oral promise by one party to another that the home will be held on trust for both of them has been held binding despite the lack of writing and consequent failure to comply with section 53 of the LPA 1925.[11] A good, if old, example is **Eves v Eves** [1975] 3 All ER 768 CA.

[11] Again, you may not have time to go into detail here, so just bring out the principle and leave details of cases out.

One can sum up by saying that the picture is a confused one. One cannot state that there is an absolute rule that equity will always intervene to prevent a statute from being used as an instrument of fraud: much depends on the values which are felt to be competing against each other and the attitudes of the judges to resolving the tension which can exist between formal statutory requirements and the need to do justice in particular cases.

 Make your answer stand out

- Look in more detail at *Rochefoucauld* v *Boustead* – what type of trust was it? Why was it imposed?
- Look at the argument of Denning MR in *Midland Bank* v *Green* in the Court of Appeal and contrast it to that of Lord Wilberforce in the House of Lords.
- Do some research on the origin of this principle: how did it originate? You could then add a little more depth to the introduction or the conclusion.
- Contrast *Lyus* v *Prowsa Developments Ltd* with *Midland Bank* v *Green* to show that you understand that different courts and judges have different approaches.
- Think of other areas where this maxim could apply – over to you!

> **! Don't be tempted to . . .**
>
> - Go into great detail on the actual cases, for example on secret trusts – instead, bring out the principles.
> - Set off on this question without explaining what lies behind the quotation.
> - Come to very definite conclusions saying, for example, that the maxim is always applied or that it never is. The area of equitable maxims is not one for very final conclusions.
> - Mention more than one case which makes the same point, as you are not adding anything to your answer and so not gaining any extra marks.

Question 5

In *Daraydan Holdings Ltd* v *Solland International Ltd* [2004] EWHC 622 (Ch) 119, Lawrence Collins J saw 'no injustice to the creditors [of an insolvent fiduciary] in their not sharing in an asset for which the fiduciary has not given value, and which the fiduciary should not have had'.

Comment critically on this statement.

Answer plan

→ Explain what the quotation means.

→ Set the question in the context of fundamental equitable principles.

→ Begin with the decision in *Lister* v *Stubbs*. Contrast this with *Attorney General for Hong Kong* v *Reid*.

→ Move on to *Sinclair Investments (UK) Ltd* v *Versailles Trade Finance (In Administration)* and show how the essential point in this case is the same as in the other two.

→ Consider *FHR European Ventures LLP* v *Cedar Capital Partners LLC* and show how the court used the fundamental equitable principles which you mentioned earlier.

→ Conclude by going back to the issue posed in the quotation.

Diagram plan

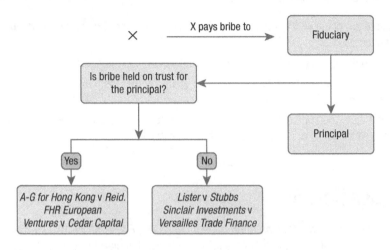

A printable version of this diagram is available from **www.pearsoned.co.uk/lawexpressqa**

Answer

[1] You really need to spend time here setting the scene before you look at the cases. Although we have not done so, you might consider, if you have time, inserting a short practical example to show what the debate is all about.

[2] The quotation in the question is not at first sight an easy one to unravel but it does go to the heart of the issue here and you will gain marks by engaging with it.

[3] This is one of those sentences which mark a vital turning point in an answer and really lift it. We are setting the cases in the context of fundamental equitable principles.

The quotation in the question refers to the issue of whether a bribe, which was received by a person acting in a fiduciary position from a third party as an incentive for the fiduciary to commit a breach of duty to his principal, should be held on a constructive trust for that principal.[1] In many cases the fiduciary will be insolvent and so the contest will be between the creditors of the fiduciary and the principal.

If the asset represented by the bribe is not held on trust for the principal then it will remain the property of the fiduciary and will be available for his creditors. However, Lawrence Collins J in the quotation, saw no injustice in holding that it should not be available for the creditors with the result that it is held on trust for the principal who has an equitable proprietary interest in it.[2]

It is important to set this issue against the fundamental rule of equity that persons in a fiduciary position must not use that position to make an unauthorised profit for themselves.[3] If they do so, they will be a constructive trustee of those profits. The leading case is ***Keech v Sandford*** [1726] 2 Eq Cas Abr HC and the principal modern authority is ***Boardman v Phipps*** [1967] AC 46 HL. When examining the cases on this area we need to bear this principle in mind.

[4] Always bring out the reasoning behind a decision. An average answer would have just given the facts of the case.

In **Lister & Co v Stubbs** [1890] 45 Ch D 1 CA, it was held that a bribe received by a fiduciary from a third party was not held on trust for the principal. The reasoning was that proprietary claims (i.e. those founded on trust) were only available where the principal seeks to recover property which belonged to him before the breach of fiduciary duty.[4] A bribe, by contrast, is not the property of the principal but is property held by the fiduciary in breach of fiduciary obligation. The principle in **Lister v Stubbs** was reversed in **Attorney General for Hong Kong v Reid [1994]** 1 AC 324 HL, which held that benefits obtained from a third party in breach of fiduciary obligation, such as bribes, belong in equity to the principal from the moment of receipt. A Crown prosecutor took bribes and then used them to buy land. It was held that, when he took the bribes, he became under an immediate duty to pay them over to his principal (i.e. his employer) and so the bribes were the property of his employer in equity. Thus the employer was entitled to claim the profits from the bribes when they were invested. Lord Templeman explicitly linked this decision to that in **Boardman v Phipps**,[5] pointing out that in that case a fiduciary acting honestly and in good faith and making a profit which his principal could not make for himself still became a constructive trustee of that profit. It followed, he said, that 'a fiduciary acting dishonestly and criminally who accepts a bribe and thereby causes loss and damage to his principal must also be a constructive trustee and must not be allowed by any means to make a profit from his wrong doing'.

[5] Here is when you earn those extra marks. You have stated above the fundamental principle of equity where a fiduciary makes a profit out of his position and now you are applying it to the actual issue.

[6] These twists and turns of the cases can be confusing, which means it is a good idea to make a plan of your answer, especially in cases like these where the case law is not straightforward.

This was in itself reversed in **Sinclair Investments (UK) Ltd v Versailles Trade Finance (In Administration)** [2011] EWCA Civ 347 CA, which changed the position back to what it was before **Attorney General for Hong Kong v Reid** and so **Lister v Stubbs** became good law again.[6] A company director (X) made a secret profit of £28 million on the sale of his shares in a company but had breached his fiduciary duty by entering into fraudulent transactions which were intended to increase the value of his own shareholding which was in fact of no value at all. Y was an investor who took an assignment of the company's claims against X and he claimed a proprietary interest in the traceable proceeds of the gains made by X. However, X had not acquired the shares with company funds and so the claim was not over funds in respect of which X owed any pre-existing duty to the company.

[7] This is a crucial point and do make sure that you are clear about it. The facts differed quite markedly from *Lister* v *Stubbs* but the essential point was the same. This of course often arises and do make sure that you can explain the essential rationale of cases clearly and concisely.

[8] Note the reference to equitable remedies and how important it is to have a secure grasp of these when answering questions on constructive trusts.

[9] This shows the advantage of having referred to fundamental principles at the start of your answer; you can reinforce them now and also at the end of your answer.

Thus although the case did not involve a bribe, it involved the same principle: could a principal claim a proprietary interest in property which had not belonged to him before the breach of fiduciary duty?[7] This was the same issue as in **Lister v Stubbs** and the Court of Appeal held that Y's claim failed as he had no proprietary interest in the money as it had never been the property of the principal (the company). The reasoning in **Lister v Stubbs** was approved. The effect was that Y only had the personal remedy of an account which would not override the payments already made to the banks.[8] **Attorney General for Hong Kong v Reid** as a Privy Council decision need not be followed in preference to a Court of Appeal decision, **Lister v Stubbs.**

Finally, in the latest decision, **FHR European Ventures LLP v Cedar Capital Partners LLC** [2014] UKSC 45 SC, the law has been changed again so that the position reverts to what it was before **Sinclair Investments (UK) Ltd v Versailles Trade Finance. Lister v Stubbs** was overruled and **Attorney General for Hong Kong v Reid** [1994] was approved.

The facts were that while advising F in relation to their purchase of a hotel, the Monte Carlo Grand Hotel, C had entered into an agreement with the sellers under which C was to receive a fixed commission of €10 million for securing a purchaser. C failed to notify F of that agreement and received the commission when F bought the hotel. F sought to recover the €10 million from C. The Supreme Court reiterated the general equitable rule that where an agent acquired a benefit, including as here a bribe, which came to his notice as a result of his fiduciary position, or as the result of an opportunity which results from his fiduciary position, he should be treated as having acquired the benefit on behalf of his principal, so that the benefit is beneficially owned by the principal.[9] Thus F could recover the €10 million from C. Lord Neuberger felt that this conclusion had the merit of simplicity: any benefit acquired by an agent as a result of his agency and in breach of his fiduciary duty is held on trust for the principal. Moreover this was supported by 'considerations of practicality and principle'.

This decision can be supported on the ground that it follows fundamental equitable principles and, as Lawrence Collins J stated in the quotation in the question, it accords with fundamental principles of justice: why should the creditors of an insolvent fiduciary share in an asset for which the fiduciary has not given value, and which the fiduciary should not have had?

Make your answer stand out

- Hicks (2011), commenting on the High Court decision in *Sinclair Investments* approved by the Court of Appeal, points out that one unresolved issue is what is meant by 'property' and says, 'Opportunity, or information used to exploit an opportunity, has been treated as the intangible property of the principal in many cases', for example, *Boardman v Phipps.* Do not just insert this quote into your answer but consider carefully what it means.

- Read Gummow (2015) and consider his point that the influence of 'restitution theorists' contributed to the decline in the influence of *Attorney General for Hong Kong* v *Reid.*

- Note the comment of Hayton (2011), commenting on the Court of Appeal decision in *Sinclair Investments,* that in consequence many trust deeds will now provide that any bribe or other secret profit received by the fiduciary will be held on trust for the relevant beneficiaries or the other contracting party.

- Ask if the constructive trust recognised by the Supreme Court in *FHR European Ventures LLP* was institutional or remedial.

Don't be tempted to . . .

- Just go through the four cases mechanically, forgetting to bring out the reasoning in them and to contrast them.
- Forget to investigate at the start exactly what the quotation in the question is saying.
- Just go through cases involving fiduciaries without attempting to address the issue of exactly who is a fiduciary.
- Fail to highlight the fundamental equitable principles which lie at the heart of this issue.

Question 6

'Estoppel must not be so governed by its own principles that it is unable to undertake its main function nor so wide and general that it is impossible to see what that function is.'

Critically evaluate this statement.

Answer plan

→ Begin by looking at what the question is about.

→ Consider the types of estoppel – make it clear that this answer will concentrate on proprietary estoppel.

→ Critically consider when proprietary estoppel can apply.

→ Analyse the decision in *Yeoman's Row* v *Cobbe.*

→ Similarly analyse the decision in *Thorner* v *Major* and contrast it with that in *Yeoman's Row* v *Cobbe.*

Diagram plan

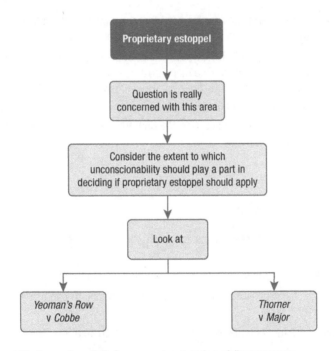

A printable version of this diagram is available from **www.pearsoned.co.uk/lawexpressqa**

Answer

The idea behind this question is that estoppel needs to steer a middle ground. It must be governed by principles but at the same time the application of those principles must not be so rigid and inflexible that estoppel is unable to exercise its proper function.

[1] Promissory estoppel and proprietary estoppel are so different that a definition covering them both would be too wide to be of use, especially in an essay like this. Better to say at once that there are two types, which then leads you on to discuss proprietary estoppel in detail, which is what this question is about.

There are two distinct types of estoppel.[1] As Hanbury (2015, p. 870) points out, 'Each has a separate origin and history.' Promissory estoppel applies in contractual relationships and essentially operates as a defence to prevent a party from going back on a promise. Its best-known application was in **Central London Property Trust v High Trees Houses Ltd** [1947] KB 130 HC. This doctrine does not create a new cause of action; instead it prevents a party going back on a representation as in **High Trees** itself. Proprietary estoppel, by contrast, is a sword: it enables rights, especially property rights, to be acquired when none existed before. It is founded on certain principles: there must be a representation by one person (X) to another (Y) which X intends Y to rely on and where Y's actual reliance is reasonable in the circumstances. An objective test applies: thus, the question is whether a promise by X can reasonably be understood as a commitment by X to Y. If so, then X will be estopped from going back on the representation and asserting his strict legal rights.

[2] Your discussion of the issue raised in the question will be much clearer if you have started by stating what the essential elements of estoppel are.

[3] However, as we will see later, the mention of promissory estoppel is not wasted even though the question is primarily about proprietary estoppel.

Provided that the above elements are present, the fundamental basis of the estoppel can be seen as unconscionability: would it be unconscionable for X, when Y has relied on X's promise to his detriment, to then depart from that promise?[2]

This question was prompted by cases involving proprietary estoppel and so this essay will concentrate on this[3] rather than on promissory estoppel.

The first issue is to ask if proprietary estoppel should be available where conduct has been unconscionable, even though the essential elements of it are not present. If this is so then there is of course the danger that estoppel will indeed be so wide and general that it is impossible to see what its function is.

In **Yeoman's Row Management Ltd v Cobbe** [2008] UKHL 55 HL, an oral agreement between the company and Cobbe provided that a block of flats owned by the company would be demolished and Cobbe would apply for planning permission to erect houses in their place with any excess of the proceeds over £24 million shared equally with the company. After planning permission had been obtained, the company went back on the oral agreement and demanded more money, as it now realised that the land was worth much more. Cobbe claimed that the company was estopped from going back on the agreement.

Lord Scott asked, 'What is the fact that the company is estopped from asserting?' There was no question that the oral agreement was unenforceable and Cobbe did not claim a specific property right, merely a hope of entering a contract. He held that the Court of Appeal, which held in Cobbe's favour, had been influenced too much by the fact that it regarded the behaviour of the company as unconscionable without requiring the essential elements of proprietary estoppel to be present.

[4] This case is outside the current debate but adds another angle to it. Mention of it ought to add to your marks.

It is submitted that another case where estoppel acted too much as a general remedy is ***Pascoe v Turner*** [1979] 1 WLR 431 HC.[4] The claimant and defendant had lived in the claimant's house. When the relationship ended the claimant told the defendant that the house and everything in it was hers. In reliance on this the claimant, to the defendant's knowledge, spent money on the house. She was given notice to quit by the claimant but the court ordered the house to be conveyed to her although it was clear that her acts of reliance were only on the basis that she had a licence to live there for life.

[5] This is a crucial paragraph which links the first part of the answer to the second. You are showing that you are actually engaging with the question and writing a balanced answer which looks at two points of view. The type of paragraph which really adds to your marks!

However, although the courts should require that a proprietary estoppel claim satisfies the criteria set out above, there is also a danger of the courts going too far the other way and setting out criteria which would mean that proprietary estoppel would no longer apply to promises of future intentions such as promises to leave by will.[5]

[6] This is an essential point: the view of Lord Scott needs to be carefully stated.

In ***Yeoman's Row Management Ltd v Cobbe,*** Lord Scott considered that proprietary estoppel should be restricted to representations of specific facts or mixed law and fact by X which stood in the way of a right claimed by Y.[6] This seemed to mean that proprietary estoppel was no different from promissory estoppel: it only applied as a defence to an action where those specific representations had been gone back on and not to enable an independent right to be asserted. In cases of promises to leave by will, Lord Scott would use the remedial constructive trust.

[7] This is important: if Lord Scott's analysis was adopted then it would mean not only that promises to leave on death would be outside the scope of estoppel but others too. *Dillwyn* v *Llewellyn* is a good case to mention, as it has always been regarded as a classic estoppel case and it would seem startling if this type of case was no longer to be decided under estoppel.

The problem is that proprietary estoppel has always applied to representations of what will happen and not just to specific present facts, as where there is a representation to someone that she will acquire property on the death of the representor, as in ***Gillett v Holt*** [2001] Ch 210 CA, and in cases such as ***Dillwyn v Llewelyn*** [1862] 4 De GF & J 517 HC,[7] where a father's encouragement to his son to build a house on the father's land meant that on the father's death the land built on was ordered to be conveyed to the son.

[8] *Thorner* v *Major* is the second recent case which is essential to mention.

However, in ***Thorner v Major*** [2009] UKHL 18,[8] the majority did not accept that estoppel should be confined to representations of present fact. D had worked at P's farm for no payment from 1976 onwards, and by the 1980s, hoped that he might inherit the farm. No express representation had ever been made, but D relied on various hints and remarks made by P over the years. The House of Lords held that these amounted to an estoppel.

[9] This rounds off the answer, as it mentions a slightly different point from that made by Lord Scott. It shows that you have really looked at what the judges actually said in these cases and will add to your marks.

Furthermore, the idea of Lord Walker in ***Yeoman's Row*** that the claimant must believe that they have been made an irrevocable promise was not accepted.[9] This would inevitably have meant that promises to leave by will would not be covered by promissory estoppel as a will can be revoked. However, in ***Thorner v Major*** it was held that the question is whether a party has reasonably relied on an assurance by the other as to that person's conduct.

In conclusion, estoppel should apply in as wide a variety of situations as possible but only if certain criteria are met. The decision in ***Thorner v Major*** is to be welcomed as keeping estoppel on the right track.

 Make your answer stand out

- By considering the extent to which detriment is an essential requirement of estoppel.
- By discussion of the remedial constructive trust.
- By examining the extent to which promissory estoppel has moved on from the *High Trees* decision.
- By including the further point made by Lord Scott – the need for certainty of subject matter as to the subject of the representation.
- By referring to cases following *Thorner* v *Major,* for example *Cook* v *Thomas* [2010] EWCA Civ 227.

Don't be tempted to . . .

- Just describe estoppel.
- Go into the question without distinguishing between proprietary and promissory estoppel.
- Just reel off cases on estoppel without looking at the underlying issues.
- Miss the point that there are two distinct issues raised by the discussion of *Yeoman's Row* v *Cobbe* and *Thorner* v *Major.*

@ Try it yourself

Now take a look at the question below and attempt to answer it. You can check your response against the answer guidance available on the companion website (**www.pearsoned.co.uk/lawexpressqa**).

> Jack gave Mary a licence to occupy a cottage on his land. Jack then sold all of the land, including the cottage, to Steve. The sale was expressly subject to Mary's licence to occupy the cottage and Steve paid a reduced price as a result.
>
> It is now two years since the sale and Steve wishes to redevelop the land which will involve demolishing Mary's cottage. Steve is prepared to compensate Mary for this but he insists that she must leave the cottage.
>
> Mary does not wish to leave. Advise her.

www.pearsoned.co.uk/lawexpressqa

Go online to access more revision support including additional essay and problem questions with diagram plans, 'You be the marker' questions, and download all diagrams from the book.

Charitable trusts

How this topic may come up in exams

This is a favourite area for problem questions on whether particular objects of a trust are charitable. Watch for where a question asks you if a trust is valid rather than if it is just charitable. If this is so you may need to use material from our discussion of three certainties (Chapter 3) and non-charitable *purpose trusts* (Chapter 10). Essay questions may focus on public benefit, especially on the Charities Act 2011, and on political trusts. A final area is failure of charitable gifts together with failure of non-charitable gifts. These could be either problem or essay questions.

■ Before you begin

It's a good idea to consider the following key themes of charitable trusts before tackling a question on this topic.

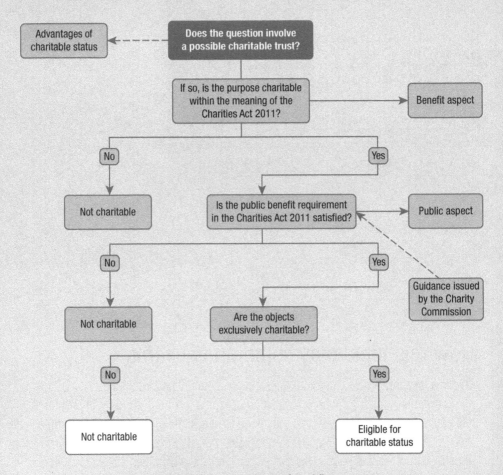

A printable version of this diagram is available from **www.pearsoned.co.uk/lawexpressqa**

? Question 1

Joan is drafting her will and wishes to leave some bequests and wants to know if they are charitable. If they are not, then she would like you to suggest revised wording to ensure that they are charitable.

(a) £50,000 to hold on trust to research into whether the works of Jane Austen were in fact written by Walter Scott.

(b) £10,000 to my trustees to support the campaign against the building of a relief road round Barset as this would have a detrimental impact on the environment and also to campaign against the building of new roads generally and in favour of rail transport on environmental grounds.

Advise her.

Answer plan

→ Begin by explaining the fundamental points of charity law as they apply to both parts of the question: the requirements for charitable objects and public benefit.

→ Distinguish clearly between the 'benefit aspect' of charity and the 'public aspect'.

→ Note the relationship between statute and case law on the one hand and the Charity Commissioners' Guidance on the other.

→ Explain and analyse in part (a) the law on trusts for the advancement of education in the area of research and also the requirement of public benefit.

→ Suggest possible changes in wording to make this gift charitable.

→ Explain in part (b) that political trusts cannot be charitable but that charities may engage in political activity in support of their charitable objects.

→ Suggest possible changes in wording to make this gift charitable.

Diagram plan

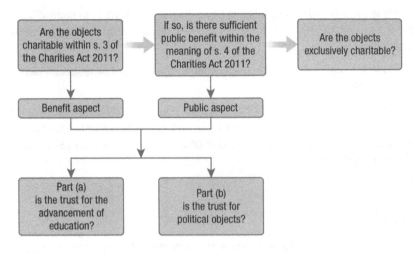

Are the objects charitable within s. 3 of the Charities Act 2011? → If so, is there sufficient public benefit within the meaning of s. 4 of the Charities Act 2011? → Are the objects exclusively charitable?

Benefit aspect | Public aspect

Part (a) is the trust for the advancement of education? | Part (b) is the trust for political objects?

A printable version of this diagram is available from **www.pearsoned.co.uk/lawexpressqa**

Answer

[1] In problem questions it is often better to plunge straight in and start answering part (a), etc. However, here it will save time if you set these essential points out first – and it will also gain you marks at the start.

[2] It is vital at the start to relate your answer to the angle of the question. It is not: 'are these objects charitable?' but 'if they are not charitable, can they be amended so that they are charitable?' Keep coming back to this point.

[3] It is vital to stress that in all cases there is an initial issue of whether the actual purpose has public benefit. This is often missed by students and so emphasising this at the start will gain you those valuable extra marks.

In these situations it is necessary to consider three points:[1]

(i) Are the objects charitable within the meaning of section 3 of the Charities Act 2011?

(ii) If so, is there sufficient public benefit?

(iii) If so, are the objects exclusively charitable?

If any of these requirements are not met then it is necessary to suggest appropriate wording so that, if possible, the trusts do have charitable status.[2]

The law on public benefit applies to both situations. Section 2(1)(b) of the Charities Act 2011 provides that any charitable purpose must be for the public benefit (referred to by the Charity Commission as the 'benefit aspect').[3] If a charity satisfies this test then the question is whether the actual benefit is available to the public or to a section of the public (referred to by the Charity Commission as the 'public aspect').[4]

Section 4(2) removes what is said to be the previous presumption that certain types of charities, including those for the relief of poverty and the advancement of religion, were presumed to be for the public benefit and so public benefit must be proved in all cases. Section 4(3) provides that 'any reference to the public benefit is a reference to the public benefit as that term is understood for the purposes of the law relating to charities in England and Wales'. The effect of this is to preserve the case law which existed before the 2006 Act. It was this Act which effected changes in charity law; the 2011 Act merely consolidates the statutory provisions relating to charity law.[5]

[5] An examiner will look carefully to see if you have mastered all these points. They are the foundation of the law on public benefit and must be set out clearly in any answer to a problem question on charitable trusts. As they appear in both parts of the question, it makes sense to set them out at the start.

[6] This follows on from the previous comment: you are relating this point to the actual question. In fact the Guidance simply states the law but with examples.

In addition, section 17 of the Charities Act 2011 obliges the Charity Commission to issue Guidance on the meaning of public benefit and by section 17(5) charity trustees must have regard to this. It is the Charity Commission which decides on applications for charitable status and so, when advising Joan, I will need to have the Guidance in mind.[6]

[7] The price to be paid for a good mark in a question on charitable trusts is a wide knowledge of the case law, as this is where the detail of the law on charities is. Here our knowledge has paid off, as we have identified relevant cases on educational charities.

[8] It is very important not to go off the point here and try to judge for yourself if this proposed bequest is charitable, as you could easily go into a long rambling discussion. Instead, deal with it as the courts would: expert evidence needs to be sought. You should do the same for any answer where you are uncertain of the actual merits of the proposed charitable gift.

(a) The first proposed bequest is '£50,000 to hold on trust to research into whether the works of Jane Austen were in fact written by Walter Scott. This could be for the advancement of education, which is charitable by section 3(1)(b) of the Charities Act 2011 but, as pointed out above, the court must be satisfied that the actual purpose is for the public benefit so that it satisfies the benefit aspect. Trusts for research can be charitable as in *Re Hopkins' Will Trust* [1964] 3 All ER 46 CA,[7] where a gift to be applied towards finding the Bacon–Shakespeare manuscripts was charitable. Wilberforce J held that research must be of educational value to the researcher, or pass into the store of 'educational material' or 'improve the sum of communicable knowledge in a field which education may cover'. In this case, he held that discovering the Bacon–Shakespeare manuscripts would be 'of the highest value to history and to literature'. The case here involves a more unusual question and so there would need to be expert evidence as to the educational value of the research and whether this is a worthwhile endeavour.[8] Thus in *Re Pinion* [1965] Ch 85 HC, a studio and its contents were given to trustees to enable them to be used as a museum but no benefit from it could be shown as its contents were stigmatised by the court as 'a mass of junk'. There is the same fundamental issue here: is this enquiry of possible public benefit?

If it is, then we must ask if the benefit is available to the public or a section of it. In **Re Besterman's Will Trust** [1980] *The Times,* 21 January HC it was emphasised that a trust for research will only be charitable if, in addition to the subject of that research being useful, there is the intention to disseminate it, and there is no mention of this in Joan's proposed bequest. This will therefore need to be amended to include details of how and where the results of any research will be communicated to the public.[9]

There is also the possibility that the research could be charitable under section 3(1)(f), 'the advancement of arts, culture, heritage or science', but the same considerations will apply here: is the research of value and the need to disseminate it.[10]

(b) The next proposed bequest is: £10,000 to my trustees to support the campaign against the building of a relief road round Barset as this would have a detrimental impact on the environment and also to campaign against the building of new roads generally and in favour of rail transport on environmental grounds.

There are two separate bequests here: one for the specific issue of campaigning against the building of the road on environmental grounds and second a more general one of campaigning against the building of new roads generally and in favour of railways instead.

The first bequest could be valid on the ground set out in section 3(1)(i) of the Charities Act 2011 as being for advancement of environmental protection or improvement. In principle this could certainly be charitable but more detail is needed on the initial question of how building the road would have a detrimental impact on the environment so that it is clear that the actual purpose satisfies the benefit aspect. Once that is satisfied, there needs to be evidence of how the benefit is available to the public or to a section of the public (the 'public aspect'). This again needs to be spelt out: what exactly will the campaign involve?[11]

The second bequest is problematic as it could be construed as political. Where the main purpose of the trust is political then it

[9] Do not forget that the question asks you for advice on suggested wording to make the gifts charitable if you feel that, at present, they are not.

[10] There is no need to go into detail on this point, as the same considerations apply as in the question of whether the bequest was educational. However, you will certainly gain credit for mentioning it.

[11] There is no need to go at a tangent here and give lengthy examples of what the campaign might involve, for example, use of social media, press, etc. Just raise the point.

[12] It is essential that you start with an explanation (not a definition, which is not possible) of exactly what political is. The advantage of using the explanation given by Slade J in this case is that you can then use it to illustrate how it was applied to the facts of the case.

will be invalid. In ***McGovern v A-G*** [1982] Ch 321 HC, Slade J said that the term 'political trusts' included trusts to:[12]

1 further the interests of a particular political party;

2 procure changes in the laws of either the United Kingdom or a foreign country;

3 procure a reversal of government policy or of particular decisions of governmental authorities whether in the United Kingdom or in a foreign country.

In this case the object of the trust seems to be to procure a reversal of government policy and would be political. However, the Charity Commissioners have issued Guidance (Campaigning and Political Activity by Charities: CC9) which states that 'political campaigning, or political activity . . . must be undertaken by a charity only in the context of supporting the delivery of its charitable purposes. Unlike other forms of campaigning, it must not be the continuing and sole activity of the charity'. The question is then whether here the political campaigning supports the delivery of the main object, which would have to be environmental protection. However, here there seems to be two objects, one dealing with a particular road and the other with roads in general, and so it cannot be said that the second one is in support of the first. Thus the gift is not exclusively charitable and Joan should delete the second object and give more detail on public benefit in the first one.

 Make your answer stand out

- Analyse the wording of each gift closely and never assume that because it may be for charitable purposes this automatically makes it charitable – apply all three requirements.
- Do further research on the 'Guidance Campaigning and Political Activity by Charities: CC9' mentioned in the question.
- Could the restriction on the 'political activities' of charities be an infringement of their rights under Article 10 of the European Convention on Human Rights, which provides for freedom of expression?
- In *Aid/Watch Incorporated* v *Commissioner of Taxation* [2010] 241 CLR 539, the High Court of Australia held that there is no longer any prohibition in Australia on charities having political purposes. Look at this case in more detail.

> **!** **Don't be tempted to . . .**
>
> - Ignore the instruction in the question that you are asked if necessary to advise on revised wording to make the gift charitable.
> - Fail to distinguish between the 'benefit aspect' and the 'public aspect'.
> - Spend too long on whether the gift can be charitable and not enough on whether it has sufficient public benefit.
> - Fail to mention (even briefly) the requirement that all trusts must be exclusively charitable.
> - Come to very definite conclusions, especially in (a).
> - Fail to analyse the exact wording of each gift.

? Question 2

Andrew's will contained the following dispositions:

(a) £10,000 to my needy brothers, Tim and Tom, to enable them and their families to have a better standard of living.

(b) £10,000 to the Malvern Brethren. This body meets on the Malvern Hills and worships various deities. Admission is by a rigorous process of scrutiny and the Brethren also publish an annual report on their work.

Advise Albert's executors on whether these dispositions are valid as charitable trusts.

Answer plan

→ Summarise the requirements for a valid charitable trust.

→ Explain in part (a) the law on trusts for the relief of poverty and public benefit.

→ Consider the decision in *Attorney General* v *Charity Commission for England and Wales.*

→ Note the distinction between the 'benefit aspect' of public benefit and the 'public aspect'.

→ Explain in part (b) the law on trusts for the advancement of religion.

→ Note the decision in *R (on the application of Hodkin)* v *Registrar General of Births, Deaths and Marriages* and assess its impact on charity law.

→ Consider if the public benefit test is satisfied.

Diagram plan

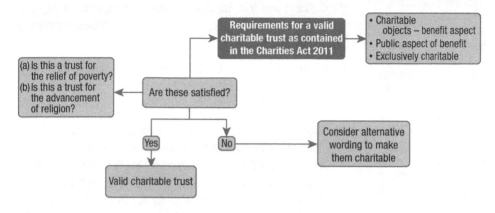

A printable version of this diagram is available from **www.pearsoned.co.uk/lawexpressqa**

Answer

In these situations it is necessary to consider three points:[1]

(i) Are the objects charitable within the meaning of section 3 of the Charities Act 2011?

(ii) If so, is there sufficient public benefit?

(iii) If so, are the objects exclusively charitable?

The law on public benefit is worth setting out at the start as it applies to both situations. Section 2(1)(b) of the Charities Act 2011 provides that any charitable purpose must be for the public benefit (referred to by the Charity Commission as the 'benefit aspect'). If a charity satisfies this test then the question is whether the actual benefit is available to the public or to a section of the public (referred to by the Charity Commission as the 'public aspect'). Section 4(2) removes what is said to be the previous presumption that certain types of charities, including those for the relief of poverty and the advancement of religion, were presumed to be for the public benefit and so public benefit must be proved in all cases. Section 4(3) provides that 'any reference to the public benefit is a reference to the public benefit as that term is understood for the

[2] An examiner will look carefully to see if you have mastered these points. They are the foundation of the law on public benefit and must be set out clearly in any answer to a problem question on charitable trusts. As they appear in both parts of the question, it makes sense to set them out at the start. Make sure also that you insert this explanation of the relationship between the 2006 and 2011 Acts into every answer. It is vital to make this clear.

[3] You should make it a rule to first refer to the charitable purposes set out in section 3 of the Charities Act 2011 and see which of them could apply. It may be that more than one could apply, so do watch for this as an ability to recognise that more than one purpose could be relevant will obviously boost your marks.

[4] Remember that you need to separate any consideration of public benefit from the first question of whether the gift is charitable at all before the benefit aspect.

[5] Students sometimes say that trusts for the relief of poverty do not require public benefit at all. Do not make this mistake.

purposes of the law relating to charities in England and Wales'. The effect of this is to preserve the case law which existed before the 2006 Act. It was this Act which effected changes in charity law; the 2011 Act merely consolidates the statutory provisions relating to charity law.[2]

In addition, section 17 of the Charities Act 2011 obliges the Charity Commission to issue guidance on the meaning of public benefit and by section 17(5) charity trustees must have regard to this.

(a) Albert wishes to leave '£10,000 to my needy brothers, Tim and Tom, to enable them and their families to have a better standard of living' and the word 'needy' could imply that this trust is for the prevention or relief of poverty, which is a charitable purpose by section 3(1)(a) of the Charities Act 2011. The question is whether 'needy' comes within the notion of poverty.[3] In *Re Coulthurst* [1951] Ch 661 CA, Evershed MR explained that 'poverty does not mean destitution . . . it may not unfairly be paraphrased for present purposes as meaning persons who have to "go short" in the ordinary acceptation of that term . . .', and in *Re Scarisbrick* [1951] Ch 622, a gift for 'needy persons' was held to be charitable. It could also be said that this trust is charitable under section 3(1)(j), 'the relief of those in need by reason of youth, age, ill-health, disability, financial hardship or other disadvantage', as Tim and Tom will be suffering financial hardship if they are needy.

The next question is whether the trusts have sufficient public benefit.[4]

The problem here is that the benefits are restricted to Albert's brothers, Tim and Tom. The courts had established that trusts for 'poor relations' can be valid (see *Isaac v Defriez* [1754] Amb 595 HC) but a distinction was drawn between these and trusts for individuals (see Jenkins LJ in *Re Scarisbrick* [1951] Ch 622 CA). In *Dingle v Turner* [1972] AC 601 HL, this distinction was expressly approved and the fact that trusts for the relief of poverty are subject to a more generous test of public benefit[5] was recognised in *Attorney General v Charity Commission for England and Wales* [2012] UKUT 420 (TCC) and the continued existence of this was accepted. However, this case is a trust for individuals and so will not meet the public benefit test.

If the trust claims to be charitable under section 3(1)(j) of the Charities Act 2011, 'the relief of those in need by reason of youth, age, ill-health, disability, financial hardship or other disadvantage', it will fare no better as it will come up against the same problem of lack of public benefit.

Given that the trust is clearly not charitable, the question of whether it is exclusively charitable does not arise.[6]

[6] But you should mention this point.

(b) Malvern Brethren will argue that they are charitable as being for the advancement of religion as they worship various deities. Section 3(1)(c) of the Charities Act 2011 provides that a trust for advancement of religion is charitable and the fact that the Brethren worship more than one deity does not affect this, as section 3(2)(a) of the Charities Act 2011 provides that, for the purposes of this Act, religion can involve a belief in more than one god. The question of what is a religion arose in ***R (on the application of Hodkin) v Registrar General of Births, Deaths and Marriages*** [2013] UKSC 77 HL. This did not concern charity law but whether a Church of Scientology chapel was a place of worship. Lord Toulson said that religion was '. . . a spiritual or non-secular belief system, held by a group of adherents, which claims to explain mankind's place in the universe and relationship with the infinite, and to teach its adherents how they are to live their lives in conformity with the spiritual understanding associated with the belief system'. This was a much wider definition than in the previous case, on this issue, ***R v Registrar General, ex parte Segerdal*** [1970] 2 QB 697 CA, and the Charity Commissioners have recognised that this extended definition of religion may mean that charity law's definition of religion may need to be modified. It is suggested that the Malvern Brethren are within this definition, given that they are a belief system as they worship various deities. Moreover they are also within the definition in the Charity Act 2011, as this specifically provides that religion can involve a belief in more than one god.[7]

[7] Until matters become clearer you should refer to both possibilities, as we have done here.

The next question is whether there is sufficient public benefit as required by section 4 of the Act, and it is worth emphasising that the Charity Commissioners have made it clear that the decision in *Hodkin* (above) does not affect the law on public benefit. In this case membership is not closed even though it is by a 'rigorous process of scrutiny'. In *Gilmour v Coats* [1949] AC 426 HL, a gift to a community of strictly cloistered and enclosed nuns was held not charitable because the benefit conferred on the public by their prayers was, per Lord Simonds, 'manifestly not susceptible of proof'. However, here an annual report is published which is presumably available to the public. Moreover, the report is on their work, which implies that the Brethren actually undertake some tasks beyond worship.

Here we could draw a comparison with *Neville Estates* v *Madden* [1962] Ch 832 HC, where a trust for the advancement of religion among members of the Catford Synagogue was held charitable on this basis even though the services at the synagogue were only open to those on its list of members. There was a benefit in the actual holding of services and this was on the facts public benefit.

[8] You will not lose marks by failing to come to a definite conclusion provided that you have examined the arguments fully. Indeed, it is often weak students who come to extremely definite conclusions.

On the facts here it is impossible to tell whether there is sufficient public benefit and we would need more information on what the report contains and what activities the Brethren undertake.[8] The admission of new members, albeit by rigorous scrutiny, may well tip the balance in favour of charitable status.

 Make your answer stand out

- Research the case of the Preston Down Trust – you can find it on the Charity Commission's website: **www.gov.uk/government/publications/preston-down-trust.**
- Consider the argument of Hackney (2008) that in fact there never was any presumption of public benefit and that benefit was assumed. What had to be proved – and still does – is that this is public benefit.
- Consider the possibility that Article 9 of the European Convention on Human Rights might be relevant in considering whether a trust for the advancement of religion might have public benefit. See Harding (2008). Look also at Iwobi (2009).
- Look in detail at the Guidance issued by the Charity Commission and apply it to the question.

❓ Question 3

You are asked to advise his executors and trustees on the validity of the following bequests contained in the will of Arthur, who has just died:

(a) £10,000 to the Barsetshire County Cricket Club.

(b) £100,000 to be held by my trustees to distribute at their discretion among the employees and ex-employees of the National Health Service for their education and training, in gratitude for the excellent treatment by the NHS of me throughout my life.

Answer plan

→ Consider whether the gifts can be for a charitable purpose and if there is public benefit.

→ If not, can there be a valid non-charitable purpose trust or a gift to the members?

→ Can there be a valid private trust and, if so, will it satisfy the test for certainty of objects?

→ Consider the possible effects of the rules against perpetuities.

Diagram plan

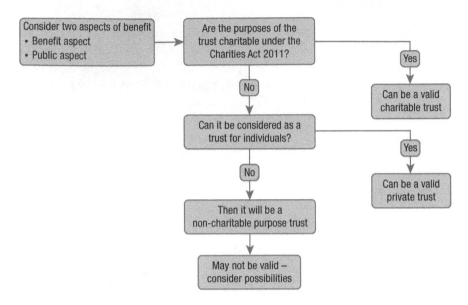

A printable version of this diagram is available from **www.pearsoned.co.uk/lawexpressqa**

[1] This is an absolutely vital sentence, as it would be all too easy to take a quick look at this question, think that it concerned charitable trusts and devote all of your answer to this. In fact the question just asks if the trusts are *valid* and so we must consider all possibilities.

[2] This may seem an obvious point but it is a good idea to be aware of this possibility and in other questions of this kind there may be the possibility of a private trust. It also shows at the start that you are thinking of all possibilities.

[3] Do not assume that any sport club is amateur or professional unless you are given this information.

Answer

We are asked whether these trusts are valid or not, and not whether they are, for example, charitable. Therefore, this answer will consider the whole range of possibilities.[1]

(a) The first gift is one of £10,000 to Barsetshire County Cricket Club. This cannot be a private trust, as it is for purposes and not for individuals.[2] Is the purpose charitable? Trusts for amateur sport are charitable by section 3(1)(g) of the Charities Act 2011 and sport is defined by section 3(2)(d) of the Act as meaning 'sport or games which promote health by involving physical or mental skill or exertion'. This certainly includes cricket. We do not know, however, if Barsetshire County Cricket Club is an amateur club.[3] If it is, then the purposes will be charitable and it is suggested that the necessary element of public benefit is found by the gift enabling people to play cricket. If the club is professional then the gift cannot be charitable as, in *IRC v McMullen* [1981] AC 1 HL, Lord Hailsham stated that the playing of games was not in itself charitable and so charitable status depends on satisfying section 3(1)(g) above.

If the gift is not charitable then it falls within the category of non-charitable purpose trusts unless the cricket club is a company, as then there will be no trust at all and it will simply be a bequest to the company.[4] If it is not a company it will be an unincorporated association and, thus, as it cannot hold property itself, any property must be held on trust for its purposes, as in *Re Finger's Will Trust* [1972] Ch 286 HC. In this case the purposes were charitable and so there was a valid charitable trust, but this is not so here. There is the possibility that the gift could be considered as either to be held on trust for the members of the club, as in *Re Denley's Trust Deed* [1969] 1 Ch 373 HC, or as a gift to the members who will hold it on a contractual basis, as in *Re Recher's Will Trusts* [1972] Ch 526 HC.[5] The wording of the gift simply mentioned the club and not the members but this is not necessarily an obstacle to the court discovering either a trust for the members or a gift to them as in *Re Lipinski's Will Trusts* [1976] Ch 235 HC, where a gift to be used 'solely' for the construction or maintenance of the association's buildings was a gift to the members.

If the court adopts either the solution in *Re Denley* or *Re Recher* then the gift may be valid, but if not, then unless the club is a company there will be an invalid non-charitable purpose trust and so the £10,000 will be held on a resulting trust for Arthur's estate.

If *Re Recher* applies there will be a gift to the members, but if there is a trust on the lines of *Re Denley,* the question is whether the gift infringes the rule against perpetuities. There are in fact two perpetuity rules and the applicable one here concerns inalienability of capital.[6] The period cannot exceed that fixed by section 15(4) of the Perpetuities and Accumulations Act 1964, as lives or lives in being plus 21 years. As no other period is specified here, this will apply. It is likely that the 'wait and see' provisions of the 1964 Act do not apply to non-charitable purpose trusts and so, as there is the possibility at the outset that the perpetuity period will be infringed, the gift will be void and the £10,000 will be held on a resulting trust for Arthur's estate.

[4] Note that this part of the question refers to a 'bequest' and not a trust as in the second part. Thus it could be a direct gift.

[5] In any answer on this area you should consider both of these possibilities although how much time you spend on them will depend on the type of question.

[6] There is no need to discuss perpetuities at length but, as many students for some reason try to avoid the topic altogether, you will gain considerable credit for an accurate account of the law.

(b) The gift of £100,000 to employees and ex-employees of the National Health Service for their education and training can first be considered as a charitable trust as the number of employees and ex-employees of the NHS give it the flavour of a trust for purposes rather than for individuals. If it is charitable, then it can be for the advancement of education which is charitable under section 3(1)(b) of the Charities Act 2011, or possibly for the advancement of health or the saving of lives under section 3(1)(d). The next question is whether there is sufficient public benefit, as all the beneficiaries are linked by their employment in the NHS.

In **Oppenheim v Tobacco Securities Trust Co Ltd** [1951] AC 297 HL, a trust was held not charitable where it was to provide for 'the education of children of employees or former employees of the British American Tobacco Co Ltd or any of its subsidiary or allied companies', even though the number of employees exceeded 110,000. Lord Simonds held that the fact that the group was large did not make the trust charitable if the connection between its members was based on some personal tie such as employment by a particular employee or employees, as here. This would seem to decide the matter, as the effect of section 4(3) of the Charities Act 2011[7] is that existing case law on charities is preserved.

Lord MacDermott dissented, holding that there was the intention to benefit a class of substantial size and importance in such a way that the interests of the class as a whole were advanced. If this view is accepted then it is arguable that there is sufficient public benefit.[8]

If this trust is not charitable on the basis of **Oppenheim,** it might be valid as a private trust provided that it satisfies the requirement of certainty of objects laid down in **McPhail v Doulton** [1971] AC 424 HL, where Lord Wilberforce held that the test was, 'Can it be said with certainty that any given individual is or is not a member of the class?' Thus it is open to anyone to come forward and show that they are an employee or ex-employee of the NHS.

[7] Note that in the interests of accuracy we have not put 'section 4(3) of the Charities Act *says*' because the actual wording of section 4(3) does not expressly say that existing case law is preserved. However, this is what it means. If you are going for high marks – or simply do not want to drop marks – make sure that you get these small points right.

[8] If you mention *Oppenheim* then you should mention Lord McDermott's dissent too, as it is often thought that his was the better view.

[9] This is clearly a point which the examiner is expecting you to mention and so you will lose marks if you end with *McPhail* v *Doulton*.

However, there must be very many employees or ex-employees of the NHS[9] and in ***McPhail v Doulton*** Lord Wilberforce said that even though a description of beneficiaries complied with the test he had laid down, it might be 'so hopelessly wide as not to form anything like a class', and gave as an example 'all the residents of Greater London'. This principle was applied in ***R v District Auditor, ex parte West Yorkshire Metropolitan County Council*** [1986] RVR 24 HC, where a trust set up for the inhabitants of the County of West Yorkshire, of which there were about 2,500,000, was held void for administrative unworkability. If this is so the trust will be invalid.

✓ Make your answer stand out

- Look at McInnes (2008), who looks at Canadian case law – this could give any answer on sport and charity law a good comparative perspective.
- Mention that section 18 of the Perpetuities and Accumulations Act 2009 exempts non-charitable purpose trusts from the provisions of this Act.
- As the Perpetuities and Accumulations Act 1964 applies to private trusts, if the 'wait and see' principle in the Act does apply it will enable the trustees to exercise their powers within the perpetuity period, and any money not distributed at that time will go on a resulting trust for Arthur's estate.
- Mention that in *Dingle* v *Turner* [1972] AC 601, Lord Cross (with whom all the other Law Lords concurred) agreed with Lord MacDermott's view of public benefit in *Oppenheim* v *Tobacco Securities*, although this was *obiter.*

! Don't be tempted to . . .

- Spend too long on any one area – recognise that this problem deals with many points, and marks will be allocated for each one.
- Assume that the gifts are charitable and fail to consider other possibilities.
- Deal with whether the gift is for a charitable purpose and then forget to consider if there is public benefit.
- Start off without a clear plan in mind, as this is an area where the issues are closely linked.

 Question 4

'We have concluded that, while the (Charities Act 2006) has been broadly welcomed by the charitable sector, it is critically flawed on the issue of public benefit.' (Post-legislative scrutiny of the Charities Act 2006 by the Public Administration Committee (2012).)

Critically consider this view of the public benefit requirement in the Charities Act 2006.

Answer plan

→ What the question is about: the two problems of confusion in what is now the 2011 Act and misleading Guidance issued by the Charity Commission.

→ Explain carefully by analysing sections 4(2) and (3) of the Charity Act 2011 how this confusion arose.

→ Look at how the confusion seems to have been cleared up by *Attorney General* v *Charity Commission* [2012] but make the case that the legislation itself still needs amending.

→ Then look at the Guidance issued by the Commission showing the problems with its application in actual cases.

→ Conclude by stating that legislation is needed to clarify the law on public benefit.

Diagram plan

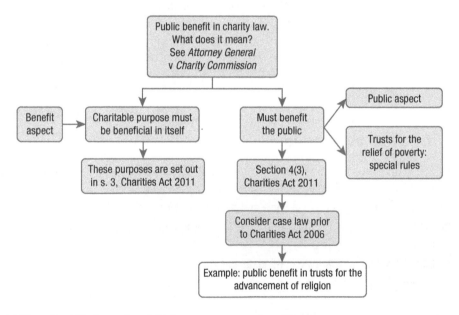

A printable version of this diagram is available from **www.pearsoned.co.uk/lawexpressqa**

Answer

[1] Here we are addressing the issue directly and in effect setting out a structure for our essay. Always aim for this type of start. Note carefully that the question only concerns the public benefit issue and so there are no marks for discussion of charitable purposes themselves.

[2] Always remember to include clarifying points such as this – they show that you are really thinking clearly.

[3] This is a crucial provision which you must remember for the exam.

[4] Your mention of section 4(2) above must be accompanied by contrasting it with section 4(3), clearly bringing out the differences between the two.

[5] This is an important argument to refer to and it connects with the next paragraph.

The argument of the Public Administration Committee that the Charities Act 2006 is 'fatally flawed' on the issue of public benefit is based on two points:[1] first, the confusion on whether the presumption of public benefit was removed by the Act; and secondly, the requirement for the Charity Commission to produce public benefit Guidance when the law on which that Guidance was based was itself uncertain. This has led, as the Public Administration Committee says, to lengthy legal battles which could perhaps have been avoided if the law had been clear. Moreover, the Committee says that it has left the 'Commission, a branch of the executive, in an impossible position'. It should be made clear that the legislation is now in the Charities Act 2011 but the legislation is the same as the 2011 Act was a consolidating statute.[2]

The first issue is the debate on whether the presumption of public benefit in cases of trusts for the relief of poverty, the advancement of education and the advancement of religion was removed by the Act so that in all cases public benefit has to be proved. This was clearly the view of the Charity Commission, as a spokesperson for the Charity Commission (quoted in Third Sector Online, 25 July 2012) said that, 'The Act stated that it is not to be presumed that a purpose of a particular description is for the public benefit.' The problem is that this referred to section 4(2), which indeed provides that in determining whether the requirement of public benefit is satisfied in relation to any such purpose, it is not to be presumed that a purpose of a particular description is for the public benefit.[3]

However, this does not go far enough as section 4(3) provides that any reference to the public benefit is a reference to the public benefit as that term is understood for the purposes of the law relating to charities in England and Wales.[4] The effect of this is to preserve the previous case law, but this means that cases such as **Oppenheim v Tobacco Securities Trust Co Ltd** [1951] AC 297 HL and **Gilmour v Coats** [1949] AC 426 HL, which laid down the law on public benefit in cases of education and religion respectively, are still good law.

Hackney (2008) argued that the law has been misunderstood and that it has not indeed changed.[5] He says that the answer is that the 'law has always been that those seeking to establish a charity have had to prove that it was of a public character: this has not been presumed in any way nor was it a matter for dogmatic assumption'. He quoted the argument of counsel in **Oppenheim v Tobacco Securities Trust Co Ltd** [1951] AC 297 at 301, 'It is for the appellant to show that it is a charity. This cannot be a valid charitable trust unless it is of a public character, i.e., for a purpose directed to the benefit of the community or a section of the community.'

This argument seems to have been accepted in **Attorney General v Charity Commission** [2012] UKUT 420 (TCC), which involved a number of charities concerned with the relief of poverty, but the Upper Chamber took the opportunity to restate the law on public benefit. It held that public benefit is part of the nature of each charitable purpose. Thus education is by itself charitable and so is the relief of poverty.[6] There could of course be cases where this was not so, one example often given being a school for pickpockets, but that does not affect the general principle. That being so, there is no question of any presumption of public benefit: that benefit is intrinsic to the charitable purpose. Thus the actual purpose must itself have benefit (known as the 'benefit aspect') such as the relief of poverty, but in addition any actual benefit must be public benefit (known as the 'public aspect').

Nevertheless the Charities Act 2011 remains in force with the two subsections – 4(2) and (3) – and so there is a strong argument for a change in statute law to reflect the actual position.

The mistaken view of the law on public benefit was compounded by the fact that by section 17 of the Charities Act 2011 the Charity Commission is obliged to issue Guidance on the meaning of public benefit and this led to the lengthy legal battles to which the Public Administration Committee referred.[7]

One involved independent fee-paying schools. Guidance issued by the Commission said that any benefit must not be unreasonably restricted by ability to pay any fees charged but this section was successfully challenged in **Independent Schools Council v Charity Commission for England and Wales** [2011] UKUT 421, where the Upper Chamber held that the use of the word 'unreasonable' in the Guidance was wrong as charity law (see e.g. **Re Resch's Will Trusts** [1969] 1 AC 514 PC) had never imposed such a requirement. There was indeed a duty on educational charities to make provision for the poor and this must be more than minimal or tokenistic. Beyond that,

[6] There is no time – and no need – in this essay to consider individual charitable purposes.

[7] You have now come to the other issue raised in the question.

the level of provision to be made for those unable to pay the full fees was to be decided by the trustees in the context of their charity's circumstances. There were no objective benchmarks about what was appropriate. As a result of this case and other problems, the Commission revised its Guidance which now simply states what the law is with examples of how it might apply.

[8] Not everyone agrees with this point and you should make this clear.

The other problem was that lack of clarity on public benefit led to allegations that the Commission was pursuing what was seen by some as a left-wing, secularist anti-religion agenda,[8] especially in the light of the rejection of the Commission's Guidance on fee paying by independent schools in the above case. This was seen also in the Commission's refusal to grant charitable status to the Preston Down Trust, which runs meeting halls for the Exclusive Brethren in Torquay, Paignton and Newton Abbot, because the Commission was not satisfied that it had been established for the advancement of religion for public benefit. The Commission said that its decision took into account such matters as the nature of Christian religion embraced by the trust and the means through which this was promoted, including the public access to its services and the potential for its beneficial impact on the wider community. However, after this decision had been given considerable publicity, the Commission changed its decision in the light of further evidence.

[9] You have rounded off your answer by referring back to the report quoted in the question. This is an excellent way to end but to do so you needed to have done your research on this report.

The Public Administration Committee[9] believes that it is essential for Parliament to revisit charity legislation and set the criteria for charitable status rather than delegating such decisions to the Charity Commission and the courts. This must be the right course of action.

 Make your answer stand out

- Look at the *Preston Down Trust* case in more detail. It was raised in Parliament. See **www.lawandreligionuk.com/2012/11/07/ charitable-status-public-benefit-and-closed-congregations-update/**.
- Read Hackney's (2008) article, quoted in the answer, in full.
- Go to the Charity Commission's website (**www.charity-commission.gov.uk**) and look at the Public Benefit Guidance. If you can use this to add in some extra detail on the thinking of the Commission that will boost your marks.
- Annual Reports of the Charity Commissioners – available on the above website.

> **! Don't be tempted to . . .**
>
> ■ Concentrate too much on the public benefit issue to the exclusion of the others.
> ■ Go through all of the heads of charity set out in section 3 of the Charities Act 2011 and in each case decide if the law has changed. This will take you too long and you will not have time to discuss the issues.
> ■ Discuss whether the Charities Act 2006 (now Charities Act 2011) has changed the law without explaining exactly what its provisions are.

📝 Question 5

'A trust for political purposes . . . can never be regarded as being for the public benefit in the manner which the law regards as charitable' (Slade J in *McGovern* v *AG* [1982] Ch 321 HC).

Critically consider this statement.

Diagram plan

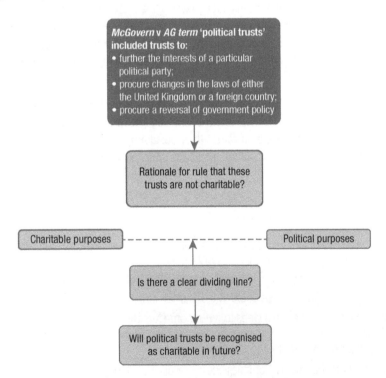

A printable version of this diagram is available from **www.pearsoned.co.uk/lawexpressqa**

Answer plan

→ Explain what the question is saying beginning with an analysis of *McGovern* v *AG* which explains what charitable means.

→ Explain that the theoretical dividing line between charitable and political purposes is not always a clear one in practice.

→ Explain what 'political' means in the context of charity law and follow this with examples from the cases.

→ Consider the problem which 'campaigning' can bring for charities and the Guidance given by the Charity Commission.

→ Conclude by mentioning the different view taken in Australia and the changing role of charities in the context of this question.

Answer

[1] Not everyone agrees with this point and you should make this clear. It is essential that you start with an explanation (not a definition, which is not possible) of exactly what political is. The advantage of using the explanation given by Slade J is that you can then use it to show how it was applied to the facts of the case.

In ***McGovern* v *AG*** [1982] Ch 321 HC, Slade J said that the term 'political trusts' included trusts to:[1]

(a) further the interests of a particular political party;

(b) procure changes in the laws of either the United Kingdom or a foreign country;

(c) procure a reversal of government policy or of particular decisions of governmental authorities whether in the United Kingdom or in a foreign country.

In this case a trust was established by Amnesty International with four main objects:

(i) the relief of prisoners of conscience and their relatives;

(ii) seeking the release of such prisoners;

(iii) the abolition of torture or inhuman treatment or punishment;

(iv) research into human rights and the dissemination of the results of that research.

[2] This case is especially good as an illustration of the law, as it gives examples of where some activities were charitable and some not.

Although objects (i) and (iv) were held by themselves to be charitable, objects (ii) and (iii) *involved* attempting to procure changes in the law and the reversal of government decisions, whether in the United Kingdom or abroad.[2] The trust was therefore held not to be charitable, on the basis that it was not exclusively charitable.

Slade J gave the following reasons why political activities are not charitable as being for the public benefit:

(i) The courts cannot judge if a change in the law is for the public benefit, because it will not normally have evidence before it to enable it to do this.

(ii) Even if the court does have such evidence, to hold that a change in the law is desirable would usurp the function of the legislature.

(iii) In the case of trusts campaigning to secure the alteration of foreign laws, not only would there be the evidential problem referred to at (i) above, but the enforcement of such a trust might prejudice the relations of this country with that of the foreign country concerned.

[3] This is an important sentence as you are setting out the main argument of your essay and then following it with some research detail of your own. These are excellent ways to boost your marks.

There is undoubtedly a theoretical dividing line between charitable and political purposes but it will be argued that it is not always a clear one in practice.[3] In a letter to the Daily Telegraph (8 August 2013), Sir Stephen Bubb, the CEO of the Association of Chief Executives of Voluntary Organisations, pointed out the long history of political campaigning by charities from the presentation of a petition to Parliament in 1787 advocating the abolition of the slave trade to the establishment of societies for the prevention of cruelty to animals in the Victorian era.

However, the boundary between political and charitable activities is not in fact always clear, especially where the trust has an educational flavour. If the objects are connected with propaganda then they will not be charitable, as in **Re Bushnell** [1975] 1 All ER 721 HC, where the object was to use a fund 'for the advancement and propagation of the teaching of socialised medicine'. The court held that the dominant or essential object of the primary trust was to promote or bring about the establishment of a state health service in accordance with the testator's own theory. Therefore, as it was not a trust to educate the public so that they could decide for themselves upon the advantages or otherwise of

[4] It would have been easy to follow *Re Bushnell* with another case where the trust was held not to be charitable but this would have made the same point and would not have boosted your marks by very much. Instead, the next case makes a contrasting point.

such a service, it was not charitable. On the other hand,[4] in **Re Koeppler's Will Trusts** [1985] 2 All ER 869 HC, a gift was construed as being for a project involving conferences on issues of current political debate but which did not involve the propagation of political opinions or any activities of a party political nature. Instead, the object of the project was a genuine attempt to find and disseminate the truth, and accordingly the gift was held to be for the advancement of education and thus charitable. In **Southwood v AG** [2000] WTLR 119 HC, the actual trust

[5] There is no need to set out the facts of this case, as it makes a similar point to those above. Instead, it is this particular point which is significant.

[6] This is a decision of the First Tier Tribunal and it shows how it is now vital keep an eye on decisions of this court as it now hears an increasing number of cases involving claims to charitable status.

[7] This is one area where you will lose marks if you do not refer to what the Charity Commission is saying.

deed was ambiguous and so the court held that it could look at the actual activities of the trust. Here they were not charitable.[5]

Problems have also arisen with the activities of university or college students' unions. These are charitable bodies, as they are connected with the advancement of education, and so their funds must not be used for political purposes, as in **Baldry v Feintuck** [1972] 2 All ER 81 HC, where the use of union funds to campaign for free school milk to be restored was held to be political. In **Webb v O'Doherty** (1991) *The Times,* 11 February HC, an injunction was granted to restrain a students' union from spending money in support of a campaign against the Gulf War. The court distinguished between campaigning by seeking to influence public opinion, which is not charitable, and mere discussion of political issues, which can be charitable.

The matter arose again in **Jonathan Bishop on Behalf of Crocels Community Media Group v The Charity Commission for England and Wales** (2016) WL 03947469.[6] The organisation had a number of objects, including improving fraternity between nations, advancing the understanding and promoting the cause of peace and innovating for the abolition or reduction of standing armies. It was held that these were not charitable purposes within the meaning of the Charities Act 2011, section 3(1). For instance, the object of advancing education on the subject of peace was a potentially charitable purpose but it was linked to a political purpose, seeking to change government policy by promoting this cause. The object of innovating for the abolition or reduction of standing armies was a clear political purpose within the meaning given to that term by Slade J in **Mc Govern v AG.**

It is this distinction between charitable and non-charitable activities, especially in the area of campaigning, which the Charity Commission seeks to draw in its Guidance *Speaking Out: Guidance on Campaigning and Political Activity by Charities* (March 2008).[7] The problem is that a charity may have identified a particular problem as part of its activities in, for example, the area of famine relief, and as a result may feel impelled to take action to remove this. The Guidance states at 3.1. that: 'So long as a charity is engaging in campaigning or political activity solely in order to further or support its charitable purposes, and there is a reasonable likelihood of it being effective, it may carry out campaigning and political activity, as set out in this guidance. The activities it undertakes must be a legitimate and reasonable way for the trustees to further those purposes, and must never be party political.' Moreover,

'A charity can make public comment on social, economic and political issues if these relate to its purpose, or the way in which the charity is able to carry out its work'. Thus, campaigning may be a legitimate activity only if arises out of the work of the charity.

The rule that charities cannot have political purposes may change in future. In ***Aid/Watch Incorporated v Commissioner of Taxation*** [2010] 241 CLR 539, the High Court of Australia held that there is no longer any prohibition in Australia on charities having political purposes. For now the rule remains and while it does it is worth noting that the debate on what is a political purpose needs to be looked at in the context of the enhanced role which governments see for charities or the 'Third Sector', as they are called.[8] The boundary between charities and political activity may be theoretically clear but it is still likely to give rise to problems in the future.

[8] This is a really excellent point to end on – it means that your answer ends on a suitably challenging note by referring earlier to developments in other jurisdictions – always a good idea to boost your marks – and then with this point which looks beyond just legal considerations.

Make your answer stand out

- Read Dunn (2008). This article looks at the role of charities in promoting social reform and the increasing role of the state in promoting social welfare. It then looks at the rules which restrict the political activities of charities.

- Ask if the list of charitable objects set out in section 3 of the Charities Act 2011 could enable a charity to engage in political activity e.g. section 3(1)(h): 'the advancement of human rights, conflict resolution or reconciliation or the promotion of religious or racial harmony or equality and diversity'.

- Mention the different approach taken in the United States. There is a very useful summary of the US cases in the judgment of Carnwath J in *Southwood* v *AG*.

- Look at investigations undertaken by the Charity Commission into particular charities, e.g. the investigation into OXFAM (1991).

- Look at the activities and objects of any charity and see if, in your opinion, the boundary between charitable and political activity is crossed.

- Could the restriction on the 'political activities' of charities be an infringement of their rights under Article 10 of the European Convention on Human Rights, which provides for freedom of expression?

Question 6

John, who died in April 2018, left the following charitable bequests in his will made in 2006:

(a) £10,000 to Hanbury College, where John took his LLB. Hanbury College provided law courses but it no longer exists. When it was dissolved in 2009 its assets were transferred to Chamberlain College, which provides a range of business courses including legal courses.

(b) £50,000 to the Association for Distressed Retired Lawyers, a registered charity. In July 2018 this was wound up. There is in existence an Association for the Relief of Retired Lawyers which is also a registered charity.

(c) £20,000 to the Swinton League for the Rescue of Sick Cats. There has never been such a body.

(d) £15,000 to the Earlsdon College for Young Ladies, an international finishing school for girls aged 16–18. There is a condition attached to the gift that it can only be used for the education of girls who are of German nationality, as John was keen to promote Anglo-German understanding. The school has, however, refused to accept the gift with this condition.

You are asked to advise his executors, Teresa and Richard, on what action they should take with regard to the above bequests.

Diagram plan

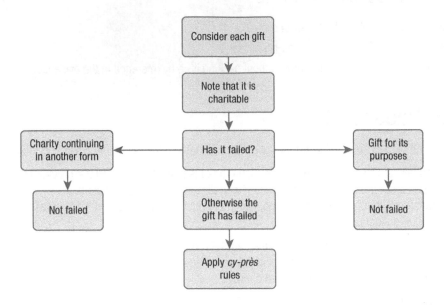

A printable version of this diagram is available from **www.pearsoned.co.uk/lawexpressqa**

Answer plan

→ Identify that the bequests are all charitable.

→ Consider whether the gifts have failed at all.

→ If the gifts have failed, is *cy-près* application possible?

→ Is a general charitable intention required and, if so, is it present?

→ If the gift has failed and if *cy-près* application is not possible, then the property will have to be held on a resulting trust for the estate.

Answer

[1] If you did not spot this point then you would have wasted time and marks by discussing in detail if each gift has charitable status. It is quite common for questions dealing with the failure of charitable gifts to actually tell you that the gift is charitable. This is because the examiner considers that there is enough in the question on the issue of failure of the gift to occupy you. You must not assume this, however, and so you need to check in each case if you are told that the gift is charitable.

The first point is that we are told that all the bequests are charitable and so there is no need to discuss if they have charitable status.[1]

(a)   The charity to which the gift was left, Hanbury College, no longer exists as a separate entity. The first question is whether the gift can be said to be for the purposes of this charity rather than necessarily to the actual charity, so that, if it is continuing under another form, the gift can still be applied to those purposes. This looks on its wording like a gift to Hanbury College rather than to its purposes. However, if it is for the purposes of the college we must then ask if these are continued under the work of Chamberlain College, which has taken over its assets. This college provides a range of courses which includes the legal courses which were run by Hanbury College and so it may be possible to say that Hanbury College is continuing in another form. In **Re Faraker** [1912] 2 Ch 488 HC, a testatrix bequeathed a legacy to 'Mrs Bailey's Charity, Rotherhithe', the object of which was to benefit poor widows. However, the charity had been amalgamated with others with the object of benefiting the poor in general of Rotherhithe. The court held that the amalgamated charities were entitled to the gift. If this principle applies here, Chamberlain College will be entitled to the gift. However, the extent to which the legal courses form part of the work of Chamberlain College is not clear. If, for example, the business courses are very large in comparison to the legal courses, then it may be that the purposes of Chamberlain College are different to Hanbury College and so it could not claim the gift on this basis. In **Re Roberts** [1963] 1 All ER 674 AC, it was held that the **Re Faraker** principle could not apply as the original trust in this case had been terminated under a power which allowed the fund to be used for purposes which might have no relation whatever to the old charity. Although our case seems nearer to **Re Faraker,** if the court takes the same view as in **Re Roberts** then the solution in that case, that of a *cy-près* scheme, could also apply here.[2]

[2] This is where you can start to earn those extra marks. The examiner has deliberately left open the question of whether the principle in *Re Faraker* applies. You should then examine the situation if it does not and go on to explore the possibility of a *cy-près* application.

Under the *cy-près* rules where a gift has failed then it may be applied for other charitable purposes *cy-près* (so near) to the original intention of the testator. Section 62 of the Charities Act 2011 lays down cases when a gift has failed and one of these, that the original purposes cannot be carried out (section 62(1)(a)(ii)), applies here, as Hanbury College no longer exists. There is a further condition required before *cy-près* application is possible, which is that the testator must have shown a general charitable intention.

Where the gift is for the purposes of a particular institution then it may be that there will be no general charitable intention, as in **Re Rymer** [1895] 1 Ch 19 HC, where there was a gift to a seminary which had ceased to exist. In **Re Roberts** Wilberforce J observed that the 'gift there was of a particularly local character by reason not only of the gift itself but by reason of the other context in the will'. Thus, whether there was a general charitable intention will depend on an examination of the rest of the will and here there are three other gifts to charity. This may indicate such an intention (**Re Jenkins' Will Trusts** [1966] 2 WLR 615 HC). If not, and if *cy-près* application is not possible, then the gift of £10,000 will be held by Teresa and Richard on a resulting trust for John's estate.[3]

[3] It is essential to round off an answer in this way. Remember that you must always find a home for the property and often it may be uncertain if in fact *cy-près* application is possible. Therefore, you should have the possible solution of a resulting trust in mind.

(b) The crucial point is that the Association for Distressed Retired Lawyers was wound up in July 2018 and John died in April 2018.[4] Thus the principle in **Re Slevin** [1891] 2 Ch 236 HC provides that the requirement of a general charitable intention need not be satisfied where the charity ceases to exist *after* the testator's death, because the property would already have vested in the recipient and so it can be applied *cy-près*. In this case money was left to an orphanage which existed at the testator's death but ceased to exist before the money was paid over. *Cy-près* application was ordered. The only requirement necessary for *cy-près* application is then that the gift has failed and, as in (a) above, section 62(1)(a)(ii) applies as the original purposes cannot be carried out as the Association no longer exists. It would seem appropriate for a *cy-près* scheme to be ordered under which the Association of Retired Lawyers can receive the gift.

[4] If you do not recognise this point your marks for this part of the answer will be very poor. If you receive a question on failure of charitable gifts check for one where you are told the date of the testator's death and the date when the gift failed. If the gift failed *after* the death of the testator then you should answer as shown here.

(c) The gift of £20,000 to the Swinton League for the Rescue of Sick Cats has obviously failed under section 62(1)(a)(ii) of the Charities

Act 2011, as the league does not exist, and so the question is whether it can be applied *cy-près*. In **Re Harwood** [1936] Ch 285 HC, a gift to the Belfast Peace Society, which had never existed, was applied *cy-près* because the testator showed a general intention to benefit societies whose object was the promotion of peace. Although **Re Koeppler's WT** [1986] Ch 423 HC doubted **Re Harwood** on the ground that promotion of peace was political and not charitable, this does not affect its application here. However, it would be wrong to simply assume that **Re Harwood** applies, as in every case it has to be shown that there is a general charitable intention.[5] If this is not the case here, the £20,000 will be held on a resulting trust for John's estate.

[5] Too often students quote *Re Harwood* and assume that this automatically means that the gift can go on a *cy-près* application. Boost your marks by showing that this is not necessarily so.

(d) Where a gift has a condition attached to it and the charity will not accept the gift with the condition, as here, then it may be possible to apply the gift *cy-près* with the condition removed. In **Re Lysaght** [1966] Ch 191 HC, a gift to the Royal College of Surgeons (RCS) to hold on trust to found medical studentships contained a condition stating, *inter alia,* that the students should not be of the Jewish or Roman Catholic faith. The RCS refused to act as trustee unless this condition was removed, which it was. A general charitable intention must, of course, also be found in these cases.[6] In **Re Lysaght** it was held that the general charitable intention was the foundation of medical studentships and so in this case it would presumably be the intention to further the education of girls aged 16–18. If not, then the gift will be held on a resulting trust for John's estate.

[6] This is really the same point as before but in another context. Always remember that *cy-près* application of property is never possible without a general charitable intention except where the principle in *Re Slevin* applies.

Make your answer stand out

- Take a clear and logical approach, especially in part (a) where you must not assume that the gift has actually failed.

- Read Garton (2007). This is a really interesting account of the history of the *cy-près* doctrine and its present-day role.

- Do some research into the latest case on this area: *Kings* v *Bultitude* [2010] EWHC 1795 (Ch) and see Picton (2011).

- Consider if the decision in *Re Harwood* was justified. If a charity to which a gift is left does not exist then how can it be said that there is any charitable intention at all?

! Don't be tempted to . . .

■ Forget that where the purposes of the charity seem to be carried on in another form then the gift may not have failed at all. Only mention *cy-près* if you think that the purposes may not be being carried on in another form.

■ Forget that for a *cy-près* application to succeed two requirements must be satisfied: the gift must have failed; and, except in the *Re Slevin* type of case, there must be a general charitable intention.

■ Just apply cases to this area without asking whether there is a general charitable intention.

@ Try it yourself

Now take a look at the question below and attempt to answer it. You can check your response against the answer guidance available on the companion website (**www.pearsoned.co.uk/lawexpressqa**).

The will of Fiona, who has just died, contains the following gifts. You are asked to advise on whether they are charitable and, if not, whether they are valid.

(a) £10,000 to Worcestershire County Cricket Club.

(b) £50,000 to the 'Campaign against War', which holds conferences and publishes papers to alert the public to the dangers of warfare.

(c) £20,000 to the 'No More By-Passes Movement' which campaigns against the building of further by-passes on environmental grounds.

www.pearsoned.co.uk/lawexpressqa

Go online to access more revision support including additional essay and problem questions with diagram plans, 'You be the marker' questions, and download all diagrams from the book.

10

The beneficiary principle and purpose trusts

How this topic may come up in exams

This topic can arise in problem questions dealing with the validity of gifts made to, for example, unincorporated associations, and also bequests in wills for the care of animals and the maintenance of monuments. A frequent essay question is to ask you if the law of trusts has, in effect, got it right here in the first place. Why, for example, should a gift to an unincorporated association cause problems at all? Look out as well for questions which link material in this chapter with the three certainties (Chapter 3) and charitable trusts (Chapter 9).

■ Before you begin

It's a good idea to consider the following key themes of the beneficiary principle and purpose trusts before tackling a question on this topic.

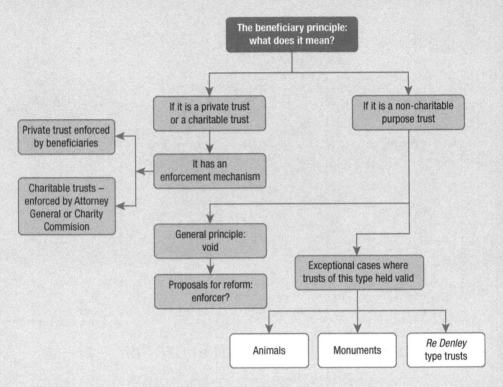

A printable version of this diagram is available from **www.pearsoned.co.uk/lawexpressqa**

Question 1

'It was decided in *Re Astor's Settlement Trust* that a trust for a number of non-charitable purposes was not merely unenforceable but void on two grounds; first, that it was not a trust for the benefit of individuals, which I will refer to as "the beneficiary principle", and, secondly, for uncertainty.' (Goff J in *Re Denley's Trust Deed* [1969] 1 Ch 373 HC.)

Critically examine these two reasons referred to by Goff J for why trusts for non-charitable purposes are held void and assess in your answer if any reforms to the law are possible to enable these types of trusts will be held valid.

Diagram plan

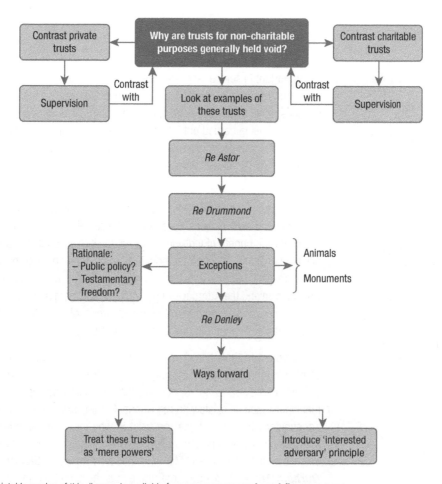

A printable version of this diagram is available from **www.pearsoned.co.uk/lawexpressqa**

Answer plan

→ Look closely at what Goff J said and contrast non-charitable purpose trusts with other types of trusts.

→ Look at the first reason why Goff J felt that these trusts could not be enforced: the beneficiary principle and how it has been applied in the cases.

→ Consider the exceptional cases where trusts for animals and monuments have been held valid, asking what rationale there is for these, if any.

→ Now look at the other reason, that these trusts are too uncertain for the court to control. This will then lead to an analysis of *Re Denley* itself.

→ End by critically considering the various ways in which it has been suggested that these trusts could be held valid.

Answer

[1] We will come to the reasons for declaring that these trusts are void in the next paragraph but first we need to raise the question, without at this stage answering it, of why these trusts are considered void at all. This theme will then lead us through the answer to the conclusion where we will examine possible ways in which these trusts may be held valid. In this way we have created a structure for our answer.

[2] In any essay on non-charitable purpose trusts it is essential near the start to make this contrast with other types of trusts, otherwise your essay has no context.

It is important to seek a rationale for the rule that trusts for non-charitable purposes are generally void. This is needed because the law as it stands prevents perfectly reasonable intentions of settlors and testators from being carried out. Moreover, the rule is subject to exceptions which themselves have no clear rationale and attempts to hold that these trusts can be valid have led to unnecessarily complex case law.[1]

The first ground for holding trusts for non-charitable purposes not only unenforceable but void was stated by Goff J as being that 'it was not a trust for the benefit of individuals, which I will refer to as "the beneficiary principle"'. By contrast, private trusts can be enforced by the beneficiaries, and charitable trusts are supervised by the Charity Commission and the Attorney General can enforce them and also 'any person interested in the charity' may take proceedings with respect to the charity (section 115(l)(c) Charities Act 2011).[2]

The problem is that there is no beneficiary who can control non-charitable purpose trusts by taking legal proceedings and the settlor will not be allowed to do so, nor of course is there any supervisory machinery such as exists with the Charity Commission. The lack of a beneficiary who can enforce the trust is why they are sometimes known as trusts of imperfect obligation. Its origin is sometimes said to be the dictum of Grant MR who said in **Morice v Bishop of Durham** [1804] 10 Ves 522 that 'there must be somebody in whose favour the court can decree performance'. In fact, however, this was a trust which failed through lack of certainty of objects. It is more accurate to say that the basis of the rule is found in the beneficiary principle: a trust must have a beneficiary who can enforce it.

[3] It is time for an actual example and the facts of *Re Astor* themselves are a perfect illustration.

The effect of this rule was seen in *Re Astor's ST* (1952 Ch 534 HC) itself, where a fund was left to be held for various non-charitable purposes including the maintenance of good relations between nations and the independence of newspapers.[3]

Although the beneficiary principle is stated to be the rationale for holding non-charitable trusts void, in fact trusts of this type were held valid in cases before *Re Astor.* For instance, in *Re Drummond* [1914] 2 Ch 90 HC, a trust was upheld where the objects were the Old Boys of Bradford Grammar School and to acquire premises for a clubhouse. Suppose that in this case the trustees did not perform the trust, then presumably the Old Boys could act if they wished to. Conversely, if the trustees did perform the trust then there would be no problem at all.

[4] We are now developing our answer by looking at the next issue: the anomalous cases where non-charitable purpose trusts have been enforced but tying this in to the main theme: what is the rationale here, if any?

The idea that the rationale is the beneficiary principle breaks down altogether in two cases where trusts for non-charitable purposes have long been held valid.[4]

One is trusts for the care of specific animals, as in *Re Dean* [1889] 41 Ch D 552 HC, and the other is a trust for the building or maintenance of a tomb or monument, as in *Re Hooper* [1932] 1 Ch 38 HC, where a testator made a gift for the care of some family graves and monuments and a tablet in a church window. In neither of these cases has the lack of an enforcement mechanism to enforce the trust caused difficulty, although these are of course very limited situations.

[5] At this point some research detail really helps to boost your marks and keeps the focus on the essential issue: the rationale for these trusts.

What is the rationale here? Brown and Pawlowski (2012) argue that in *Re Dean* it was simply that the court felt it was socially acceptable for testators to leave gifts in their wills to look after their favourite pets as otherwise the cost would fall on the testator's family or the public.[5] This is really a public policy ground and can be said to derive from the much broader principle of testamentary freedom: that a testator should be free to dispose of her estate as she pleases, a principle upheld by the House of Lords in *Blathwayt v Baron Cawley* [1976] AC 397 HL.

Nevertheless, the beneficiary principle remains important in cases other than these anomalous ones and now we turn to the second point made by Goff J in *Re Denley's Trust Deed*, [1969] 1 Ch 373 HC that these trusts are uncertain. One aspect of uncertainty is that the actual objects of the trusts are uncertain, a problem dealt with in the case of private trusts by applying the 'individual ascertainability' rule laid down in *McPhail v Doulton* [1971] AC 424 HL, where Lord Wilberforce held that the test was, 'Can it be said with certainty that any given individual is or is not a member of the class?' One example here is *Re Astor,* where the maintenance of good relations between nations and the independence of newspapers was uncertain. The other aspect of uncertainty, linked to the first, is that if the trust is too uncertain then the court cannot control it, a point referred to by Grant MR in *Morice v Bishop of Durham* and which has troubled the courts ever since.

[6] The facts of *Re Denley* are clearly important in this answer and you will lose marks if you do not consider them in some detail.

However, it is possible with some judicial ingenuity to hold that some apparently non-charitable purpose trusts are in fact private trusts and so valid. This occurred in *Re Denley's Trust Deed*.[6] A plot of land was conveyed to trustees 'for the purpose of a recreation or sports ground primarily for the benefit of the employees of the company' and also for the benefit of such other persons as the trustees might allow. This was held valid as a trust for the employees and the possible problem with the phrase 'such other persons as the trustees might allow' being too uncertain was solved by holding that that this was a mere power[7] which then trustees could if they wished exercise in their favour, and as such the trustees did not need to know all possible objects in whose favour it was exercisable (*Re Gulbenkian's Settlements* (1970) AC 508.

[7] This is an excellent example of using your knowledge from another area, covered here in Chapter 3, to boost your marks.

The judicial ingenuity displayed by Goff J certainly enabled what seemed to be a perfectly valid trust to escape from being held void, but should this be necessary? There are in fact two possible ways in these trusts can be, at least in some circumstances, enforced.[8]

[8] This should be where you really earn your extra marks. This area has been controversial for a long time and there have been various proposals for reform. It is essential that you are aware of these.

One is to hold that these trusts could take effect as mere powers, as occurred in *Re Denley*, and if the principle was used more widely in the case of these trusts it would have the advantage that the enforceability point did not matter: a power is discretionary anyway and does not have to be carried out.

The other and more radical solution is the introduction of an 'interested adversary principle', where persons or institutions might be identified

[9] Here you are thinking laterally and using your knowledge from another area. Do this whenever possible: it is a perfectly valid approach as the law of trusts is a unity and it will undoubtedly impress an examiner.

as being watchdogs to act in enforcing the trust. A bold decision of the courts might bring this about and the developing law on trusteeship may help.[9] In **Schmidt v Rosewood Trust Ltd** [2003] AC 709, an action concerning disclosure of trust documents, Lord Walker held that 'the right to seek the court's intervention does not depend on entitlement to a fixed and transmissible beneficial interest'. Thus, it might be possible to develop this line of argument to give the courts power to supervise a non-charitable purpose trust.

✓ Make your answer stand out

- Read and refer to Hayton (2001) who considers how this area can be developed in a more satisfactory way.
- Read and refer to Matthews (1996), another attempt at charting a way forward. This essay also gives a stimulating and clear account of the present law.
- Look at Brown (2007). This has some very interesting research detail on the extent to which trusts for animals, monuments and masses are used today and a suggestion that a promise given by a nominated person and contained in a 'deed of commitment and enforcement' could be a way of enforcing them.
- Mention, if only with a brief example, how the perpetuity principle has affected the operation of non-charitable purpose trusts.

! Don't be tempted to . . .

- Leave out the theoretical issues and plunge into the cases at once.
- Say too much about the powers of the Charity Commission to control charitable trusts. Just a mention of this point is needed as the question is not about charitable trusts.
- Just give examples of cases where these types of trusts have been held to be invalid. You must discuss the background to the law first.
- Forget to discuss possible ways forward at the conclusion of your answer.

Question 2

Jim, by will, directed his trustees, Frank and Brendan, to hold the following bequests on trust:

(a) £10,000 to hold on trust to look after my dog, Felix.

(b) £20,000 to care for and maintain the monument to myself which will be erected in the park of my home town Barset.

(c) **£5,000 to the priest of St Peter's Church, Worcester, to say masses for the repose of my soul.**

(d) **£50,000 to promote the admirable sport of fox hunting.**

Consider whether these bequests are valid.

Answer plan

→ Consider in each case whether the gift could be charitable.

→ If it is not, then explain the general attitude of the law to non-charitable purpose trusts and mention the rationale for this.

→ Analyse each situation to establish if it comes within any of the exceptional cases where a trust for non-charitable purposes can be valid.

→ Consider whether the trust is affected by the rules against perpetuities.

→ Finally, look at any other reasons why the trust might fail, e.g. illegality.

Diagram plan

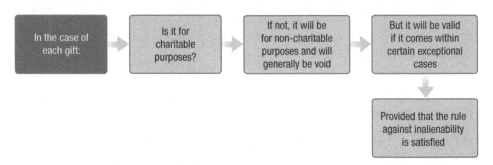

A printable version of this diagram is available from **www.pearsoned.co.uk/lawexpressqa**

[1] Although the conclusion turns out to be that the gift is not charitable, in a question like this you will be expected to first ask if it *could* be charitable.

[2] There is also the point that there is no public benefit but, as the purpose is not charitable anyway, there is no need to consider this.

Answer

(a) The gift of £10,000 to look after the testator's dog Felix is not for charitable purposes,[1] as it does not come within any of the purposes set out by section 3 of the Charities Act 2011. Trusts for animal welfare are charitable by section 3(1)(k) of the Act but this is a trust for a particular animal.[2] It is therefore a trust for non-charitable purposes. These are generally void (**Re Astor** [1952] Ch 534 HC), as they are trusts of imperfect obligation in

[3] In addition to stating the law on why these trusts are generally invalid, you will gain credit if you explain briefly why this is so. This is a controversial area and the examiner will expect you to be aware of the rationale for the principle stated in *Re Astor*.

[4] Many students for some reason try to avoid the topic of perpetuities altogether and you will gain considerable credit for an accurate account of the law.

[5] You will see that we actually give the facts of three cases for this point. This is because the law is not settled and so we are looking for possible principles on which to base our answer.

that there is no one to compel performance of them.[3] However, trusts for the care of specific animals form an exception to this principle and are valid, as in *Re Dean* [1889] 41 Ch D 552 HC, where money was left for the maintenance of the testator's horses and hounds. However, such gifts must be limited to the perpetuity period. There are in fact two perpetuity rules and the applicable one here concerns inalienability of capital which prevents capital being tied up for too long a period.[4] The period cannot exceed that fixed by section 15(4) of the Perpetuities and Accumulations Act 1964, as lives or lives in being plus 21 years. As no other period is specified here, this will apply. In *Re Dean* itself the court seemed to ignore the perpetuity point as the gift was valid even though it was for 50 years provided that any of the horses and hounds should live that long.[5] However, in the Irish case of *Re Kelly* [1932] IR 255 HC, the court stated that the life span of animals could not be taken as the measuring point for the perpetuity period and that lives meant human lives. In *Re Haines* [1952] *The Times*, 7 November, however judicial notice was taken of the proposition that a cat cannot live for more than 21 years and this validated the trust, but this is a trust for a dog and so it is suggested that expert evidence will be needed on how long a dog can live for. It is likely that the 'wait and see' provisions of the 1964 Act do not apply to non-charitable purpose trusts and so if there is the possibility at the outset that the perpetuity period will be infringed, as a dog is capable of living for more than 21 years, then the perpetuity period will apply and the gift will be void. Thus, the £10,000 will be held on a resulting trust for Jim's estate.

[6] This is a good point which will earn you extra marks as once again you are showing your awareness of the *possibility* of charitable status.

(b) The gift of '£20,000 to care for and maintain the monument to myself which will be erected in the park of my home town Barset' will not be charitable unless the monument is of such artistic value that it comes under section 3(1)(f) of the Charities Act 2011 as being for the advancement of arts, culture or heritage.[6] If not, it will be a non-charitable purpose trust and in principle void under the principle in *Re Astor*. However, a trust for the building or maintenance of a tomb or monument has been held valid, as in *Re Hooper* [1932] 1 Ch 38 HC, where a testator made a gift for the care of some family graves and monuments and a tablet in a church window. On this basis the gift can be valid, although it must comply with the perpetuity period and no period is mentioned. As we have mentioned above, it is not possible to wait and see if, for example, the monument does not last for more than the perpetuity period and so this gift will be void.

(c) The gift of '£5,000 to the priest of St Peter's Church, Worcester to say masses for the repose of my soul' may be valid as a charitable trust under section 3(1)(b) of the Charities Act 2011 as being for the advancement of religion. In **Bourne v Keane** [1919] AC 815, the House of Lords established that gifts and trusts for the saying of masses were not void as being for superstitious uses as had at one time been the case but it did not decide that such trusts were charitable.[7] Thus there was a view that they came within the same category as trusts for animals and monuments as valid non-charitable purpose trusts, but in **Re Hetherington** [1989] 2 All ER 129 HC, it was held that a trust for the celebration of masses was charitable because 'the public celebration of a religious rite edifies and improves those who attend it'.[8] The fact that the masses could be said in private was not a bar to charitable status as there was, in effect, one purpose, the saying of masses, capable of implementation in two different ways. One, public masses, is charitable, the other, private masses, is not. The court applied the principle that where a gift has a single purpose which could be performed by either charitable or non-charitable means, it should be construed as a gift to be performed by charitable means. A further ground for holding that the gift was charitable was that it was for the advancement of the priesthood as the gifts made provision for priests. The perpetuity point does not arise, as the rule against inalienability of gifts does not apply to charities on the basis that as charities are for the public benefit their continuance is to be encouraged.[9]

(d) The gift of £50,000 'to promote the admirable sport of fox hunting' will not count as a charitable trust as it does not come within any of the charitable purposes set out in section 3 of the Charities Act 2011. It is sometimes said that in **Re Thompson** [1934] Ch 342 HC, the court held that a trust for the promotion of fox hunting was valid presumably as a non-charitable purpose trust.[10] In fact, the case concerned a gift to be applied to the promotion of fox hunting with a gift of residue to Trinity Hall,

[7] This is an area of law which has developed over the years and your answer will gain more marks if you set this out.

[8] Notice how you are building up your argument: the first case, *Bourne* v *Keane,* held that gifts for the saying of masses could be valid but in *Re Hetherington* it went further and held that in principle they were charitable. This is the type of approach which will impress an examiner.

[9] This point is not always understood, even by the courts, and so you will boost your marks by stating it correctly.

[10] The examiner will be checking to see if you fall into the common error of saying that this case held that trusts for the promotion of fox hunting are valid. As you can see, it did not.

Cambridge. The issue was whether the trust was void, as there was no beneficiary, but the court held that it was not, as the purpose was sufficiently certain. A trust for the promotion of fox hunting would now be void anyway, as it promotes an illegal purpose contrary to the Hunting Act 2004. Thus, this gift will fail and there will be a resulting trust of the £50,000 for Jim's estate.

 Make your answer stand out

- Read Parry (1989) who analyses the decision in *Re Hetherington* and looks at the history of the law on trusts for the saying of masses.
- Mention some criticisms of the rule in *Re Astor* that trusts for non-charitable purposes are void, and possible ways in which the law could be changed so that they were valid. See, for example, Brown (2007) for one idea. This article is also useful in providing a very helpful and clear account of the law.
- Explain that the cases where trusts for non-charitable purposes have been held valid are regarded as an anomaly and that the categories will not be extended.

! Don't be tempted to . . .

- Fail to consider at the start of each answer if the gift could be charitable.
- Omit to state that a gift will be valid without considering the perpetuity period.
- Fail to find a home for the property if the trust fails.

Question 3

'It would astonish a layman to be told that there was a difficulty in his giving a legacy to an unincorporated non-charitable society which he had, or could have, supported without trouble during his lifetime' (Brightman J in *Re Recher's Will Trusts* [1972] Ch 526 at 536).

Examine what these difficulties are and critically consider whether the solutions to them adopted by the courts are satisfactory or whether a new approach to the problem of gifts to unincorporated associations is needed.

Answer plan

→ Outline the fundamental problem – trusts for non-charitable purposes are void.

→ Identify and analyse problems which flow from these: for example, the fact that the society is not incorporated and the rule against inalienability.

→ Explain how the decision in *Re Denley* might provide a solution.

→ Explain how the decision in *Re Recher* might provide a solution.

→ Conclusion – evaluate possible reforms of the law to make it easier to make gifts to unincorporated non-charitable bodies.

Diagram plan

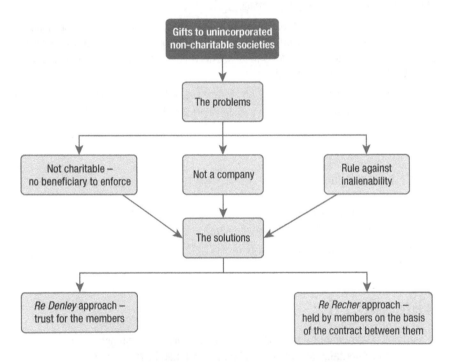

A printable version of this diagram is available from **www.pearsoned.co.uk/lawexpressqa**

Answer

The reason why there is a problem with gifts to unincorporated non-charitable societies is that these gifts can infringe a number of rules. The crucial point is that as they are not charitable and as they are not private trusts for the benefit of identifiable beneficiaries, they take effect as non-charitable purpose trusts which are generally void.[1] The basis of the rule is found in the beneficiary principle: a trust must have a beneficiary who can enforce it.[2] As Harman J said in **Re Wood** [1949] Ch 498 HC, 'a gift on trust must have a *cestui que trust*'. Thus, as there are no identified beneficiaries to enforce it as in the case of a private trust nor the Charity Commission in the case of a charitable trust, the trust is void. There are certain exceptions to this principle, for example trusts for the care of specific animals, but these do not affect gifts to societies.[3]

The next problem, which follows from the first, is that the society is not incorporated. If it was incorporated as a company then the gift would vest in that company immediately and there would be no question of a trust. As the society is not incorporated there cannot be a gift to it as it cannot hold property, and so any gift can only be for its purposes which are not charitable. The result is that we come back to the problem that there cannot be a trust for non-charitable purposes. In **Re Finger's Will Trust** [1972] Ch 286 HC, a testatrix left shares of her residuary estate to various charities. One of these was an unincorporated association but as the gift was for charitable purposes it was valid. Had they not been charitable, it would have failed.[4]

The final problem is that trusts in these cases must comply with the rules against inalienability.[5] The inalienability rules are concerned with the tying up of money for an excessive time. As such they are applicable to non-charitable purpose trusts which could tie up a fund. The effect is that such a trust will be void unless from the beginning it is certain that persons will have become absolutely entitled by the end of a period fixed at lives or lives in being plus 21 years, and it should be noted that the 'wait and see' provisions of the Perpetuities and Accumulations Act 1964[6] do not apply to purpose trusts (see section 15(4)). It is possible to fix a shorter time. If the gift had been charitable then the rule against inalienability would not have applied and if the gift had been to a company then it would have been irrelevant as the gift would have vested in the company at once.

[7] This is the kind of linking sentence which you must always aim for in an answer. You have set out the problems and, as you are approaching halfway through the essay, it is time to turn to the possible solutions.

Given these problems, the courts have devised various solutions in an attempt to have some at least of gifts made to unincorporated non-charitable societies held valid.[7]

The first is that of Goff J in *Re Denley's Trust Deed* [1969] 1 Ch 373 HC, where he was able to construe what appeared to be a trust for purposes as one for individuals. A plot of land was conveyed to trustees 'for the purpose of a recreation or sports ground primarily for the benefit of the employees of the company' and also for the benefit of such other persons as the trustees might allow. This was held valid as a trust for the employees because they were entitled to the use of the land.

[8] This extra thinking will gain extra marks.

This decision has, however, been difficult to classify. Was the trust one for individuals, in which case there is no problem, or is it a kind of hybrid trust, being partly private and partly for purposes?[8]

Another approach, and one which applies particularly to gifts to societies, is to hold that the gift is to the members of the society who will hold it, not on trust, but on the basis of the contract between them. In *Re Recher's Will Trust* [1972] Ch 526 HC, a gift made to the London and Provincial Anti-Vivisection Society was held to be a beneficial gift to the members, not so as to entitle each of them to an immediate share but as an addition to the funds of the association subject to the contract between the members as set out in the rules. This approach was followed in *Re Lipinski's Will Trusts* [1976] Ch 235 HC, where a testator bequeathed half of his residuary estate in trust to an association to be used solely in constructing or maintaining the association's buildings. This was held valid as a gift to the members subject to the contract between them as members, even though the word 'solely' might have indicated that a trust was intended for the purpose specified.

[9] An answer will always gain marks if it shows that you are aware of recent developments. This is an especially useful case to mention, as it illustrates the application of both the trust and the contract approaches explained earlier.

A more recent decision,[9] *Re Horley Town Football Club; Hunt v McLaren* [2006] EWHC 2386 (Ch), shows a development of this approach. This concerned a surplus arising on a sale of land held in trust as an endowment for an unincorporated association. It was held that the beneficial interest vested in the current full members and was held on a bare trust for them. This entitled them to call in a general meeting for the assets to be transferred to them as individuals. This decision follows the line of authority in *Re Recher* in basing the solution on contract, but the device of a trust is used to solve the problem of exactly where the legal ownership of the property lies pending any distribution between the members.

One problem with the approach in **Re Recher** is that a gift to the members may offend the rule against inalienability if there is something in the gift or its circumstances or the rules of the association which prevents the members from dividing the gift between them on the basis that they are solely entitled in equity. This is what caused the gift to fail in **Re Grant's Will Trusts** [1979] 3 All ER 359 HC, where a gift was made to the Chertsey Labour Party but the members could not change the rules and divide the gift between themselves because the rules were subject to control by the National Executive Committee of the Labour Party.

Therefore, there is no doubt that, as Brightman J said in **Re Recher,** a layman would indeed be astonished by the difficulties in making gifts to an unincorporated non-charitable society. One possible solution[10] is to allow a trust for non-charitable purposes to have an enforcer, who could in the case of a will be the residuary legatee, who would be able to take action if the terms of the gift were felt to be infringed. This would be a sensible reform, given that there is no objection on the grounds of public policy to these gifts and every reason for enforcing them.

[10] A conclusion will always impress the examiner if it contains some new idea to lift the answer at the end. This is much better than a lame summary of what you have already said.

Make your answer stand out

- Refer to Brown (2007). This article gives a very helpful summary of the law and of its practical effects and then goes on to consider proposals for change.
- Look into what the basis of the decision in *Re Denley* was: see Matthews (1995).
- The decision in *Re Horley Town Football Club* is analysed by Luxton (2007).
- Consider the possibility that gifts to unincorporated non-charitable associations could be valid under the Quistclose principle (see Chapter 7).

! Don't be tempted to . . .

- Fail to make the distinction between charitable and non-charitable purposes clear.
- Miss the point that gifts to companies will vest at once.
- Fail to explain the inalienability rule.
- Quote too many cases on one area.

❓ Question 4

You are asked to advise on what should be done with surplus funds in the following cases:

(a) The Hanbury Park Association of Retired Lecturers in Land Law and Equity was founded to provide benefits for the spouses of these persons after they had died. It was a large and popular organisation with a lively membership which held a number of social events that were attended by members of the public and where funds were raised by an entry fee and the sale of raffle tickets. In addition, an anonymous donation of £5,000 was received which was believed to be from a grateful ex-student. However, the Association has only one member left, who is the Chairman. The surplus funds amount to £20,000.

(b) A collection was held for victims of a flood disaster in 1947 with the object of 'cheering them up' by providing them with holidays. However, all the victims of the flood have now died and a surplus of £5,000 remains. The trustees seek advice on what to do with this money.

Answer plan

→ Are the organisations charitable? If so, consider application of the funds *cy-près.*

→ Note that neither organisation is a company and so we must deal with the law on unincorporated associations.

→ In the case of the Hanbury Park Association, consider where the money came from in each case: the entry fee, the proceeds from the sale of raffle tickets and the donation, and apply the relevant law.

→ In the case of the fund for flood disaster victims, consider the possibility of the money going to the Crown as *bona vacantia* or being held as a private trust.

Diagram plan

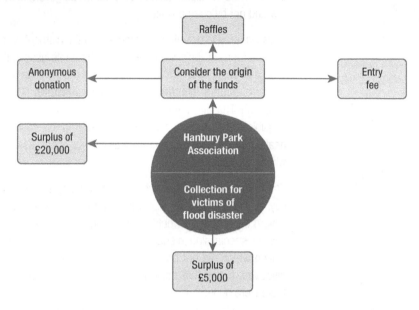

A printable version of this diagram is available from **www.pearsoned.co.uk/lawexpressqa**

Answer

[1] Check in a question of this kind whether you are told that the funds were not held for charitable purposes. If so, you should leave this first paragraph out. In this case, although it is fairly obvious that the organisation is not charitable, you should spend a paragraph, but no more, on this point.

[2] Never in any answer just refer to 'charitable purposes' but always to 'charitable purposes as defined by section 3(1) of the Charities Act 2011', as you are making it clear that you are concerned with the legal definition of charity.

(a) The first question is whether the association is charitable.[1] If it is then it will be possible for the surplus funds to be applied *cy-près* for other charitable objects provided that there was a general charitable intention and that the gift has failed within the meaning of section 62 of the Charities Act 2011. However, there is no evidence that the association was established for charitable purposes as defined by section 3(1) of the Charities Act 2011,[2] as there is no evidence that it was for the relief of poverty or the advancement of education. In addition, the class of beneficiaries is too small to have any public benefit. Thus, we must assume that it was not charitable. The other point is that the association

10 THE BENEFICIARY PRINCIPLE AND PURPOSE TRUSTS

[3] This again is a point to include if you are not told the status of the organisation. Almost certainly the organisation will not be a company, as this is a trusts exam and not a company law exam, but still watch for it.

[4] The opening paragraph was, as it were, clearing the ground and now you can come to the main issue.

[5] It is worth showing the examiner that you know this, as it makes a clear starting point for your answer. However, you should then move on quickly to consider the question posed here.

[6] It is likely that you will not be told what the rules are so that you have to continue and consider the various solutions adopted by the courts. Even so, you must always mention that the association's rules are the starting point.

[7] Although this is not likely to be the answer, you should mention the resulting trust solution, as it was adopted in many cases.

[8] This gives you an opportunity to deal with these separately. The examiner obviously intended you to do this, otherwise they would not have been mentioned.

is obviously not a company[3] and so it is an unincorporated association. Thus the distribution of its funds will be governed by trust law and not by company law.

Thus we need to examine the case law on the distribution of the surplus funds of unincorporated non-charitable associations.[4] The usual rule is that the actual funds of an association are held by the members (*Neville Estates Ltd v Madden* [1962] Ch 832 HC). The alternative, that they are held on trust, is only possible if the trust is charitable.[5] However, in this case we are dealing with a claim to the surplus assets of the association when it is dissolved.

The first step must be to see what the rules of the association say, as these form a contract between the members and so will govern the matter.[6] It would seem strange that an association of lawyers specialising in equity and land law should have an association which did not provide for what was to happen if it was dissolved, but we are not told of any and so must assume that there were none.

The anonymous donation could be held to go on a resulting trust[7] for those who contributed it, as in *Re Gillingham Bus Disaster Fund* [1958] 2 All ER 749 HC, where a surplus remained from a fund raised mainly from street collections and other non-identifiable sources. The court held that the money was to be held on a resulting trust for the donors because, as Harman J said, 'the donor did not part with his money out and out absolutely' but only to the extent that his wishes as declared by the trust could be carried into effect. Thus, when 'this has been done any surplus still belongs to him'. This is a most unfortunate solution, as the money may simply remain in court as the donor may never come forward. A preferable solution is that adopted in *Re West Sussex Constabulary's Benevolent Fund Trust* [1970] 1 All ER 544 HC, where it was held that the donors, as they were anonymous, must have intended to have parted with their money out and out. The relationship was one of contract, not trust, and so the sum would go to the Crown as *bona vacantia*.

This solution could apply to the money paid to attend fundraising events and raffle tickets,[8] where it was held in the *West Sussex* case on similar facts that the relationship was one of contract not trust: those who paid for the entertainment had had their entertainment and so no longer had any claim to the money. Thus, again, the money will go to the Crown as *bona vacantia*.

However, the *bona vacantia* solution is also unsatisfactory, as the contributors can never have intended their money to end up in the hands of the Crown. The other solution would be to follow **Re Bucks Constabulary Widows' and Orphans' Fund Friendly Society (No 2)** [1979] 1 WLR 936 HC and hold that as all the funds are assets of the association they should be held for the members alive at the date of the dissolution. The problem here is that Walton J held that, where there is only one member of an association left, as here, then the association must cease to exist and the surviving member cannot claim the funds. In that case the only destination of the assets would be as *bona vacantia* to the Crown.

[9] This is now the leading case to refer to in this area.

However, in the recent case of **Hanchett-Stamford v Attorney General** [2008] EWHC 30 (Ch),[9] the last surviving member was allowed to claim the funds. The claimant was, on her husband's death, the last surviving member of the Performing and Captive Animals Defence League, which was an unincorporated non-charitable association. She wished the assets, amounting to nearly £1.5 million, to be held on trust to select a charity with similar objects to whom the funds could be given. Lewison J could not see the logic in saying that 'if there are two members of an association which has assets of, say, £2m, they can by agreement divide those assets between them and pocket £1m each, but if one of them dies before they have divided the assets, the whole pot goes to the Crown as *bona vacantia*'. In addition, he took account of Article 1 of the First Protocol of the European Convention on Human Rights. This provides that no one is to be deprived of their possessions except in the public interest and subject to the conditions provided by law.[10] It is suggested that on the basis of this, the surviving member can claim the surplus funds.

[10] This is the kind of extra detail which will gain you marks.

(b) The problem with the fund raised for victims of flood disasters is that it does not seem to have been charitable, as the provision of holidays may not be considered a charitable purpose as defined by section 1(1) of the Charities Act 2011. There is no evidence that the fund was for the relief of poverty, and funds raised for victims of disasters cannot give benefits to victims which exceed their needs. This problem arose with funds contributed to the Penlee Lifeboat Disaster Fund in 1981 (see **Re Picarda** [1982] 132 NLJ 223). If the fund is not charitable then it could go to the Crown as *bona vacantia,* as it will now be impossible to trace the subscribers. If they could be traced, it would be held on a resulting trust for them. The solution in the Penlee Lifeboat case was to simply treat the fund as a private trust which, as it is for the benefit of individuals, makes sense both legally and in practice as it allowed the money to be distributed among the families. In this case it could be distributed among the descendants of the victims.

[11] Do not forget this last point. We cannot be certain that it is *not* charitable.

Finally, if the fund is charitable[11] then it will be possible for the surplus funds to be applied *cy-près* for other charitable objects, provided that there was a general charitable intention and that the gift has failed within the meaning of section 62 of the Charities Act 2011.

Make your answer stand out

- Read and refer to Baughen (2010), which analyses the decision in *Hanchett-Stamford* v *Attorney General.* This is an important decision and you can expect questions on it in an exam.
- Mention, by way of comparison, the position on the distribution of the surplus funds of pension schemes – see *Davis* v *Richards and Wallington Industries Ltd* [1990] 1 WLR 1511 and *Air Jamaica Ltd* v *Charlton* [1999] 1 WLR 1399.
- See if you can find any details on what actually happened to the money contributed in *Re Gillingham.*

! Don't be tempted to . . .

- Forget to deal first with the possibility that the organisations are established for charitable purposes.
- Fail to identify that they are not companies and so are unincorporated.
- Deal with only one possible solution to the question of where the surplus goes.
- Come to very definite conclusions. We cannot be certain, for example, that the trust for flood victims is *not* charitable.

Try it yourself

Now take a look at the question below and attempt to answer it. You can check your response against the answer guidance available on the companion website (**www.pearsoned.co.uk/lawexpressqa**).

Emily is trustee of a trust set up by her late husband Phil which contains the following gifts:

(a) £50,000 to the Worcester branch of the English Nationalist Party.

(b) £5,000 to the priest at the Roman Catholic Church Droitwich for masses to be said for the repose of my soul.

(c) £10,000 to maintain and breed from my horses.

Advise Emily on the validity of these bequests.

www.pearsoned.co.uk/lawexpressqa

 Go online to access more revision support including additional essay and problem questions with diagram plans, 'You be the marker' questions, and download all diagrams from the book.

11

Trusteeship and variation of trusts

How this topic may come up in exams

This is a fertile area for essay questions with obvious ones on the nature of trustee-ship, the idea of a fiduciary, the relationship between the Trustee Acts and the trust instrument and, if it is in your syllabus, variation of trusts. Problems can be on particular duties and powers of trustees, with likely candidates being investment, inspection of trust documents, maintenance and advancement.

Obvious links are with constructive trusts (Chapter 8) as a constructive trust can be imposed where a trustee is in breach of fiduciary duty, and remedies for breach of trust (Chapter 12) as these will be relevant once you have decided that the trustee has broken a term of the trust.

■ Before you begin

It's a good idea to consider the following key themes of trusteeship and variation of trusts before tackling a question on this topic.

Diagram plan

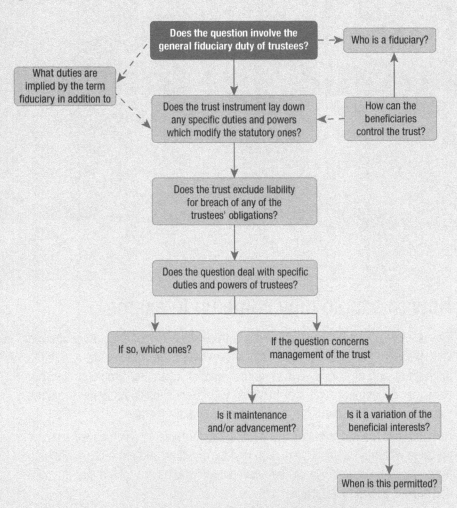

A printable version of this diagram is available from **www.pearsoned.co.uk/lawexpressqa**

❓ Question 1

Tim and Ted are trustees of a fund of £500,000 established by the will of Edgar to be held for each of Edgar's children in equal shares on their reaching the age of 25. There are three children, Ben, aged 17, Sue, aged 19 and Jack, aged 22. Tim is a solicitor and Ted is a family friend.

Jack is a trainee investment manager and tells Tim and Ted that shares in a property company in South America represent a 'fantastic investment opportunity' and that they should act quickly and give him a cheque for 'as much as they can' out of the trust funds. Tim and Ted write to Ben and Sue saying, 'What do you think of this?' and asking for an 'urgent reply'. They both reply at once. Ben says, 'Why not?' and Sue says, 'This is a wonderful idea!'

Tim and Ted hand over a cheque for £300,000 drawn on the trust made out to Jack personally. Jack did not invest the money as promised but instead spent all the money on a racehorse which collapsed and died in its next race.

Advise Sue and Ben on any action which they can take and against whom.

Answer plan

→ Explain the significance of the general duty of care in section 1 of the Trustee Act 2000.

→ Explain the rules in the Trustee Act 2000 on investment.

→ Critically consider how the rules on delegation apply, especially in the context of investment powers.

→ Explain possible remedies of the beneficiaries.

→ Consider any possible defences available to the trustees.

Diagram plan

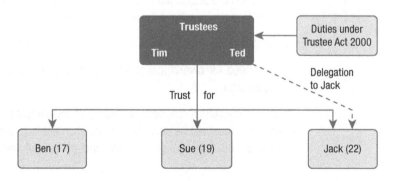

A printable version of this diagram is available from **www.pearsoned.co.uk/lawexpressqa**

[1] This shows the examiner at once that you are aware that there are two areas to this question and so makes an excellent start. There is no point in looking at possible remedies until you have identified if there have been any breaches of trust. Then go on and make a habit of asking if there are any express powers contained in the trust instrument. This not only shows a logical approach but is also exactly what you would do in practice. Finally, make a note to mention the possibility of an exclusion clause as well at the start. There is no need for any more detail on this in this answer.

[2] Although this question deals with a particular area, that of liability for breach of trust in the exercise of the power of investment, it is important to begin with this general principle and then go on to deal with specific areas.

[3] This is important: make the contrast between section 3, which deals with what the trustees can legally do, and section 4 which deals with the actual criteria when investing.

Answer

This question first asks us to consider if there have been any breaches of trust and then, if so, to look at what remedies are available and against whom. The question does not say that there are any express powers in the trust instrument and so this answer is on the basis that the trustees' powers are statutory. Nor are we told that there is any clause purporting to exclude the liability of trustees.[1]

Section 1 of the Trustee Act 2000[2] provides that a trustee must exercise such care and skill as is reasonable in the circumstances, having regard in particular to the following:

(a) Any special knowledge or experience which he has or holds himself out as having.

(b) If he acts in the course of a business or profession, to any special knowledge or experience that it is reasonable to expect of a person acting in the course of that business or profession.

In this case Tim is a solicitor, whereas Ted is a family friend. Solicitors are not investment experts but they should know the law and it is suggested that this may place a higher standard on Tim. On the other hand Ted, as a family friend, may have extra knowledge of the circumstances and needs of the beneficiaries.

Section 3 of the Trustee Act provides that a trustee may make any investment that he could make if he was absolutely entitled under the trust. Thus the trustees did have power to make the investment[3] suggested by Jack of shares in a property company in South America. However, when trustees are investing they must have regard to the standard investment criteria in section 4, which are

(a) the suitability to the trust of particular investments; and

(b) the need for diversification of investments, so far as this is appropriate.

These criteria reflect the portfolio theory of investments whereby investments must not be considered in isolation but looked at in the context of the portfolio as a whole and an overall investment strategy.

In this case the trustees proposed to invest £300,000 out of a total trust fund of £500,000 in an overseas company. This is clearly a speculative investment which might be appropriate in some trusts but here there is a family trust which will end at the latest date in eight years when Ben, the youngest beneficiary, reaches 25. A speculative investment, which may take years to realise its potential, does not seem to satisfy the criteria in section 4.[4]

[4] Note this practical point relating the very general rules in sections 3 and 4 to the facts. It shows how you can analyse a situation and will gain you extra marks.

Finally, section 5 provides that trustees must obtain and consider 'proper advice' about the way in which the power on investment should be exercised, having regard to the standard investment criteria. Proper advice is defined as the advice of a person reasonably believed by the trustees to be qualified to give it by reason of their ability in and practical experience of financial matters relating to the proposed investment. Clearly Jack, who was an investment trainee aged only 22, does not come into this category. Although trustees need not obtain advice if they reasonably conclude that in the circumstances it is unnecessary or inappropriate to do so, this obviously does not apply here.

[5] Although the investment was never made, the trustees still intended to make it and so this issue needed to be explored.

Thus even if the investment proposed by Jack had been made, it would have been in breach of trust.[5]

However, the trustees simply delegated the investment decision to Jack by handing him a cheque made out to him personally. Section 11 of the Trustee Act 2000 provides that trustees may delegate all decisions except those contained in a list set out in the section. Investment is not in this list and so may be delegated. However, by handing over the cheque to a person who cannot reasonably be considered a suitable agent, the trustees are clearly in breach of their statutory duty of care laid down in section 1. In addition, they have in effect employed Jack as an agent and they can be liable for his acts. Section 23 of the Trustee Act 2000[6] provides that a trustee is not liable for the acts or defaults of the agent unless he has failed to observe the standard of care when appointing the agent or keeping the arrangement under review. Clearly both trustees are liable for Jack's acts. Having established that there has been a breach of trust, we now turn to consider the remedies.

[6] We have mentioned two sections of the Trustee Act 2000, whereas many students would only have mentioned one. They are both relevant and so your marks will be increased.

[7] This point does not need any detail as the answer is obvious!

One which is not open to the beneficiaries is a tracing remedy under which they can follow the trust property, as the proceeds of the trust fund were all invested in a racehorse which is now dead.[7] Thus any remedy will be a personal remedy against the trustees for their breach of trust.

However, Jack, one of the beneficiaries, actually instigated the breach of trust and so he cannot claim any compensation, and under section 62 of the Trustee Act 1925 his interest in the trust may be impounded to satisfy the claims of the other beneficiaries.

It may be argued that any action by Ben and Sue is barred as they consented to the breach of trust. However, Ben is 17 and so, as he was not of full age when he wrote his letter of apparent consent, he can still claim. Sue is 19 and of course over full age but she could argue, first, that the letter from Tim and Ted did not give all the relevant facts as it just said 'What do you think of this?' and, second, that she was put under pressure as they asked for an 'urgent reply'. Thus it is suggested that they can both claim.

Tim and Ted may try to use the defence in section 61 of the Trustee Act 1925 under which the court may relieve a trustee from liability if he has acted honestly and reasonably and ought fairly to be excused both for the breach and for omitting to obtain the directions of the court. In **Nationwide Building Society v Davisons-Solicitors** [2012] EWCA Civ 1626, it was emphasised that the standard of trustees under section 61 was reasonableness not perfection, but it is suggested that in view of Tim and Ted's conduct outlined above they would not be held to have acted reasonably and so could not rely on section 61.

[8] It is essential that you mention the actual remedy in a question such as this as this is what the question has been leading up to.

Assuming that Ben and Sue claim against Tim and Ted, the measure of liability will be to restore to the trust all the property (the £300,000) which was wrongly taken from it, with interest.[8]

[9] Problem questions in this area often involve two or more trustees and if this is so then you must state and apply this rule.

Tim is a solicitor whereas Ted is a family friend. Although all trustees are individually liable for their own actual breaches, they are jointly and severally liable to compensate the beneficiaries and the fundamental equitable rule is that no regard is taken of fault.[9] Accordingly, a beneficiary can sue one or some or all of them and recover the entire loss from those trustees against whom he brings the action (**Bahin v Hughes** [1886] LR 31 Ch D 390). Thus Ben and Sue may claim against either or both trustees.

Make your answer stand out

- Explore the implications of Tim being a solicitor.
- Research the Law Commission in its Report *Trustees' Powers and Duties* No 260 (1999) especially Part III (Duty of Care) and Part IV (Trustees' Powers of Delegation). These will add value to your answer by giving extra detail on why the Trustee Act 2000 was passed and what the law was before.
- Read Clements (2004). This is a very valuable survey of the background to the Trustee Act 2000.
- Consider *Re Evans* [1999] 2 All ER 777, which dealt with section 61 of the Trustee Act 1925.
- End your answer by referring to *Re Partington* [1887] 57 LT 654, where the breach was committed solely on the advice of one trustee who had to indemnify his co-trustee and explain that this is not so here.

! Don't be tempted to . . .

- Fail to check the ages of the beneficiaries at the start.
- Ignore the remedies for breach of trust issue.
- Jump straight to the remedies for breach of trust issue and fail to start by asking if there has been a breach of trust at all.
- Miss the point that one trustee is a solicitor. You would not have been told this for nothing.

❓ Question 2

John died on 1 September 2018 and has left £400,000 to Pete and Mike to hold on trust for his two children, Cat and Helen, in equal shares for them on reaching the age of 21. You are asked to advise Pete and Mike on whether they should agree to any of the following requests made to them by the beneficiaries:

(a) Cat is 19 and a promising opera singer. She has asked for £120,000 to be paid to her now so that she can go to Paris for specialist opera tuition for a year and to meet her accommodation and living expenses whilst there. She intends to ask her boyfriend Phil to accompany her.

(b) Helen is 14 and is a promising hockey player. She has asked the trustees to pay the fees of £5,000 a year at a specialist hockey academy in India for five years so that she can improve her skills as a hockey player and at the same time continue with her academic studies there.

Answer plan

→ Explain that Pete and Mike as trustees have statutory powers and do not appear to have any additional ones conferred by the trust instrument.

→ Note that the relevant provisions of the Inheritance and Trustees' Powers Act 2014 apply.

→ Distinguish between powers and duties and explain what each means.

→ Note the ages of the beneficiaries as Cat is over 18 and so is automatically entitled to income.

→ Analyse powers of advancement in relation to Cat.

→ Analyse powers of maintenance and advancement in relation to Helen.

Diagram plan

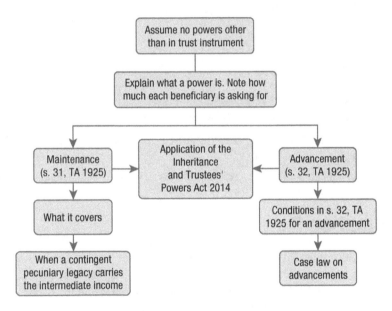

A printable version of this diagram is available from **www.pearsoned.co.uk/lawexpressqa**

Answer

This question is concerned with the statutory powers of trustees, in sections 31 and 32 of the Trustee Act 1925, of maintenance and advancement as amended by the Inheritance and Trustees' Powers Act 2014 which applies as John died after the Act came into force on

[1] There may still be cases where the death occurred before this date and so you will gain marks for pointing out when this Act came into force.

[2] Make it a habit to begin any answer to a problem question on this area by explaining the relationship between statutory powers and those in the trust instrument. You should then, as here, check whether there are in fact any relevant powers in the trust instrument. Finally you should mention as we have done that trustees have powers and what this means. Put all of these three points in at the start of your answer and you have laid a solid foundation for a really good mark.

[3] Always note the ages of beneficiaries: this is one reason why you should do so.

[4] Note carefully that all the capital can now be advanced as the 2014 Act applies.

[5] State exactly what section 32 says and then go on to the cases.

[6] Beware, as always, of making generalised assumptions but in questions on this area you may find that you need to say something on these lines. Do not spend too long on this point as we cannot come to a definite answer.

1 October 2014.[1] These are additional to any powers contained in the trust instrument and are also subject to the general provision in section 69(2) of the Trustee Act 1925 that the statutory powers conferred on trustees only apply in the absence of a contrary intention. As we are not told of any specific powers in the trust instrument, we will assume that there are none and assume that the trustees' powers are in sections 31 and 32. The other general point is that the trustees have a power[2] and not a duty, and as powers are discretionary they do not have to agree to any request for maintenance and advancement.

(a) Cat is 19 and the statutory power to pay maintenance ceases at the age of 18[3] and she is entitled to the income unless there is a contrary intention, of which there is no evidence here. However, this is clearly a request for capital and Cat is not entitled to this until she is 21 and so she must ask the trustees to exercise the power of advancement. Section 32, as amended by section 9 of the Inheritance and Trustees' Powers Act 2014, allows trustees to make advancements up to the total sum of the capital,[4] provided that any beneficiary with a prior interest must consent in writing to the advancement. In order for this consent to be valid the relevant beneficiary must be of full age. However, this does not apply here as there is no beneficiary with a prior interest.

It is also worth noting that if an advancement is made to Cat and this is of less than the total sum that she is entitled to under the will, then she must bring the amount of the advancement into account when the fund is distributed (section 32(1)(b)), otherwise she would be paid twice.

The question is then whether the trustees should exercise their power of advancement. Section 32 refers to 'advancement or benefit'.[5] Advancement has been held to refer to establishing the beneficiary in life through, for example, buying or furnishing a house, and the word 'benefit' seems to give a wider meaning to the term (**Re Kershaw's Trusts** [1868] LR 6 Eq 322 HC). It is suggested that if there is evidence that this course will indeed enable Cat to pursue a career as an opera singer then an advancement could be made but the sum of £120,000 does seem high.[6] In **Re Pauling's Settlement Trusts (No 1)** [1964] Ch 303 HC, the court held that where trustees prescribe a particular purpose for which the money is to be used they cannot leave the beneficiary entirely free to spend it for that purpose or in any other way that she chooses and so the trustees should make sure that the sum of £120,000 will be used for this purpose.

The other point is that the advancement should not be used to benefit others, as in this case Phil, Cat's boyfriend, but Cat might use **Re Kershaw's Trusts** as a precedent where an advancement to the beneficiary's husband to enable him to set up a business in England and so prevent the family from separating was held valid. She might argue that if a small part of the £120,000 paid to her then goes to Phil, it will prevent them from separating.

(b) Helen has asked for £5,000 a year for five years, which will take her to the age of 19. As she is entitled to £200,000 at 21, this sum might come out of income, in which case the trustees could exercise their power of maintenance.[7] This is a power to pay such income as the trustees think fit for the maintenance, education or benefit of an infant beneficiary. The term 'as they shall think fit' replaced the previous standard of reasonableness in the Trustee Act 1925 and the effect is to make any decision on maintenance one for the trustees to be exercised in good faith.[8] Trustees may pay the income to the infant (minor's) parent or guardian, if any, or otherwise apply the money (section 31(1)(i) of the Trustee Act 1925). Thus, the money could be paid direct to the academy.

However, section 31(3) provides that maintenance can only be paid when a person is entitled to the income. Here there is a contingent pecuniary legacy as the sum is contingent on the beneficiaries attaining the age of 21.[9] A contingent pecuniary legacy does not carry the intermediate income unless any of the following apply:

(i) The legacy was given by the father of the minor or some person *in loco parentis* to the beneficiary, provided that no other fund is set aside for the maintenance of the legatee (**Re West** [1913] 2 Ch 345 HC) and the contingency is the attainment of the legatee's majority (**Re Jones** [1932] 1 Ch 642 HC).

[7] Where a beneficiary is entitled to both maintenance and advancement, it seems sensible to start by asking if the sums might come out of maintenance even if it turns out that this will not be sufficient. Note the simple but vital point that you need to work out how much capital Helen is entitled to.

[8] This sentence is the kind of useful extra research detail to aim for.

[9] This can be a notoriously complex area but, as in this problem, the answer will not turn out to be too difficult. You will lose marks if you do not at least tackle it.

(ii) The testator shows an intention to maintain the legatee (***Re Churchill*** [1909] 2 Ch 431 HC).

(iii) The testator sets the legacy aside so as to be available for the legatee as soon as the contingency arises (***Re Medlock*** [1886] 55 LJ Ch 738 HC).

It appears that (i) above will apply unless there is another fund set aside for Helen's maintenance and there is no evidence that this is so. Thus, the trustees will have power to pay the sum requested out of income or, if there is insufficient income, out of capital. The only point is that the trustees may be reluctant to enter into a commitment for some years ahead but as the power of maintenance ceases at 18, Helen will have the income paid direct to her during her last year at the academy as of right and so the commitment will only be for four years. It is suggested that the trustees could agree to this request.[10]

[10] Note the way in which we have combined payment of income with that of maintenance. This approach will increase your marks.

✓ Make your answer stand out

- Read and refer to *Southgate* v *Sutton* [2011] EWCA Civ 637, which is considered in the answer to Question 4. The effect was to confer on the trustees a wider power to make advancements. Read and refer to Ker (1953) on intermediate income. This may help you to understand what can be a difficult area.
- Read the Report of the Law Reform Committee (1982) Cmnd 8733 Paragraphs 4.43 and 4.44 on the effect of inflation on advancements. You may be able to include a brief mention of this in your answer.
- Read and refer to *X* v *A* [2006] 1 WLR 741: an interesting case providing an illustration of when an advancement can be refused.

! Don't be tempted to . . .

- Forget to make a note at the start of the ages of the beneficiaries and when they will be entitled to maintenance and advancement.
- Forget when beneficiaries are entitled to income anyway.
- Leave out the first paragraph setting out three basic points.
- Leave out any mention of contingent pecuniary interests as if you do your answer will be incomplete and you will lose marks.

 **Question 3**

Critically examine the present law on the control by the courts of the discretionary decisions of trustees and assess whether it gives adequate protection to the interests of beneficiaries.

Answer plan

→ Set out the crucial passage in Lord Walker's judgment in *Pitt* v *Holt*.

→ Look carefully at when trustees make discretionary decisions.

→ Look in detail at the general principles on the extent to which the courts can control discretionary decisions.

→ Look in detail at the law on disclosure of trust documents, showing how it has evolved.

→ Evaluate the effect of the decision in *Schmidt* v *Rosewood Trust Ltd* on this area.

→ Conclude by asking whether the law is satisfactory.

Diagram plan

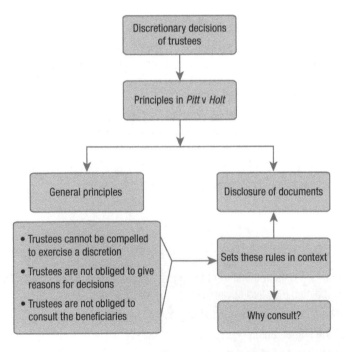

A printable version of this diagram is available from **www.pearsoned.co.uk/lawexpressqa**

Answer

The principles on when the courts can control the discretionary actions of trustees were set out by Lord Walker in *Pitt v Holt* [2013] UKSC 26:[1] 'Trustees must act in good faith, responsibly and reasonably. They must inform themselves, before making a decision, of matters which are relevant to the decision. These matters may not be limited to simple matters of fact but will, on occasion (indeed, quite often) include taking advice from appropriate experts, whether the experts are lawyers, accountants, actuaries, surveyors, scientists or whomsoever.'

[2] You could spend time on this particular area but it would be a diversion from the main theme.

Lord Walker's judgment was delivered in the context of litigation involving undoing of mistakes by trustees and the so-called rule in *Re Hastings-Bass* [1975] Ch 25 HC[2] but it was intended to have wider application.

Trusts have duties, which are mandatory, and powers, which are discretionary. Trustees are under a duty to collect in the trust assets and to invest but under a power to pay maintenance to beneficiaries and to advance trust capital to them. In addition, where the trustee is exercising a duty, such as that of investment, there is also a power to decide exactly how that duty should be exercised.

[3] The link to wide discretionary trusts is an absolutely crucial point in the success of this essay.

Moreover there has been a considerable growth in wide discretionary trusts from the decision in *McPhail v Doulton* [1971] AC 424, which upheld their validity[3]. In this context, Davies (2004) points out 'as with *Donoghue v Stevenson* some 40 years earlier, control mechanisms are scarcely able to limit them' as the only persons allowed to seek the intervention of the courts are those with defined beneficial interests and in the case of very wide discretionary trusts there might be few if any of these.

Where trustees have a discretion then the courts will not compel trustees to exercise it, otherwise there would be no discretion. In *Tempest v Lord Camoys* [1882] LR 21 Ch D 571 CA, trustees were given a discretion to buy and sell land. One trustee wished to buy land but his co-trustee did not agree and the court refused to order him to.

Moreover, the courts will not compel trustees to give their reasons for exercising or not exercising a discretion. In *Re Beloved Wilkes Charity* [1851] 3 Mac. & G. 440 HC, trustees had a duty to select a boy to be educated for Holy Orders in the Church of England. They were obliged to give preference to suitable boys from certain parishes but they selected a boy from another parish apparently after the boy's brother, a Minister, had approached the trust on his behalf. The trustees refused to give any reason for their decision and the court would not compel them to. This rule is based on the confidential nature of trustees' obligations which the courts feel they cannot exercise if they are subject to checks to see how they have exercised them (*Re Londonderry's Settlement* [1965] Ch 918 CA).[4]

[4] It is vital to add depth to your answer by looking at the reasons why the law has evolved, especially where, as here, there is a strong argument that it is now unfair.

The limits of trustees' obligations towards the beneficiaries are seen in *Hawkesley v May* [1956] 1 QB 304 HC, where the court held that although trustees had a duty to disclose to the beneficiaries on attaining 21 that they had an interest in the capital and income of the trust fund, they were not under any duty to advise on their legal position.

Nor is there any general duty to consult the beneficiaries except where statute provides, as in the case of trusts of land (section 11 Trusts of Land and Appointment of Trustees Act 1996).

[5] Here we are going back, as it were, and showing how an old case is illustrated by a principle that has only recently been stated in detail.

The actual decisions of trustees are subject to scrutiny by the courts under the general principles set out by Lord Walker in *Pitt v Holt*. An old example of taking account of irrelevant matters is *Klug v Klug* [1918] 2 Ch 67 HC,[5] where one trustee, the beneficiary's mother, refused to approve the exercise of a power of advancement because she was annoyed by the daughter having married without her consent. In *Turner v Turner* [1984] Ch 100 HC, the court intervened where the discretion was not exercised at all. The trustees, who had no knowledge of trust matters, signed deeds of appointment on the orders of the settlor who said in evidence that he still regarded himself as 'captain of the ship' and who had established the trust for tax purposes whilst retaining *de facto* control. These appointments were set aside. However, these earlier decisions were not set in the context of any general statement of the law on when the court could investigate the discretionary decisions of trustees.

[6] This is vital: the law on disclosure of trust documents must be seen against the general law on control of discretionary decisions by trustees of which it forms part.

Here *Pitt v Holt* is welcome but even though this represents a tightening up of the extent to which the courts can control decisions of trustees, if beneficiaries are denied access to trust documents then their means of control are blunted.[6]

In *Re Londonderry's Settlement,* the Court of Appeal refused the beneficiary access to documents that would show why the trustees chose to distribute the fund in the way that they did. Disclosure had been sought of minutes and agendas of trust meetings and correspondence between the trustees and their agents. The court held that trustees of a discretionary family settlement such as this could not discharge their duties if, '[A]t any moment there is likely to be an investigation for the purpose of seeing whether they have exercised their discretion in the best possible manner.'

It is arguable that the court failed to clarify the basis on which beneficiaries could assert a right to see documents. Nor did it clearly address the fundamental question of exactly what are trust documents. The court's reasoning in **Re Londonderry's Settlement** emphasised the need for confidentiality in trustees' decision making, especially in family type trusts. Here we return to **Pitt v Holt**,[7] as it is arguable that a principle allowing the courts to exercise greater control over the decisions of trustees is stymied by a rule that denies access to the trustees' reasons for their decisions.

[7] Do emphasise the change in the law made by *Pitt* v *Holt*.

Schmidt v Rosewood Trust Ltd [2003] AC 709 PC concerned an application by a discretionary beneficiary and the object of a power of appointment to require the production of trust documents. The Judicial Committee rejected the proposition that the right to seek the court's intervention depended on entitlement to a fixed and transmissible beneficial interest and that the beneficiaries had to have a proprietary interest in the documents.[8] Instead Lord Walker held that '(the) correct approach is to regard the right to seek disclosure of trust documents as one aspect of the court's inherent jurisdiction to supervise and, if necessary to intervene in, the administration of trusts'. He said that there were three areas on which the court will need to form a discretionary judgment: should a discretionary object of a trust be granted relief at all; what classes of documents should be disclosed, either completely or in a 'redacted' (i.e. edited) form; and what safeguards should be imposed by the court.

[8] Here we get to the heart of the matter: the fact that in this case the court recognised the need for a different approach.

In conclusion although recent decisions have increased the control of the discretionary decisions of trustees, there are still too many outdated decisions limiting the rights of beneficiaries which can lead to an atmosphere of unnecessary secrecy when a more transparent approach by trustees would lead to better protection of the interests of beneficiaries and also better decision making by trustees.[9]

[9] Note the two points made here: try for an engaging end to an essay question even where, as here, the conclusion is only one paragraph.

Make your answer stand out

- Read and refer to Davies (2004) 'The integrity of trusteeship' in full. It is a most valuable summary of the law and contains a clear account of *Schmidt* v *Rosewood Trust Ltd*. Note in particular his criticism of the decision because: 'It is not however obvious what an applicant for a disclosure order will have to demonstrate before the order is issued.'
- Read and refer to Griffiths (2008). 'The author looks at the shift from confidentiality to accountability and is important in a wider context.
- Look at cases post-*Schmidt* v *Rosewood Trust Ltd*, such as the New Zealand decision in *Foreman* v *Kingstone* [2004] 1 NZLR 841.
- Read and refer to Lee (2018) who looks at *Pitt* v *Holt* in the specific context of seeking to set aside mistakes of trustees.

! Don't be tempted to . . .

- Forget to deal with the general issue of control by the courts of trustees.
- Just look at the details of the law on disclosure of documents only.
- Ignore any underlying reasons for the decisions of the courts – a good example is *Re Londonderry's Settlement*.

Question 4

'The court has discretion to approve an arrangement under the Act, even though the settlement may make it crystal clear that the settlor or testator does not want any departure from any of the strict terms of the trust' (Mummery LJ in *Goulding* v *James* [1997] 4 All ER 239 CA).

Critically consider the jurisdiction of the courts to vary beneficial interests under a trust especially in the light of this observation by Mummery LJ on the operation of the Variation of Trusts Act 1958.

Answer plan

→ Set the scene by explaining when trusts can be varied and when the consent of the beneficiaries is needed.

→ Set out the provisions of the Variation of Trusts Act dealing with when the court can approve a variation in the beneficial interests under a trust.

→ Emphasise the fundamental point that the court cannot approve a variation unless it is for the benefit of those on whose behalf it is sought.

→ Critically consider cases where the intentions of the settlor seem to have been overridden by the courts in consenting to a variation.

→ End by looking at the parallel jurisdiction of the courts under section 57 of the Trustee Act 1925 and how it has been exercised in *Southgate* v *Sutton.*

Diagram plan

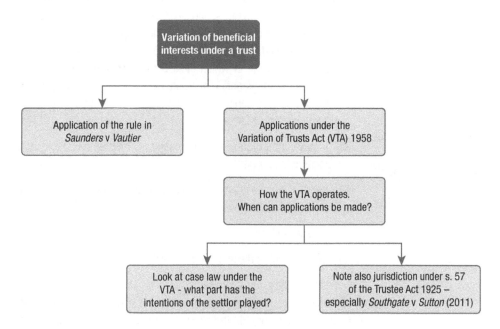

A printable version of this diagram is available from **www.pearsoned.co.uk/lawexpressqa**

Answer

It is first important to clarify exactly when the interests of beneficiaries under a trust can be varied.[1] If the beneficiaries are of full age then they will need to give their consent personally[2] to any variation of their beneficial interests where, for example, the shares to be taken by each beneficiary are to be altered. This is clearly fair. In fact, if all the beneficiaries are of full age and capacity and absolutely entitled, then they can all agree under the rule in **Saunders v Vautier** [1841] 41 ER 482 to terminate the trust and claim the fund absolutely. However, not all the beneficiaries may agree to the proposed variation, as in **Southgate v Sutton** [2011] EWCA Civ 637, or there may be discretionary beneficiaries, in which case **Saunders v Vautier** will not apply. However, the Variation of Trusts Act (VTA) 1958 does give the court power to give consent to a variation on behalf of a number of classes of persons.[3] These are:

(a) infants and persons who by means of (mental) incapacity are incapable of assenting;

(b) persons who have only an expectation of succeeding, such as a potential future spouse;

(c) persons unborn; and

(d) persons with a discretionary interest under a protective trust.

How should the court exercise its powers? The only guidance given to the courts is contained is section 1 of the VTA which provides that (apart from category (d)) the court shall not approve any variation on behalf of any person unless this would be for 'the benefit of that person'[4] and in deciding this the courts have taken a wide view of what constitutes 'benefit'.

The classic objection to any legislation on variation of trusts is, as Mummery LJ pointed out in **Goulding v James** [1997] 2 All ER 239, that the settlement 'may make it crystal clear that the settlor or testator does not want any departure from any of the strict terms of the trust'.[5] Thus by varying the trust the court may be going against the wishes of the settlor in creating the trust. Has this in fact been the case?

[1] Read the question carefully and you will see that it asks you to 'Consider the jurisdiction of the courts to vary beneficial interests under a trust *especially* in the light of this observation . . . ' Thus it is not asking you only to consider the observation of Mummery LJ, although you must certainly do this, but also to consider the jurisdiction of the courts to vary trusts *in general*. If you had concentrated only on the point made by Mummery LJ then you would have lost marks.

[2] This fundamental point needs to be stressed at the outset.

[3] It is vital to make it clear that the VTA only applies in a limited number of cases.

[4] This is the crucial phrase: omit it and you will lose marks.

[5] Now that you have set the scene, you can focus on the observation of Mummery LJ mentioned in the question.

[6] It is impossible to give an answer which discusses the issues in the required depth and demonstrates some critical analysis if at the same time you mention a great many cases. Note the approach adopted here: only two cases are discussed but these are discussed in detail and they are analysed.

[7] It is essential to mention this to explain that not in all cases are the settlor's wishes ignored.

[8] Here we begin to look at the two cases in detail.

[9] If you are aiming for high marks then this is the kind of paragraph to include. You have, as the previous paragraph shows, researched this case and now you are using this research to critically analyse the decision.

[10] This is excellent research detail: we have contrasted the approach of the High Court with that of the Court of Appeal. Try to do this in other answers.

The cases show some variation in approach.[6] In **Re Steed's Will Trust** [1960] Ch 407, Evershed MR emphasised that the intentions of the settlor must be considered.[7] Here a testator had left his property to his housekeeper on protective trusts to prevent her from 'being sponged upon by one of her brothers'. The court refused to sanction the removal of the protective element, which would mean that she would be absolutely entitled to the trust property, because this would undermine the testator's intention that she should not be exposed to risk. However, in **Re Remnant's Settlement Trusts** [1970] Ch 560,[8] a will contained a forfeiture clause, under which children who practised Roman Catholicism or married a Roman Catholic would forfeit their interests. The testator had two children, one of whom stood to forfeit her interest as she had married a Roman Catholic and had become a Roman Catholic herself. The other sister was a Protestant. The court approved the deletion of the forfeiture clause and Pennycuick J observed that 'a forfeiture provision of this kind might well cause very serious dissension between the families'. In fact both sets of families agreed to the deletion of the clause.

If we are to treat fidelity to the intentions of the settlor as an important consideration then this decision is hard to understand.[9] It was not unlawful to include this forfeiture clause and the will was made just after the daughter had married a Roman Catholic. Thus it seemed clear that the settlor intended that her daughter's marriage to a Roman Catholic should result in the forfeiture of her interest.

In **Goulding v James** itself Mrs Froud, the testatrix, had set up a trust under which her daughter, J, took a life interest in her residuary estate followed by an absolute gift of the estate to her grandson, M, on his attaining the age of 40. If M predeceased J, or if M failed to reach 40, the estate would pass to such of the testatrix's great-grandchildren as should be living at the date of M's death. The variation proposed by J and M would give each of them an absolute, 45 per cent share in the estate and the remaining 10 per cent would be held on trust for any great-grandchildren.

The result would be to give much more generous provision for the unborn great-grandchildren than the value of their current interest in residue. However, the High Court refused the application,[10] on the ground that the proposed variation would be contrary to the testatrix's strongly held wishes. Her intention was that J should not be able to touch the capital of the estate at any time as she disliked J's husband, and M's interest should be postponed until he reached the age of 40 as she regarded him as immature. However, Mummery LJ approved the application on appeal. He pointed out that the question of benefit had to be considered in relation to the interests of the beneficiaries on whose behalf approval was sought, in this case the unborn great-grandchildren, and the approximately five-fold increase in the value of their share was clearly for their benefit.

In fact, most variations will merely remove some technical obstacle in the trust document rather than thwarting the settlor's intentions, but it now seems clear that where the proposed variation is for the benefit of those on whose behalf approval is sought then the fact that it conflicts with the settlor's intentions is a less important factor.

In order to give a complete picture of the law in this area it should be mentioned that section 57 of the Trustee Act 1925 gives power to the court to approve proposals by trustees concerning the management or administration of trust property where this 'is in the opinion of the court expedient'. This is traditionally used to approve, for instance, changes to investment powers of trustees. However, it does not give jurisdiction to vary the beneficial interests (**Chapman v Chapman** [1954] AC 429 HL). However, in **Southgate v Sutton** [2011], the Court of Appeal approved what really amounted to a variation in the beneficial interests in an application under section 57,[11] where it agreed to the creation of a subtrust of separated funds for the benefit of the US beneficiaries as distinct from the UK beneficiaries. The object was to avoid a double tax burden on the US beneficiaries. It could be argued that a partition of the fund would vary the beneficial interests as the beneficiaries would enjoy the income of part of the fund instead of enjoying a share of the income of the whole fund as previously, but the court sanctioned the arrangement. To sum up, it seems from the cases that the courts are increasing their jurisdiction to vary beneficial interests under trusts and that fidelity to the wishes of the settlor is a less significant factor.[12]

[11] The inclusion of this case will add value to your answer and increase your marks in two ways: it shows an ability to 'think outside the box' and demonstrate that you are aware of the significance of another statutory provision, and it also shows knowledge of recent case law.

[12] You do need to round off this answer but at the same time you must avoid just summarising what you have said. A one sentence conclusion as here can be fine.

Make your answer stand out

- Have a clear structure – do not just mention the issue of the intentions of the settlor where a variation is sought but, as the question asks, set this in the context of this area of law as a whole.
- Select some cases and research these in depth.
- Research how and why the VTA was passed: look at the HL decision in *Chapman* v *Chapman* [1954] AC 429 HL and the debates in Parliament when the Variation of Trusts Bill was being considered.
- Read and refer to Luxton (1997): this looks at *Goulding* v *James* [1997] 2 All ER 239 CA, and at the extent to which the court in that case may have laid down rules restricting the exercise of the discretion of the courts in consideration of applications under the VTA.

 Don't be tempted to . . .

- State all of the cases where the court can give its consent on behalf of certain persons to a variation in the beneficial interests. Some of them are complex and would not add to this answer.
- Fail to emphasise the fundamental criterion: that any variation must be for the benefit of those on whose behalf it is sought.
- Spend too long on the details of the VTA at the expense of analysis of the cases.
- Mention too many cases at the expense of a critical analysis of the issue.

@ Try it yourself

Now take a look at the question below and attempt to answer it. You can check your response against the answer guidance available on the companion website (**www.pearsoned.co.uk/lawexpressqa**).

> Jack is a beneficiary under a family trust set up by his late Uncle John. The beneficiaries are Uncle John's children, nephews and nieces, amounting in all to twenty beneficiaries. The trustees are Uncle John's widow, Maria, and a family friend, Norman.
>
> Jack has become increasingly unhappy about the amount of money that has been given to Belinda, a niece of Uncle John, by the trustees. Jack suspects that Norman and Belinda are having an affair.
>
> Advise Jack on whether he has any grounds to challenge the decisions of the trustees and what documents belonging to the trustees he is entitled to inspect.

www.pearsoned.co.uk/lawexpressqa

Go online to access more revision support including additional essay and problem questions with diagram plans, 'You be the marker' questions, and download all diagrams from the book.

12

Remedies for breach of trust

How this topic may come up in exams

This topic can arise in two types of problem questions. One involves the situation where property may have been received in breach of trust, often linked to possible assistance in a breach of trust. The other is where a person in a fiduciary position misapplies trust property and you have to apply the techniques of tracing. You will find examples of both here. Another remedy is that of money payments where there has been a breach of trust, which is considered in a question in Chapter 11. A final possibility is an essay question which could ask you about the relationship between the different remedies which might involve the Supreme Court decision in *AIB Group (UK) Plc* v *Mark Redler & Co Solicitors*.

■ Before you begin

It's a good idea to consider the following key themes of remedies for breach of trust before tackling a question on this topic.

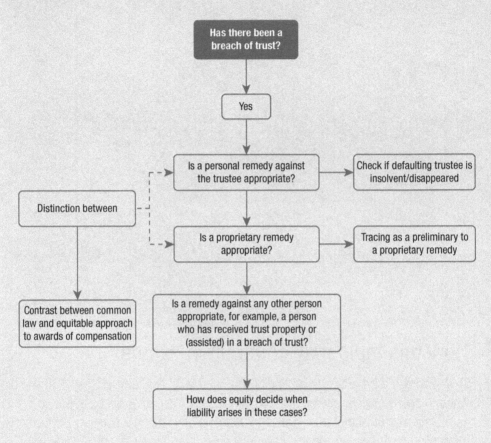

A printable version of this diagram is available from **www.pearsoned.co.uk/lawexpressqa**

? Question 1

John, Ted and Mal run 'Trig's Gigs', which provides equipment for gigs and other entertainments. The van which carries the equipment was purchased for £9,000, John, Ted and Mal contributing £3,000 each. However, the van was registered in John's name. The van had the words 'Trig's Gigs' painted on the side.

John sold the van to Ed for £8,000. Ed also provides equipment for gigs and he had seen John, Ted and Mal using the van at gigs. John asks Ned, a friend who has helped at gigs where Trig's Gigs provided the equipment, to drive the van to Ed's house, as John has lost his driving licence, and Ned does so. John is never seen again.

Ted and Mal ask your advice on any remedies which they may have explaining the relevant law fully.

Answer plan

→ Identify that Ted and Mal have a beneficial interest in the van, as it was bought with money provided by them.

→ Identify that Ed may be liable as a constructive trustee on the basis of knowing receipt of trust property.

→ State and explain the law on the test for liability in knowing receipt cases.

→ Outline common law remedies.

→ Then move on to consider Ned's liability, setting out the relevant tests and explaining first that there is some debate on exactly what this liability should be called.

Diagram plan

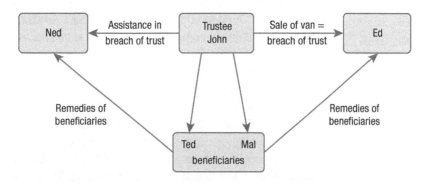

A printable version of this diagram is available from **www.pearsoned.co.uk/lawexpressqa**

Answer

[1] This is a good point for extra marks; equity only presumes a resulting trust in these cases and so you should look for any evidence that in fact none was intended.

[2] Although they did not consent to the sale in this case, it might not be so straightforward in other cases and so you should watch for this point.

[3] Students often waste time at this point. Do not be one of them!

[4] Do notice how this argument has been developed: we have not just said that Ed will be liable if he has notice of the beneficiary's rights but explained exactly why notice is important. It is this logical approach, mentioning all relevant points, which will enable you to pick up those extra marks.

[5] This is an important point and means that rather than just use one test for liability in your answer, you can pick up marks by a more general survey of the law before you come to the most recent authority.

[6] It is at this point that you come to the most recent authority and this is the one which you should apply to the facts.

John bought the van for £9,000 but, of this, Ted and Mal each provided £3,000. Thus, as they provided part of the purchase price, equity will presume that a resulting trust arises under which John holds the van on trust for all of them in proportion to their contributions. This presumption can be displaced by evidence that only a loan was intended[1] (**Dyer v Dyer** [1788] 2 Cox Eq Cas 92 HC) but there is no evidence of that here.

Although there seems to have been no trust deed, it is clear that the van was held for the purposes of the trust and so is trust property. When John sold the van to Ed he committed a breach of trust, as it is clear that Ted and Mal did not consent to the sale.[2] Ted and Mal would be able to pursue personal remedies against John for an account of profits but as John cannot be traced this would be pointless.[3]

Ed has bought the van and so he has received trust property. The question is whether an action *in rem* may be brought to recover the trust property as a result of which Ed can be made to hold it on a constructive trust for Ted and Mal. However, a beneficiary cannot recover trust property where it is in the hands of a *bona fide* purchaser of the legal estate for value without notice of the beneficiary's equitable right. The question is then whether Ed did have notice of Ted and Mal's rights.[4]

The courts have found difficulty in establishing an all-embracing principle for determining when a stranger who has received trust property can be liable.[5] In **Baden Delvaux Lecuit v Société Générale pour Favoriser le Développement du Commerce et de l'Industrie en France** [1983] BCLC 325 HC, Peter Gibson J proposed five categories which stretched to 'knowledge of circumstances which would put an honest and reasonable man on enquiry'. There has, in more recent years, been a move away from this. Megarry V-C in **Re Montagu's Settlement Trust** [1987] Ch 264 HC emphasised that the question was whether the recipient had knowledge and not notice and that liability should not be imposed unless the conscience of the recipient was affected. His choice of words as a test for liability was whether the recipient was guilty of a 'want of probity'. The present law is probably best summed up by the decision in **BCCI (Overseas) Ltd v Akindele** [2001] Ch 437 CA,[6] where Nourse LJ held the categories in **Baden** were more appropriate to cases of assistance in a breach of trust but he approved of the approach in **Re Montagu,** with its emphasis on knowledge. He held that there should be a single test of knowledge: did 'the recipient's state of knowledge . . . make it unconscionable for him to retain the benefit of the receipt'? This, he felt, would enable there to be common-sense decisions in the context of commercial transactions.

If we apply this to the facts here we see that Ed also provides equipment for gigs and he had seen John, Ted and Mal using the van at gigs. Moreover, the van had 'Trig's Gigs' painted on the side. On these facts it seems that, although we have no direct evidence that Ed actually knew that the van was the property of Trig's Gigs, there is equally no evidence that Ed thought that the van was the sole property of John. On this basis, it is suggested that Ed's state of knowledge would make it unconscionable for him to retain the van[7] solely and beneficially and so he will hold it on trust for Ted and Mal. Ed's primary duty will be to restore the van to Ted and Mal. If Ed unreasonably delays in doing this then, under the rule in **Saunders v Vautier** [1841] 41 ER 482 HC, Ted and Mal could terminate the trust, as they are absolutely entitled provided that they are both of full age, and recover the van.

[7] It is vital to apply the exact words on any test for liability to the conduct which is in issue – this shows a clear analytical approach and will certainly add to your marks.

There could be possibilities of common law actions open to Ted and Mal but they do not seem to be applicable here.[8] The common law action for money had and received, as in **Lipkin Gorman v Karpnale Ltd** [1991] 2 AC 548 HL, obviously cannot apply as the claim does not involve money, and a possible action based on unjust enrichment is really applicable where the recipient is an innocent volunteer and here Ed is a purchaser.

[8] Make it a habit in questions on receipt of trust property to mention the possibility of actions at common law. Even if, as here, they will not apply, you have shown the examiner that you are aware of them and can use them if appropriate.

The other question is whether Ned can be made liable in an action by Ted and Mal for knowing assistance in the breach of trust by John in selling the van to Ed. Here, Ned is a friend of John's who has helped at gigs where Trig's Gigs provided the equipment, and Ned agrees to drive the van to Ed's house as John has lost his driving licence.

[9] This is an important point which an examiner will expect you to mention.

Here there is no acquisition of trust property and the general view is that it is incorrect to speak of a person who assists in a breach of trust as a constructive trustee. The remedy is a personal one against the wrongdoer and is called liability for 'dishonest assistance' in a breach of trust.[9] In **Novoship (UK) Ltd v Nikitin [2014]** EWCA Civ 908 CA, it was held that although the remedy of an account of profits is also available against a dishonest accessory, the extent of his liability is determined by common law principles of remoteness as although he is an equitable wrongdoer he is not subject to a pre-existing duty as a trustee is.

In ***Royal Brunei Airlines Sdn Bhd v Tan Kok Ming*** [1995] 2 AC 378 DC, Lord Nicholls held that the accessory's liability should depend on whether he had been dishonest. He disposed of the debate on whether it mattered if the trustee had been dishonest[10] and held that the liability of the person who assisted in the breach of trust did not depend on the trustee's own state of mind. In fact in this case it seems clear that John was fraudulent.

[10] Note that the question asks you to 'explain the relevant law fully' and this is an indication that you are expected to explain points in some detail even where the answer is actually clear. However, you should not use this as an excuse to bring in irrelevant issues.

In ***Twinsectra Ltd v Yardley*** [2002] AC 164 HL, Lord Hutton held that a person will not be dishonest unless it is established that his conduct had been dishonest by the ordinary standards of reasonable and honest people and that he realised that by those standards his conduct was dishonest. ***Abou-Rahmah v Abacha*** [2006] EWCA Civ 1492 clarified this by explaining that the test for dishonesty is pre-dominately objective in that although the defendant must have known that he was acting contrary to normal standards of honesty, he need not have been actually conscious that he was doing wrong.

[11] Note two points: you need to make use of all the information given. Note how the point about the driving licence can be integrated into the answer. The other one is that you only need to come to a conclusion on the issue of Ned's possible liability as you have already dealt with that of Ed.

On this basis, Ned may not have known that he was acting in a way that was 'contrary to normal standards of honesty', as John did not tell him why he was to drive the van to Ed's house and it could have been that Ed simply wished to borrow the van. John's explanation that he could not drive it as he had lost his licence seems plausible on the facts and it is suggested that Ned will not be liable.[11]

 Make your answer stand out

- Do read the judgment of Nourse LJ in *BCCI* v *Akindele*: this contains an excellent review of the law and a discussion of the extent to which constructive notice and dishonesty has been required. You could then use some of this in your answer.
- Consider whether the test of unconscionability is really very helpful – is this term sufficiently clear?
- There is a general survey of the whole law on knowing receipt in Mitchell and Watterson (2010, pp. 115–58). They look, for example, at exactly what duties a constructive trustee, such as Ed in this question, might owe to the beneficiaries.

- There is a very useful survey of the law on liability for dishonest assistance which you could read and refer to before Ridge (2008).
- Is the language of a constructive trustee inappropriate in cases of knowing receipt as well as knowing assistance? In what real sense is Ed, for example, a trustee?
- Have a look at *Barlow Clowes International Ltd (in liquidation)* v *Eurotrust International Ltd* [2005] UKPC 37. Does this decision on liability for dishonest assistance differ from that in *Twinsectra* v *Yardley* and, if so, how?
- Read Whayman (2018) on tracing claims which contains some fresh thinking on the nature of these claims.

! Don't be tempted to . . .

- Start by discussing possible remedies which Ted and Mal have without first identifying that there is actually a trust. If there is no trust there can be no remedies for breach of trust.
- Do not confuse liability on the part of Ed for possible knowing receipt and on the part of Ned for possible knowing assistance. Deal with these issues separately.
- Do not refer to Ned as constructive trustee without at least explaining the controversy about whether he should be described in that way.

? Question 2

Nick is a trustee and also treasurer of 'Green Fingers', a small charity established to encourage gardening among young people. He is also sole trustee of a family trust set up under the will of his late wife, Edith, for the benefit of their three children, Ben, Ned and Sue.

Nick pays in £2,000 of the funds of Green Fingers into his own bank account, which previously had £5,000 in it, and then pays in £3,000 from the family trust. The total funds in his bank account are now £10,000. Nick then withdraws £8,000 to purchase a racing yacht which wins first prize of £10,000 in the 'Round the Isle of Thanet' yacht race. Nick pays this sum into his account which now stands at £12,000. He writes himself a note: 'This is to make good what I took out. All settled now.' He then withdraws £5,000 and gives it to his son, Fred, who buys premium bonds with it and wins £100. Nick then withdraws £5,000 and gives it to his local hospital to go towards its heart scanner appeal. The balance remaining is £2,000, which Nick spends on a horse which he intends to race. Unfortunately, the horse dies at the start of its first race. Nick has now retired to a monastery in Tibet to 'try to make amends for my past misdeeds'. His total assets are £100 in a bank account.

The beneficiaries under both of the trusts have now discovered the losses and ask for your advice on whether and how they can recover the lost funds.

Answer plan

→ Identify that breaches of trust have occurred.

→ Explain the possibility of a personal action for an account against Nick but point out that it will be of little use in view of the amount involved.

→ Then move on to explain what the tracing process is.

→ Explain the fundamental requirements for tracing.

→ Now analyse the situation in detail, applying the tracing rules at each stage.

Diagram plan

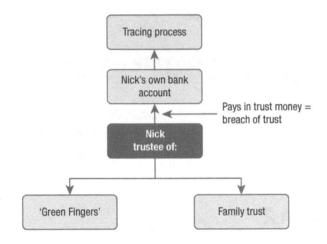

A printable version of this diagram is available from **www.pearsoned.co.uk/lawexpressqa**

Answer

[1] It is of course obvious that Nick has acted in breach of trust but you still need to say this.

The first point is that Nick has acted in breach of trust in parting with the funds of two trusts[1] and so we need to consider the possible remedies for breach of trust available to the beneficiaries. The starting point is to consider any possible remedies against Nick personally. He has £100 in his account and this is available to the beneficiaries under a personal action for an account. This is a restitutionary remedy and so the £100 must be restored to the trust funds.[2]

We then need to look at the possibility of proprietary actions to recover trust property which has been wrongly parted with, or to recover other property representing it. The process by which this takes place is known as tracing.[3]

There are certain requirements to be satisfied in order to be able to trace.[4] First, there must be a fiduciary relationship which there is here as there are two trusts. Second, those seeking to trace must have an equitable proprietary interest which they have as beneficiaries.

The first breaches of trust are where Nick pays in £2,000 of the funds of Green Fingers (we shall refer to this as Trust A)[5] into his own bank account which previously had £5,000 in it. He then pays in £3,000 from the family trust, which we shall refer to as Trust B. The total funds in his bank account are now £10,000.

Nick then withdraws £8,000 to purchase a racing yacht, which still appears to exist. Can Trust A or B trace into this?

In **Re Hallett's Estate** [1880] 13 Ch D 696 CA, the rule was established that when making withdrawals from an account a trustee is presumed to spend his own money first. However, once the amount in the account falls below the amount of trust funds then it is assumed that part of the trust funds must have been spent. Here there was £5,000 in his bank account before he had paid in any money from trust funds and so, of the £8,000 used to buy the yacht, £5,000 is his own money. The reason for this rule is to protect beneficiaries where sums are left in a trustee's account as it makes it more likely that money left will belong to the beneficiaries and can be claimed by them.[6]

However, this leaves £3,000, which must have come from the funds of one or both of the trusts. To decide which of the funds it came from, we apply the rule in **Clayton's Case** [1816] 35 ER 781 HC, which provides that, in the case of an active continuing bank account, the trustee is regarded as having taken out of the fund whatever had been first put in. 'First in, first out.' Thus, as this is certainly an active bank account, if for the wrong reasons, this rule will apply and as the money from Trust A was first in, this will be the account that the money to

[7] There will usually be something left over, as here, so that you can apply the rules starting with *Clayton's Case*.

[8] If you mention *Clayton's Case* then you must also mention this authority.

buy the yacht will come from first. However, as there is only £2,000 in this account, the other £1,000 must have come from Trust B.[7]

The authority of the rule in Clayton's Case was weakened in *Barlow Clowes International Ltd (in liquidation)* v *Vaughan* [1992] 4 All ER 22 CA,[8] when it was not applied to claims by investors to share in the assets of a company which had managed investment plans for them. The investments were in a collective scheme by which investors' money was mixed together and invested in a common fund and it was held to be wrong that those who invested first could expect least. The court held that the rule in **Clayton's Case** is only one of convenience and would therefore be displaced here, and instead investors would share rateably in the company's assets in proportion to the amounts due to them. If this principle applied here, it could be argued that the loss to the trust fund should be borne rateably by the two trusts, and so the loss of £3,000 will be borne in the proportion of 40:60 between Trust A and Trust B.

The yacht wins first prize of £10,000 in the 'Round the Isle of Thanet' yacht race. Nick pays this sum into his account, which now stands at £12,000. Of this, £2,000 is money belonging to Trust B, which is still in the account. It can be argued that the prize of £10,000 belongs to the trusts, as it is the traceable proceeds of the yacht which was bought with their money (see **Re Tilley's Will Trusts** [1967] Ch 1179 HC). On the other hand, it was held in **Roscoe v Winder** [1915] 1 Ch 62 HC that where a trustee makes any later payments into his bank account these are not treated as repayments of the trust money unless the trustee has shown an intention to do this. In this case Nick writes himself a note: 'This is to make good what I took out. All settled now.' Thus on the basis of both rules it seems clear that the £10,000 will belong to the trusts. So on the basis of 40:60, it can be argued that Trust A receives £4,000 and now stands at this figure and Trust B receives £6,000 and now stands at £8,000 adding the £2,000 already in the account.[9]

[9] A tip: if by now you are getting bemused by the arithmetic, then give it up, as it is more important to be able to apply the principles and if you get the sums wrong it may mean that you get the law wrong too.

Nick then withdraws £5,000 and gives it to his son Fred who buys premium bonds with it and wins £100. If the rule in **Clayton's Case** applies, this will come from Trust A which will now be exhausted, and £1,000 will come from Trust B. As Fred was given the money he will be a volunteer, albeit innocent, and tracing will be possible against him. Thus he will be liable to restore the £5,000 plus the win of £100

(*Re Tilley's Will Trusts*). When the money is restored it is suggested that Trust A and B will be put back to where they were before.

Nick then withdraws £5,000 and gives it to his local hospital to go towards its heart scanner appeal. In *Re Diplock* [1948] Ch 465 CA, it was held that tracing was not possible where money has been paid by innocent volunteers who were charities on improving their own land and it may be that this will apply here. This rule used to be explained on the basis that tracing would be inequitable but it is now considered to rest under the principle that there has been a change of position[10] (see *Lipkin Gorman* v *Karpnale Ltd* [1991] 2 AC 548 HL). If *Clayton's Case* applies, then this will come from Trust A, which will now be exhausted, and £1,000 from Trust B.

Finally, the balance remaining is £2,000, which Nick spends on a horse which he intends to race. Unfortunately, the horse dies at the start of its first race. As the property is no longer identifiable, the right to trace is lost. This £2,000 will come from Trust B as Trust A is exhausted.

In the end, all that is left is the £5,100 which on the facts will probably go to Trust B.[11]

[10] The idea that tracing will not be possible where money has been innocently received and spent by a charity often appears in exam questions but you will gain marks by pointing out that the law has moved on from regarding the loss of the right to trace as based on the fact that it would be inequitable to do so.

[11] You do not need a long conclusion as you have been summing up as you went along.

 Make your answer stand out

- Explain that there can be no tracing at common law as mixing money in an account makes it unidentifiable at common law (*Agip (Africa) Ltd* v *Jackson* [1990] Ch 265).

- Mention *Russell-Cooke Trust Co* v *Prentis (No 1)* [2002] EWHC 2227 (Ch) as another means of deciding how to allocate loss between more than one fund which has been wrongly applied.

- Consider the application of the rule in *Re Oatway* [1903] 2 Ch 356 – would the different principle which it establishes to that in *Roscoe* v *Winder* produce a different result in the case of trust money spent on the yacht? Note that this is a case of mixed funds.

- Look at *Foskett* v *McKeown* [2001] 1 AC 102 and especially at the speech of Lord Millett. He held that where trust money is mixed with the trustee's own money then the beneficiary is 'entitled to locate his contribution in any part of the mixture' and to subordinate the claims of the defaulting trustee and their successors to those of the beneficiary.

> **❗ Don't be tempted to . . .**
>
> - Set out all the rules on tracing first and only then apply the law. You will lose marks and get into a real muddle!
> - Confuse common law and equitable tracing – make it clear that you are dealing with equitable tracing.
> - Say that tracing is a remedy in itself.

Question 3

Analyse the principles for assessing equitable principles of compensation for breach of trust and consider the extent to which they differ from common law principles for assessing compensation for breach of a duty.

Answer plan

→ Contrast equitable and common law remedies.

→ Illustrate equitable compensation by reference to the facts of *AIB* v *Redler.*

→ Explain in detail how falsification of the account works.

→ Consider the decision in *Target Holdings Ltd* v *Redferns.*

→ Now return to the actual decision in *Redler* and explain it in relation to *Target Holdings.*

→ End by returning to the issue and asking if there is a degree of convergence between common law and equity in this area.

Diagram plan

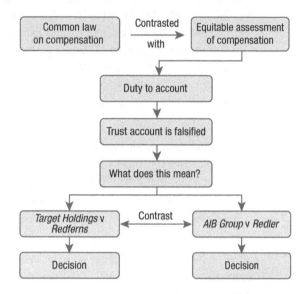

A printable version of this diagram is available from **www.pearsoned.co.uk/lawexpressqa**

Answer

At a high level of generality, the principles adopted by both equity and common law for assessing compensation for a breach of duty are the same: the primary duty is to perform the obligations whether arising in equity under a trust or at common law arising under a contract or in tort. If these primary obligations are broken there is then a secondary duty to compensate for loss suffered or to return any gain unlawfully made. It is of course true that in equity the breach may also be remedied by specific performance of injunction but our focus is on compensation.[1]

[1] It is vital not to get sidetracked into a general discussion of equitable remedies.

However, there are differences in the approach of equity and the common law, as illustrated by ***AIB Group (UK) Plc v Mark Redler & Co Solicitors*** [2014] UKSC 58 SC. The defendant solicitors were instructed by AIB who wanted to lend £3.3m to X taking a first mortgage of £4.25m over X's home.[2] There was a prior mortgage over the home from Barclays of about £1.25m which secured two different loans to X, one of about £1.2m and the other of about £300,000 and

[2] You will need to integrate the principles in this case into a more general discussion of the remedies but make sure that you set the facts out at the start of your answer.

the advance from AIB would be used to redeem both these. The solicitors acted for both AIB and X and held the £3.3m on bare trust for AIB to give effect to its instructions. The cause of all the trouble was that the solicitors only paid £1.2m to Barclays, leaving around £300,000 outstanding and so AIB did not get the first charge over the property it had expected. X then defaulted on the loan and the property was sold, but for only £1.2m as the housing market had declined. The claimant's total loss was around £3m after Barclays' first charge had been paid.

The solicitor's error was in relation to a sum of around £300,000 but the Bank sued the solicitors for the whole of its advance of £3.3m less about £800,000 that it had recovered, alleging that this loss had resulted from their breach of trust even though most of it was due to a fall in the property market.

[3] This is quite an adventurous approach as we have given the facts of the case but will only explain the decision when we have explored the background to this point. If you do take this approach, which will certainly strike the examiner as original, do not forget to return to the decision and leave yourself enough time to explain it!

If this had been a claim for negligence at common law then the matter would have been clear: the liability would be limited to the loss caused by the breach, in this case £309,000. However, equity has traditionally taken a different view and we need to look at the approach of equity in other cases before returning to this case.[3]

[4] Any discussion of equitable compensation and indeed other remedies must consider the right of the beneficiary to accounts. This is really the starting point here.

Trust remedies are based on the duty of the trustee to account, that is, to produce accounts for the beneficiary to examine[4] and this at once strikes one as entirely different from the common law where the emphasis is on the causal link between breach and loss. As the trust assets are the beneficiary's in equity, then she has the right to know what state they are in. In *Ultraframe (UK) Ltd v Fielding* [2007] WTLR 835, Lewison J said: 'The taking of an account is the process by which a beneficiary requires a trustee to justify his stewardship of trust property.' This in itself can be an everyday matter but often an account is sought as a prelude to seeking an equitable remedy for breach of trust.

[5] Note the argument: first, the taking of an account and then falsifying the account. Do not let the term 'falsifying' put you off! It is a technical Chancery procedural one.

Where the trustee misapplies trust money the trust account is falsified.[5] This means that the sum misapplied is disallowed. For example, suppose that a trustee makes an unauthorised investment of £10,000 from the trust in shares which later are only worth £5,000. On one analysis the loss to the trust is £5,000 but that is not how equity sees it. The beneficiaries will argue that the account should be falsified so that the actual purchase of the shares by the trust, being unauthorised, is disallowed. However, the fact is that the shares were purchased and so equity treats them as having been purchased with his own money and so they belong to the trustee. This means that when the accounts are examined again £10,000 will be missing from the trust fund and the trustee will have to replace this. It ought to be added, although not strictly relevant to this discussion, that if the shares have increased in value then the beneficiaries can elect to keep them.

This was the position in equity until **Target Holdings Ltd v Redferns** [1996] AC 421 HL. Money was lent by a finance company (X) to developers (Y) on the security of two properties which were fraudulently overvalued. Redferns acted for both parties and received the mortgage advance on a bare trust for the claimant to release it to Y when the transfers of the properties were executed. However, in breach of trust they released it early. This was the type of breach which could have led to falsification of the accounts.[6] Y subsequently went into liquidation, and X sold the properties for much less than their value. X claimed against Redferns for their loss on the transaction but failed.

The House of Lords held that the rule in assessing compensation for breach of trust in commercial dealings such as this, especially as the solicitor was only a bare trustee,[7] is that a trustee is only liable for losses caused by the breach and not for losses which would have occurred anyway, which seems to be getting close to the common law position. Thus, although the solicitors, the trustees, acted in breach of trust by releasing the funds early, the claimants obtained the mortgage securities later anyway. The early release of the funds did not decide if the mortgage would go through, and it was this which caused the loss.

The decision seems defensible but the remarks of Lord Browne-Wilkinson have caused debate. He felt that X should have to prove a causal link between its loss and the breach of duty by the solicitors, which looks even more like the common law position. He distinguished between bare commercial type trusts, such as that in **Redferns,** where the issue of reconstituting the trust fund did not arise, as the transaction had been completed and so the purpose of the trust had ended, with other trusts, such as a family type one which was still running and where the trust fund would need to be reconstituted.

[6] It is important that you make this link with the previous discussion on falsification of the accounts. More generally, when you are writing answers, always ask yourself: am I linking what I am writing now with what I wrote before?

[7] Make sure that you point this out and that you know what a bare trustee is.

[8] We have now returned to the decision in *Redferns*. It can be a useful examination technique to set the scene with the facts of a case, then set it in context, and then return to the decision to see how it fits into that context.

In *AIB Group (UK) Plc v Mark Redler & Co Solicitors* the Supreme Court broadly accepted the analysis in *Redferns*.[8] Lord Toulson held that the fact that the claimant sold the house at a much-reduced figure than it was worth when the loan was granted was not a loss caused by the breach of trust as this loss would have occurred even if the solicitors had acted properly. Thus it was only entitled to equitable compensation sufficient to put it in the position if it had received a first legal charge.

[9] This was the essential point in *Redler* so make this clear.

So equitable compensation rather than falsification of the account was the preferred solution.[9] Lord Reed approved the words of McLachlin J in the Canadian case of *Canson Enterprises Ltd v Broughton & Co* [1991] 85 DLR (4th) 129, who said that: 'If the trust has come to an end, the trustee can be ordered to compensate the beneficiary directly.' This will apply to bare trusts, as in *Redler* and *Redferns,* but where the trust is a continuing one with a number of beneficiaries this model will not work.

Does then mean that there is a degree of convergence between assessment of compensation at equity and common law? Although trustees are still liable to account, which is a specifically equitable construct, the principles which the courts will use to assess loss arising when that account has been made have certainly changed. So where the beneficiary would have suffered some or all of the loss claimed even if no breach of trust had been committed, the law does not require the trustee to provide a windfall. This looks like the common law insistence between breach and causal loss.

[10] Try for conclusions like this which may not actually answer the question but pose another question which shows that you are thinking about the issues.

On a broader level, the decision in *AIB Group (UK) Plc v Mark Redler & Co Solicitors* can be seen as a convergence not only of equitable and common law remedies but of common law and equity themselves.[10]

✓ Make your answer stand out

- Demonstrate that you are absolutely clear on the fundamental issues in this area. They take some time to unravel so make sure that you do this well.
- Explain the rules on remoteness and foreseeability when assessing common law damages with the position in equity.

- Read and refer to Turner (2015) who analyses the decision in *AIB Group (UK) Plc* v *Mark Redler & Co.*
- Read Millett (1998). This is a stimulating survey of the debate and contains an extremely clear exposition of the law on claims by beneficiaries against trustees. It also has the merit of providing an alternative view to those of the judges in *Redferns* and *Redler.*
- Note the issue raised in the last sentence of the essay and consider it further.

! Don't be tempted to . . .

- Miss the basic distinction between common law and equitable remedies.
- Just describe the law but instead look critically at it. This applies especially to the decisions in *AIB Group (UK) Plc* v *Mark Redler & Co Solicitors* and *Target Holdings* v *Redfern.*
- Spend too long on the facts of the above cases without relating them to the issue in the question.
- Write about equitable compensation in areas other than breaches of trust under section 2 of Lord Cairns Act (Chancery Amendment Act) 1858. The question only asks you about remedies for breach of trust.
- Mention too many areas superficially.

@ Try it yourself

Now take a look at the question below and attempt to answer it. You can check your response against the answer guidance available on the companion website (**www.pearsoned.co.uk/lawexpressqa**).

Len is an accountant and has often advised Frank, who has a business, on tax and other matters and acts as a trustee for various bodies. Last week Frank came to Len and said, 'I need to find a place for this money very quickly. Can you put it in your own account for me?' Len was reluctant to do so but eventually agreed. The next day Frank asked Len to invest the money in an offshore company based in the Isle of Man and Len did so.

Len has now found out that Frank is to be prosecuted for fraud in respect of this money. The Isle of Man company has gone into liquidation and Len has heard from Frank's trustee in bankruptcy that he may seek to recover the money from him.

Advise Len on his legal position.

www.pearsoned.co.uk/lawexpressqa

Go online to access more revision support including additional essay and problem questions with diagram plans, 'You be the marker' questions, and download all diagrams from the book.

A Mixture of
questions

How this topic may come up in exams

In many exams in equity and trusts questions are set which incorporate a variety of
topics and this chapter contains a selection of these. You will almost certainly get
questions which range across the whole area of equity and it is easier to look at
these after you have familiarised yourself with particular subject areas.

Some cases appear in more than one question as they are really excellent illustra-
tions of equitable principles and these can be used in more than one context. Learn
these cases really well rather than learning many cases superficially. You can then
use them to gain a really good mark and, at the same time, reduce the number of
cases you have to learn. A bonus all round!

■ Before you begin

It's a good idea to consider the following key themes before tackling a question that ranges across a variety of topics in equity and trusts.

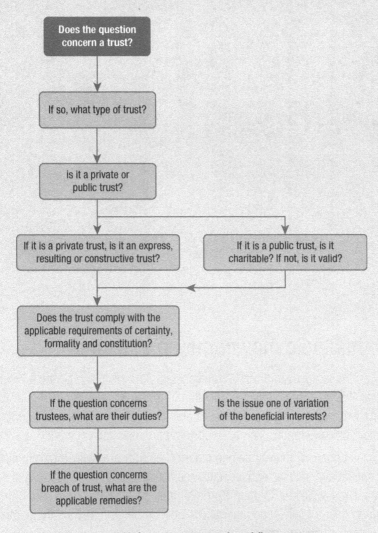

A printable version of this diagram is available from **www.pearsoned.co.uk/lawexpressqa**

❓ Question 1

John owned a house 'The Laurels' and 500 shares in Hanbury Park Ltd. He told his daughter, Mary, 'Now that you are 18 it is time to think of your future. One day you will have this house so I will take care of it for you until you are 25 and then transfer it to you.' The next day John contacted a firm of builders about a possible extension to the house to enable him to house his model railway.

Later that day he met Mike, an old friend, and said to him, 'You know, I have more wealth than I need. I would like to do something to help others and so I am going to transfer my shares into your name for you to hold on trust at your discretion for my old workmates. You know who they are.' John then told his accountant, Peter, to deal with the formalities for a transfer of his shares to Mike. Peter sent a form to John to sign but did not explain what it was about and John put it away until he had a chance to ask Peter for more advice.

John is also a beneficiary under a trust of £500,000 set up by his Uncle Jack. He telephoned Uncle Jack and said, 'I do not need the money in the trust fund. Please hold on trust for my sister Amy.'

A week later John made his will in which he left all his property to the League of Friends of Sick Cats and appointed his Aunt Molly and Mary as executors.

John died. Advise his executors now about who is entitled to:

(a) 'The Laurels';

(b) the 500 shares in Hanbury Park Ltd; and

(c) John's interest in the trust fund.

Answer plan

→ Separate the different intended gifts and note who the executors are.

→ Consider the intended trust of the house: identify and apply three certainties and formal requirements, and the possible application of the rule in *Strong* v *Bird*.

→ Now consider the intended trust of the shares: identify and apply any formal requirements, consider the question of certainty of objects and whether the trust is constituted.

→ Finally, consider the intended transfer of the beneficial interest in the trust fund: identify and apply formal requirements.

Diagram plan

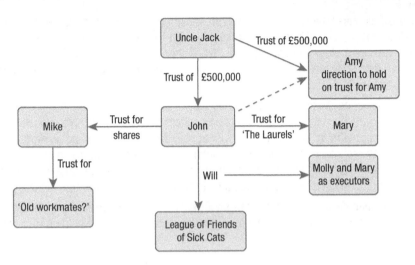

A printable version of this diagram is available from **www.pearsoned.co.uk/lawexpressqa**

[1] Many students, realising that this question concerns a possible trust, would rush to consider the formalities point. But wait . . . marks can be gained by spending time first on whether there is a trust at all and looking at the three certainties.

[2] This is not a question just about certainties but also about a number of other issues. So resist the temptation to go into detail on this point, and wrap up this part of your answer fairly quickly.

[3] Formalities should *always* be mentioned *after* you have checked if the three certainties are present. There is no point in discussing if the trust satisfies the formal requirements if there is no trust!

Answer

(a) The first question is whether John has declared a trust of 'The Laurels' in favour of Mary.[1] There is certainty of subject matter (The Laurels) and objects (Mary), so the only question is whether John actually intended to declare himself a trustee. He says that he will take care of the house for Mary until she is 25 and then transfer it to her. The question is whether the words 'take care' of the house coupled with a clear statement that he will transfer it to her at 25 are enough. This is borderline and all we can say[2] is that if the courts decide that there is no trust then of course Mary's claim fails and the house will pass on John's death to the charity. If there is a trust then as it is a trust of land it must comply with section 53(1)(b) of the LPA 1925. This provides that 'a declaration of trust concerning land or any interest therein must be manifested and proved by some writing signed by some person who is able to declare the same or by his will'. If not, the trust will not be enforceable.[3] The actual declaration of trust need not be in writing. The words 'manifested and proved' require only written evidence.

[4] Always check before beginning an answer on constitution if the intended donee is also the executor under a will of the donor. If so, this is a sure sign that you will be expected to apply *Strong* v *Bird*.

[5] Mentioning this case immediately marks your answer out as a good one. Most students would only mention *Strong* v *Bird* but as the problem concerns a trust you need to link the rule in *Strong* v *Bird* to trusts and this is what this case does.

[6] Where the question involves the possible application of *Strong* v *Bird* you should watch also for any indication of a lack of a continuing intention by the transferor.

[7] Aim for pithy conclusions like this which encapsulate your answer in one sentence.

[8] Remember the drill: certainties first!

[9] A small point but one you must never forget! Many students, seeing that the answer is obvious here as John actually says that he is creating a trust, will just say that there is certainty of intention. But if you do you will lose marks. Always give evidence for your conclusions.

[10] The question said that John simply referred to 'my shares', instead of being more specific.

The problem here is that John has declared the trusts orally, which will not satisfy section 53(1)(b), and so, as Mary cannot enforce it, the house will remain part of John's estate and will pass to the charity.

However, Mary is also an executor of John's estate [4] and so we must investigate if the rule in **Strong v Bird** (1874) LR 18 Eq 315 HC will assist her. This provides that if an incomplete gift is made during the donor's lifetime and the donor has appointed the donee, his executor, then the vesting of the property in the donee completes the gift. **Strong v Bird** dealt with a debt owed to the executor but in **Re Stewart** [1908] 2 Ch 251 HC [5] the rule in **Strong v Bird** was extended from cases of forgiveness of debts to those where there has been an incomplete transfer of property to a person who is also appointed executor under the will of the transferee. The effect is that the transfer may now be valid.

However, in addition, the rule in **Strong v Bird** requires that there must be a continuing intention to make the gift.[6] In **Re Gonin** [1979] Ch 16 HC, a mother wished to leave her house to her daughter but instead she wrote a cheque for £33,000 in the daughter's favour, which was found after her death. The court held that there was no continuing intention on the mother's part that the daughter should have the house, as the giving of the cheque indicated that she had changed her mind. So in this case the fact that the next day John contacted a firm of builders about a possible extension to the house to allow him to house his model railway may indicate that John has changed his mind about the trust for Mary. The evidence is inconclusive but, if **Strong v Bird** applies, Mary can claim the house. If it does not, she cannot.[7]

(b) John then says to Mike: I am going to transfer my shares into your name for you to hold on trust for my old workmates. You know who they are.' There is certainty of intention,[8] as John says that Mike is to hold on trust [9] and the subject matter will be clear provided that the only shares in his estate are the 500 shares in Hanbury Park Ltd.[10] If not, evidence may be brought to identify them. If there is no certainty of subject matter then all the shares will form part of John's estate on his death and will pass to the charity. The problem is then certainty of objects as John refers to 'my old workmates'. This is a discretionary trust, as indicated by the word 'discretion' in the gift, and so the test for certainty of objects is that laid down in **McPhail v Doulton** [1971] AC 424 HL: can it be said with certainty whether a person is or is not a beneficiary? It is submitted that evidence could be brought to show who John's 'old workmates' are. If, however, the test of certainty is not satisfied, then Mike will hold the shares on a resulting trust for John and, as they will then form part of John's estate, they will pass to the charity on his death.

Assuming that there is a valid trust then, although the declaration of trust is not in writing, this does not affect the enforceability of the trust, as section 53(1)(b) of the LPA 1925 only applies to trusts of land.

However, there is a problem with constitution of the trust as the subject matter, the shares, is not transferred to Mike. If John had done everything in his power to effect the transfer then, under the principle in **Re Rose** [1952] Ch 499 CA, it would bind him, but here Peter, John's accountant, sent a form to John to sign and John put it away until he had a chance to ask Peter for more advice. However, in **Pennington v Waine** [2002] EWCA Civ 227, it was held on the facts of that case that, although the transferor had *not* done all in her power to effect a transfer of shares it did still bind her. In this case the transferor had actually signed a share transfer form to this effect and had given it to her agent who took no further action. Here, however, John has not even signed the transfer form and it is submitted that this distinguishes the present case from **Pennington v Waine**[11] and so the trust was never constituted; and thus the shares form part of John's estate and pass to the charity.

[11] Note how we have stressed the essential point of difference between this case and *Pennington* v *Waine*. Clear analysis like this will always gain marks.

(c)   Finally, John telephoned his Uncle Jack, telling him to hold his interest instead under a trust fund of £500,000 for his sister Amy. In **Grey v IRC** [1960] AC 1 HL, it was held that this is a disposition of a beneficial interest under a trust and as such it must comply with section 53(1)(c) of the LPA 1925, which provides that the disposition of an equitable interest or trust must be in writing signed either by the settlor or the settlor's authorised agent. Failure to comply with section 53(1)(c) makes the disposition void. As the disposition was oral, it does not comply with section 53(1)(c) and so, as it is void, John's interest in the trust fund will still form part of his estate and will pass to the charity.

Make your answer stand out

- Look in more detail at the reasoning in *Pennington* v *Waine* and especially at the judgments of Arden LJ and Clarke LJ and contrast their reasoning.
- Read the judgments in this case and see if you can identify any policy reasons for the decision which you can highlight in your answer.
- Read and refer to the note on *Re Gonin* at (1977) 93 LQR 448.

! Don't be tempted to . . .

- Plunge into the answer too quickly. This really is one area where careful planning will help your answer as you need to disentangle the different areas of law which appear in the question.
- Spend too much time on any one area. In particular, avoid the temptation to spend too long on the certainties' point at the start.
- Make sure that you go back to the fundamental question at the end: will the property go to the charity or to the intended beneficiaries?

❓ Question 2

Anita has recently taken over as Chair of the Trust which provides pensions for employees and former employees of the Malvern Hills Mining Corporation. She asks you for advice on the following points:

(a) The trust has a standard clause stating that 'trustees are under no liability for loss or damage to the trust fund or its income unless such loss or damage shall be caused by the actual fraud of the trustees'. She has heard that some of the beneficiaries under the trust are considering claiming against the trust for negligence in its investment strategy and asks your advice on the extent to which this clause would protect the trustees in the event of negligence being proved.

(b) The accountant to the trust, Horace, has absconded taking with him £10,000 in bribes paid to him by investment companies in return for Horace agreeing to recommend to the trust that it invests with them. Anita asks you if the sum of £10,000 representing these bribes can be recovered from Horace who is now insolvent.

Diagram plan

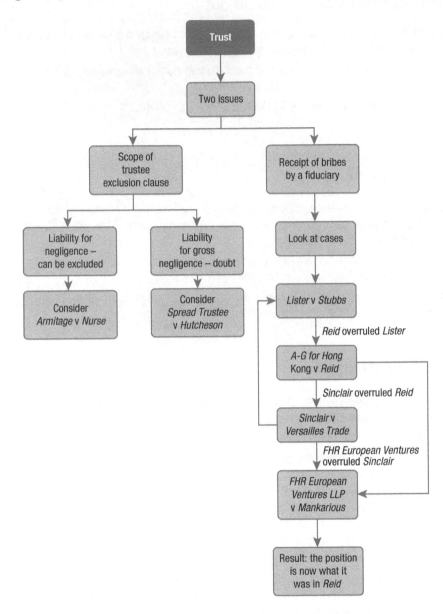

A printable version of this diagram is available from **www.pearsoned.co.uk/lawexpressqa**

Answer plan

→ Identify that this is a trustee exclusion clause and explain the decision in *Armitage* v *Nurse.*

→ Go on to distinguish between ordinary negligence and gross negligence; consider the decision in *Spread Trustee Co Ltd* v *Hutcheson.*

→ Refer to the dissent of Lady Hale in the above case.

→ Identify the remedies of the employer in cases where the employee has received a bribe.

→ Note that Horace is insolvent and so we need to consider trust remedies.

→ Trace the evolution of the case law in this area.

→ Conclude that Horace is not liable to hold the amount of the bribe on trust.

Answer

[1] There is a trap in this question for the unwary: you could easily discuss the issue of actual liability for negligence but of course you are not being asked this. Instead you must concentrate on the validity of the exclusion clause.

(a) This is a trustee exclusion clause[1] and the leading case is **Armitage v Nurse** [1998] Ch 221 HC, where the wording of the clause was very similar to the one in this case. **Armitage v Nurse** concerned property including agricultural land and the beneficiaries' alleged negligence in its management. Millett LJ held that 'there is an irreducible core of obligations owed by the trustees to the beneficiaries and enforceable by them which is fundamental to the concept of a trust' and liability for this could not be excluded. As he pointed out, 'If the beneficiaries have no rights enforceable against the trustees there are no trusts.' Thus liability for actual frauds could not be excluded, but a clause could 'exclude liability for breach of trust in the absence of a dishonest intention on the part of the trustee whose conduct is impugned'.

[2] At this point you need to broaden your answer out. An average answer would just refer to *Armitage* v *Nurse* and say that the clause is valid. However, to do better, express your views on the ongoing debate about whether there is a separate category of gross negligence and, if so, whether it is possible for liability for this to be excluded by trustees.

It seems from the facts that no actual dishonesty by the trustees is alleged and so the clause could be valid but we need to go further. The actual degree of negligence alleged in this case is not clear: is it ordinary negligence or gross negligence?[2] This is important as there is a continuing debate on whether a trustee exclusion clause can exclude liability for gross negligence or only for ordinary negligence. In **Armitage v Nurse,** Millett LJ held that trustee exclusion clauses could cover gross negligence and held that a sharp distinction has always been drawn between negligence, however gross, on the one hand, and fraud, bad faith and wilful misconduct on the other. Clearly a clause could not exempt from liability for the latter.

[3] This case must always be discussed in an answer on trustee exclusion clauses.

In **Spread Trustee Co Ltd v Hutcheson** [2011] UKPC 13,[3] the beneficiaries claimed that the trustee had been grossly negligent in failing to identify and investigate breaches of trust on the part of previous trustees. A clause in the trust instrument exempted the trustee from liability for breaches of trust arising from his own gross negligence. It was held that the parties could lawfully agree to exclude a trustee's liability for breaches arising from negligence or gross negligence. Lord Clarke in effect agreed with Millett LJ in **Armitage v Nurse** and said: 'To describe negligence as gross does not change its nature so as to make it fraudulent or wilful misconduct.'

[4] Your hard work in researching cases can really pay off here where you can gain extra marks. A mediocre answer would mention *Armitage* v *Nurse* and leave it at that. A better answer would show awareness of recent cases such as *Spread Trustee* v *Hutcheson* but only mention the reasoning of the majority. A really outstanding answer would go on to look at the dissenting judgments.

However, Lady Hale dissented and felt that trustee exclusion clauses should not cover liability for gross negligence.[4] She pointed to the Law Commission's Consultation Paper No 124, *Fiduciary Duties and Regulatory Rules* (1992), which said that 'it seems that a trustee may not exclude liability for "wilful default". There is however uncertainty as to whether liability for gross negligence can be excluded' (paragraph 3.3.6). She also gave the example of a case where the guardian of the estate of a minor might seek to rely on a clause exempting him from liability for gross negligence, which she felt any English lawyer would regard as unacceptable.

[5] Do not forget to end your answer by coming back to the original question – the advice to Anita.

The advice to Anita[5] must be that if only negligence and not fraud is alleged, as seems to be the case, then the trustees are protected by the clause, but the law is still developing and it may be that in future we will reach the stage where clauses exempt from liability for ordinary negligence but not gross negligence.

(b) The accountant to the trust, Horace, has absconded taking with him £10,000 in bribes paid to him by investment companies in return for Horace agreeing to recommend to the trust that it invests with them, and Anita asks if the sum of £10,000 representing these bribes can be recovered from Horace. There is no doubt that it could be recovered under ordinary civil law.[6] The receipt by Horace of a bribe is a breach of an implied contractual term that he will act in good faith (to his employer), and the employer can claim an account of any secret profits which the employee made from the breach. One example is **Boston Deep Sea Fishing and Ice Co v Ansell** (1888) 39 Ch D 339 HC,

[6] This is very important. There is no point in rushing in and considering the possible imposition of a constructive trust if the money can be recovered as, in effect, a simple debt. You need to show that you are aware of this.

[7] Although the previous paragraph was vital, you now need to recognise the significance of this: in fact, in problems in trust exams, those against whom claims are made are often insolvent. This will help you focus on trust remedies, as contractual ones, although needing a mention, will be useless as there will be no money to satisfy the claim.

[8] Do stress this point.

[9] Make sure that you do not get so carried away by discussing the cases that you forget a conclusion!

where a managing director of a company, who had made secret profits out of his position, was liable to account for them to the company.

However, we are told that Horace is insolvent[7] and so we need to consider if we can claim a proprietary remedy so that Horace will have received the bribe as a fiduciary and so be liable as a constructive trustee to return it to the trust. If we can, then the claim of the Malvern Hills Mining Corporation will have priority over Horace's ordinary creditors.[8]

Horace was in a fiduciary position when he received the bribe, as he was the accountant to the trust. However, in *Lister & Co v Stubbs* (1890) 45 Ch D 1 CA, it was held that a bribe received by a fiduciary from a third party was not held on trust for the principal. The reasoning was that proprietary claims (i.e. those founded on a trust) were only available where the principal seeks to recover property which belonged to him *before* the breach of fiduciary duty. A bribe, by contrast, is not the property of the principal but is property held by the fiduciary in breach of fiduciary obligation. Here the relationship between the fiduciary and principal is that of debtor and creditor, not trustee and beneficiary.

However, this principle was reversed in *Attorney General for Hong Kong v Reid* [1994] 1 AC 324 PC, which held that benefits obtained from a third party in breach of fiduciary obligation, such as bribes, belong in equity to the principal from the moment of receipt. On this basis we could argue that Horace does hold the bribe on a constructive trust and so it can be claimed from him. Although *Sinclair Investments (UK) Ltd v Versailles Trade Finance (In Administration)* [2011] EWCA Civ 347 changed the position back to what it was before *Reid*, the Supreme Court in the most recent case, *FHR European Ventures LLP v Cedar Capital Partners LLC* [2014] UKSC 45SC, held that the approach in *Attorney General for Hong Kong v Reid* was the correct one.

Thus under the authority of this case the Malvern Hills Mining Corporation should be able to claim a proprietary remedy against Horace.[9]

✓ Make your answer stand out

- Trace the evolution of the case law in both situations and in both do not just list the cases but show how the law has changed and developed from case to case.
- Research why the Trustee Act 2000 did not regulate the use of trustee exclusion clauses.
- Note *Barnsley* v *Noble* [2016] EWCA Civ 791, where a clause excluding liability for breach of the self-dealing rule by executors was valid. The clause was in common use and covered liability for losses, not gains. Although not directly applicable here, a brief mention of it will add depth to your answer.
- Read and refer to an article on the decision in *FHR European Ventures LLP* v *Cedar Capital Partners LLC*: Gummow [2015] and note how it links the decision to fundamental equitable principles.

❗ Don't be tempted to . . .

- Mention only one case in each situation: in both (a) and (b).
- Forget that negligence can be ordinary negligence or gross negligence and that there is an ongoing debate on whether trustee exclusion clauses can apply to gross negligence.
- Overlook that in (b) Horace is insolvent – there is no point in considering trust remedies here unless contract remedies will not work.
- Just list the cases on receipt of bribes; instead show how the law has developed.

🖎 Question 3

The maxims of equity 'are a useful method of paraphrasing a complex body of law: they are guidelines rather than rules' (Virgo (2018) p. 23).

Do you agree with this view of the significance of maxims as a predictive factor in judicial making in equity?

Answer plan

→ Outline what the idea of equitable maxims is and explain that you will select from them to illustrate your answer.

→ Look at two other views of authors on the maxims and use all of these views in your answer as reference points.

- 'He who comes to equity must come with clean hands.'
- 'Equity will not assist a volunteer.'

- 'Equity will not allow a statute to be used as an engine of fraud.'
- 'Equity looks to the intent and not the form.'
→ End by coming back to the quotation.

Diagram plan

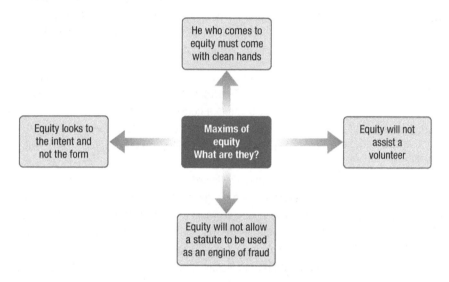

A printable version of this diagram is available from **www.pearsoned.co.uk/lawexpressqa**

Answer

This statement of Virgo gives a more positive view of the view of equitable maxims than do some other writers. Watt (2009, p. 93) sees little importance in them when he observes that, 'The appeal of maxims, so far as judges are concerned, is that they are capable of bearing what weight the judge chooses to ascribe to them'. Hanbury (2015) gives them greater importance and accords with the view of Virgo:[1] 'They are not rules which must be rigorously applied in every case but are more in the nature of general guidelines illustrating the way in which equitable jurisdiction is exercised' (p. 25). Thus Hanbury and Virgo, whilst accepting that maxims are not to be taken as rules which guide decision making in equity, would contend that they describe, although not define, some of the main principles that guide equitable intervention. This contrasts with Watt's view that they are in

[1] Reference to other slightly different views here will add to your marks.

[2] This sentence gives a structure for our answer.

[3] This question is about equity today, so you should not give a long historical account. It is essential, however, to put the maxims in their historical context.

[4] This sentence is the pivot on which this answer hangs: what would be really dreadful would be an answer which went through every maxim and said what it was, gave an example, and then went on to the next one. There would be no discussion or engagement with the issues raised by the question and the answer would almost certainly fail. You need to select from the maxims.

[5] This is also vital: you can pick up marks by using one illustration for more than one maxim and gain extra marks.

[6] This is a particularly good maxim to choose to illustrate an answer as there is plenty of scope for discussion and many opportunities to display your knowledge of case law and so earn extra marks.

[7] This sentence scores in two ways: it shows how the maxims relate to each other (and gets you away from that dreaded list of maxims!) and also gains you credit by your reference to an important judgment.

effect a cloak for the judge to use when coming to a decision which he would have come to anyway. We will refer to these slightly differing views of the maxims in our answer.[2]

The maxims are brief, pithy phrases which remain easily in the mind but in fact judges these days do not often use them. Their historical importance is greater because they began to be formulated in the time of Lord Nottingham C (1673–82)[3] and were one of the reasons why equity changed from being based on the general notion of conscience to a more formal and predictable system.

There are many maxims and I will illustrate this answer by referring to four in detail.[4] *Tinsley v Milligan* [1994] 1 AC 340 was a claim to a beneficial share in a house because of contributions made to its purchase and the majority of the House of Lords applied the presumption that such contributions will lead to the presumption of a trust in favour of the person who made them. However, the house was in the claimant's name only in order to facilitate a fraudulent claim to housing benefit by the defendant, and the minority applied the maxim 'he who comes into equity must come with clean hands' to hold that once the court was aware that the claimant did not have clean hands it should refuse any relief even though the claimant could succeed without relying on the illegality, as she could here. From one angle this shows the truth of the statement by Watt that maxims are really capable of bearing whatever weight the judge chooses to give them. On the other hand, all the judges were guided by equitable principles: the minority by a maxim and the other by a principle of equity, the common intention constructive trust, which itself rests on the maxim that equity looks to the intent and not the form because the formal legal ownership will not reflect equity's view of the beneficial interests.[5]

Another significant maxim is that equity will not assist a volunteer.[6] Thus where a trust is not constituted, equity will not, with certain exceptions, assist a beneficiary who has not provided consideration to enforce it (known as a volunteer) and this underlies the law on constitution of trusts. This is actually an example of another maxim, equity follows the law, as was pointed out by Arden LJ in *Pennington v Waine* [2002] EWCA Civ 227.[7] Thus the common law insists on the presence of consideration for the making of a contract but equity goes further than the common law, as it regards 'marriage consideration'

[8] What we need to do is bring in a case where equity has applied the maxim that it does not assist a volunteer. In order to make our point we need a case where there is a specifically *equitable* form of consideration and this is why we have used marriage consideration.

as consideration,[8] and the husband, wife and issue of the marriage together with more remote issue, for example grandchildren (*Macdonald v Scott* [1893] AC 642 HC), are within 'marriage consideration'. Thus they can enforce a promise to transfer property to be held on trust.

However, if the parties are not within marriage consideration then they will be volunteers, as in *Re Plumptre's Marriage Settlement* [1910] 1 Ch 609 HC, where beneficiaries seeking to enforce the covenant to transfer property on trust were not the issue of the marriage but the wife's next of kin. The court held that, as they were not within the marriage consideration, they were volunteers and thus could not enforce the covenant. One could say that this maxim rests on more solid foundations as although there are exceptions in its application, it does provide a foundation for equity's rules on constitution of trusts. As such it supports the view of Virgo and Hanbury, who see some merit in the continued existence of the maxims.

Another equitable maxim is 'equity will not allow a statute to be used as an engine of fraud'. In *Rochefoucauld v Boustead* [1897] 1 Ch 196 CA, the claimant was having difficulty repaying a mortgage on land and the defendant bought it, orally agreeing to hold it as trustee for her. However, he took the land as his own. The claimant was held entitled to an account of profits made on the land because, although the trust was in the claimant's favour, it did not satisfy the requirements of what is now section 53(1)(b) of the LPA 1925 (not being in writing), and it would be a fraud on the defendant's part to take the profits for himself.

[9] It is vital at this stage to refer back to the question, not only to remind you about what it is about but also to tie your answer into it.

[10] Note that we did not say: 'the land registration system' as such, as title was not registered – a small point but you can lose marks for even relatively minor inaccuracies.

The courts have applied this maxim as a general guideline (rather than as any kind of rule to be rigorously applied).[9] This is shown by *Midland Bank Trust Co Ltd v Green (No 1)* [1981] AC 513 HL, where an unregistered option to buy a farm was not binding against a purchaser even though the farm had only been conveyed to her to avoid the option, Lord Wilberforce observing that 'it is not fraud to rely on legal rights conferred by an Act of Parliament'. Thus the policy consideration of preserving the integrity of the system of registering rights against land[10] overrode the application of the maxim.

A final maxim to consider is 'equity looks to the intent and not the form'. Thus, equity will hold that a trust has been created even though the word 'trust' was not used, as in **Paul v Constance** [1977] 1 All ER 195 CA. A bank account was opened in Mr Constance's name only because he and his partner, the claimant, would have been embarrassed by having a joint account in different names. Various sums were paid into it and Constance said to the claimant, 'the money is as much yours as mine'. These words, and evidence of the transactions in the account, established that Constance intended to declare himself a trustee of the money in it for himself and the claimant.

[11] The inclusion of this case gives balance to your answer (by contrast with the previous case).

However, where it is clear that there is no intention to create a trust then of course equity will not intervene: see **Jones v Lock** [1865] 1 Ch App 25 HC,[11] where a father produced a cheque made out in his name for £900 and said, 'Look you here, I give this to baby', and placed the cheque in the baby's hand. The court held that there was no evidence of a declaration by Jones that he now held the cheque on trust for the baby. Here there is a consistent thread of thought which supports the view of Virgo and Hanbury that the maxims do have some use as guidelines.

[12] We have engaged with the question in our conclusion and slightly disagreed with Watt's view. An excellent end.

Thus an examination of the cases shows that the maxims still apply in the application of equitable principles and that although Watt is correct in implying that they do not have a clear predictive value in judicial decision making, he is overstating the case by saying that they are capable of bearing whatever weight the judge chooses. The view of Virgo and also Hanbury who see them as useful guidelines is to be preferred.[12]

 Make your answer stand out

- Look at the judgment of Arden LJ in *Pennington* v *Waine*, which shows how the maxim 'equity will not assist a volunteer' really just follows the common law.
- Read and refer to Watt (2009) especially pp. 92–104. You will find that his discussion of the place of equitable maxims can really 'lift' your answer.
- Read Gardner (1995), who argues that reasoning based on a maxim can lead to unarticulated value judgments. Read further and then consider whether you agree.

> **!** **Don't be tempted to . . .**
>
> ■ Fail to show how cases you mention illustrate how the maxims work.
> ■ Look at the maxims in isolation. Instead, show how they relate to each other.
> ■ Give too many cases. Instead, give fewer cases but in more depth.
> ■ Fail to show how the cases demonstrate differences in approach by the courts.

Question 4

'So equity is alive in the UK Supreme Court – and, I hope, well' (Lord Neuberger, President of the Supreme Court, giving the Lehane Lecture 2014, Supreme Court of New South Wales, Sydney 4 August 2014).

Select two equity cases decided by the Supreme Court and assess whether in the light of them equity is indeed alive and well in the Supreme Court.

Answer plan

→ State the cases you have chosen and give a rationale for your choice.

→ *Jones* v *Kernott*: explain the background and distinguish between acquisition and quantification issues where a beneficial interest in the home is claimed.

→ Explain the debate on what type of intention should be required to acquire a beneficial interest and on its extent, and refer to the judgments on this in *Jones* v *Kernott*.

→ Explain the decision in *Williams* v *Central Bank of Nigeria* in the context of limitation periods.

→ Explore if this decision has wider implications in the area of knowing receipt of trust property and knowing assistance in a breach of trust.

→ End by asking if either of these cases has asked more questions than given answers.

Diagram plan

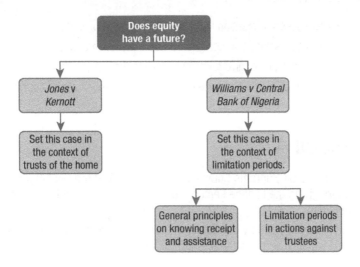

A printable version of this diagram is available from **www.pearsoned.co.uk/lawexpressqa**

Answer

The cases selected to assess whether equity is alive and well in the Supreme Court are **Jones v Kernott** [2011] UKSC 53 SC, dealing with trusts of the family home and **Williams v Central Bank of Nigeria** [2014] UKSC 10 SC, dealing with constructive trustees and limitation periods for bringing actions for breach of trust. They illustrate different areas of equity and in particular, whereas **Jones v Kernott** is concerned with equity in the domestic context, **Williams v Central Bank of Nigeria** focuses on equity in the commercial world.[1]

[1] Giving a rationale like this (why you have chosen these cases) will add to your marks as you explain that this is not just random choice.

Jones v Kernott dealt with claims to a beneficial interest in the home. The issue is deciding, in sole name cases, whether a person who is not the legal owner of property, usually the family home, should have a beneficial interest in it (the acquisition issue) and, if so, how that interest should be quantified (the quantification issue).[2] The courts have also dealt with a parallel situation in joint name cases where the legal title to the home is held jointly and the only issue is how the extent of any beneficial interests is to be quantified.[3]

[2] The terms 'acquisition issue' and 'quantification issue' are useful shorthands in this area.

[3] It is important that you mention that there are two different situations. Many students do not.

Although **Jones v Kernott** and also **Stack v Dowden** [2007] UKHL 17 HL were joint name cases, there was confusion over whether they had changed the approach in sole name cases where **Lloyds Bank v Rosset** [1991] 1 AC 107 HL had emphasised finding a common intention about whether a beneficial interest could be acquired. In **Jones v Kernott** Lady Hale and Lord Walker said that 'we recognise that a "common intention" trust is of central importance to "joint names" as well as "single names" cases . . . Nevertheless it is important to point out that the starting point for analysis is different in the two situations.' This clarifies that in sole name cases the approach is different. This was not clear after **Stack v Dowden**[4] and indeed in **Abbot v Abbott** [2007] UKPC 53 PC, Lady Hale seemed to suggest that her reasoning in **Stack** could apply in single name cases.

[4] This is important in essay questions asking you to discuss particular cases. You need to set them in their context, which means discussing other cases too, as here.

It would have helped if the Supreme Court in **Jones v Kernott** had then laid down what the law is in sole name cases where the issue is the acquisition of a beneficial interest.[5] The fact that it did not led the district judge in **Capehorn v Harris** [2015] EWCA Civ 955 CA to 'impute' an intention to the parties and to the Court of Appeal stressing in that case that claims to a beneficial interest required an agreement which could, however, be inferred. A further case, **Curran v Collins** [2015] EWCA Civ 404 CA, emphasised the importance of detrimental reliance by the party claiming the common intention. None of this divergence in approaches would have been necessary had the matter been clarified in **Jones v Kernott.**

[5] Aim for critical points like this one.

On the issue of quantifying the extent of the beneficial interests, **Jones v Kernott** adds little to **Stack v Dowden** where the parties have not reached any clear agreement. Can an intention be inferred from the conduct of the parties or can it be imputed by the courts? If it is imputed, then this is asking what intentions the parties would have had and is close to imposing what the courts consider to be a fair solution.[6] Lady Hale in **Stack v Dowden** said that the courts must search 'for the result which reflects what the parties must, in the light of their conduct, be taken to have intended' and she emphasised that it is not for the court to impose 'its own view of what is fair upon the situation'. However, in **Jones v Kernott** she, and Lord Walker, seem to have gone further when they said that the fallback position was that 'if the courts cannot deduce exactly what shares were intended, it may have no alternative but to ask what their intentions as reasonable and just people would have been had they thought about it at the

[6] It is crucial in questions in this area to be absolutely clear on what the debate on imputed intention is about.

[7] Note that we can boost our marks by looking at what another judge in the case said. If going for high marks, research the main cases and highlight significant features of the judgments.

[8] We need some conclusion at this point. One could of course take the opposite view and argue that *Jones* v *Kernott* did clarify the law.

[9] Note the clear distinction in the answer between the two relevant parts of the statute. This is where you really need to be clear.

[10] This is a vital point and can often be used to add to your marks: decisions will have implications for the particular issue raised but will also have wider implications. You can pick up these wider implications by reading around the subject. This is the way to boost your marks.

time'. Thus the courts are recognising that it may be necessary to impute an intention. Lord Wilson went further, saying that, 'Where equity is driven to impute the common intention, how can it do so other than by searching for the result which the court itself considers fair?'[7]

Jones v *Kernott* asks more questions than it answers.[8] This is still a confused area and this must be considered a disappointing decision.

In **Williams v Central Bank of Nigeria,** the claimant had been persuaded to guarantee a loan to a company of some US $6.5 million, in relation to a transaction for buying foodstuffs with Nigerian currency. He was to share the profits. A solicitor who had been entrusted with this money paid $6 million of it to the defendant bank's account in England, and kept $500,000 for himself. The claimant claimed that the bank should account for the money since it had dishonestly assisted in the breach of trust or had knowingly received the trust funds.

The events had occurred in 1986 and seemed to be time-barred by section 21(3) of the Limitation Act 1980, which prescribes a six-year period for any action by a beneficiary to recover trust property or in respect of any breach of trust. However, section 21(1)(a) provides that no limitation period shall apply to actions in respect of any fraud or fraudulent breach of trust to which the trustee was a party or privy.[9]

The Supreme Court held that actions based on dishonest assistance in a breach of trust and knowing assistance in a breach of trust were not covered by section 21(1)(a). Instead section 21(3) applied and so they were time-barred.

The court distinguished between the liability of a true trustee, and the liability which a stranger incurred solely by reason of his participation in the misapplication of trust assets. A true trustee could include a constructive trustee where a person had lawfully assumed fiduciary obligations in relation to trust property without a formal appointment (but of course that was not the case here).

The importance of this decision is twofold:[10] first on the question of limitation itself as it imposes a six-year time limit on claims based on knowing receipt and assistance; but secondly it leaves open the question of how these are to be treated in future. The idea that a person guilty of knowing receipt and assistance is not a trustee was strongly argued by Lord Millett in **Paragon Finance Plc v DB Thakerar & Co** [1999] 1 All ER 400 CA, where he argued that a stranger to the trust, 'is not in fact a trustee at all, even though he may be liable to account as if he were'. Given that this is now the law, the next stage is to consider 'knowing receipt' and 'knowing assistance'. In **Novoship (UK) Ltd v Nikitin** [2014] EWCA Civ 908 CA, it was held that there should be no difference 'between the availability in principle of remedies relating to profits made by a knowing recipient on the one hand and profits made by a dishonest assistant on the other'.

[11] Again a conclusion needed and again you could of course come to another conclusion.

Is **Williams v Central Bank of Nigeria** another Supreme Court decision raising more questions than it answers?[11]

✓ Make your answer stand out

- Distinguish clearly between the different issues when discussing *Jones* v *Kernott* : acquisition and quantification and sole name and joint names cases.
- Explain the underlying issues, for example, in your conclusion to *Jones* v *Kernott* you could mention briefly the extent to which the law should recognise the rights of cohabitees and the possibility of legislation.
- Read Lee (2015) on the implications of *Williams* v *Central Bank of Nigeria*.
- Examine the terminology used by the Supreme Court in *Williams* v *Central Bank of Nigeria* when considering liability for knowing receipt and dishonest assistance and ask if it is helpful.

! Don't be tempted to . . .

- Just write all that you know about the cases: locate them within their area of law.
- Say too much on the issues in *Jones* v *Kernott* – an area which students always find of interest – at the expense of a discussion on *Williams* v *Central Bank of Nigeria*.
- Mention only these two cases: to assess their significance you will need to look at others.
- Miss out a conclusion which engages with the words of the question.

Question 5

'Equity is a roguish thing. For law we have a measure . . . equity is according to the conscience of him that is the Chancellor, and as that is longer or narrower, so is equity. 'Tis all one as if they should make the standard for the measure of the Chancellor's foot' (*Table-Talk of John Selden*, 1856).

Is this still true of equity today? Discuss critically.

Diagram plan

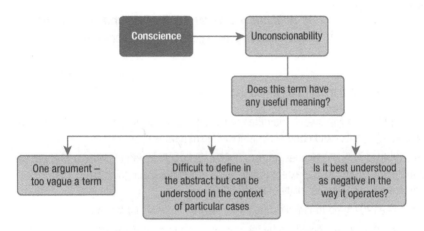

A printable version of this diagram is available from **www.pearsoned.co.uk/lawexpressqa**

Answer plan

→ What is meant by conscience?

→ Contrast this with unconscionability.

→ Critically consider whether it is possible to arrive at a workable definition of conscience, and contrast different ideas.

→ Consider cases where the notion of unconscionability has been applied and evaluate whether this term has helped in developing the law or not.

→ Conclusion – is the term unconscionability of any value to lawyers?

Answer

The assumption which underlies this question is that any attempt to use 'conscience' as a means of deciding liability is doomed to failure.[1] Although the notion of 'conscience' as a vehicle for determining liability is unsatisfactory, in reality the courts have not used this for many years and indeed it was arguably never used, with the concept of 'unconscionability' springing from conscience being used instead.

The term 'conscience' can be seen as the inner private voice of a person. If conscience was ever used in that sense to decide cases then the jibe in the quotation would be correct. However, it was not. In early equity, cases were heard by the Chancellor, who was an ecclesiastic and applied 'conscience' based on natural or universal justice.[2] Later, around the time when the Chancellors were lawyers, conscience meant the King's (or Queen's) conscience as the Chancellor was known as the Keeper of the King's (or Queen's) conscience. Lord Nottingham said in **Cook v Fountain** (1676) 3 Swans 585 at 600, that the courts were not conscience '*naturalis or interna*' but the conscience by which he would proceed was '*civilis et politica*'. Thus, conscience was not seen in the sense of an internal, private voice but in the context of society.

The courts today use the term 'unconscionability' and not 'conscience' and it is suggested that this is really the same idea of conscience as mentioned by Lord Nottingham (above). The question is then whether it is capable of having any certain meaning or whether it depends on, in that over-used phrase, 'the length of the Chancellor's foot'.

The late Professor Birks felt that it did not, likening lawyers who dealt in unconscionability to the ornithologist who was content with 'small brown bird' as describers of 'avian form' (Birks, 1996, pp. 16–17). Lord Nicholls in **Royal Brunei Airlines Sdn Bhd v Tan Kok Ming** [1995] 2 AC 378 at 392 HL, observed that 'if unconscionability is to be the touchstone for liability . . . it is essential to be clear on what . . . unconscionable *means*' (his emphasis). This is precisely the point. In fact 'unconscionability' as a tool of equity passed into disuse for many years and has only fairly recently gained renewed prominence.[3]

[1] This start pulls us away at once from what would be a tiresome essay on the over-familiar theme of whether equity is less certain in its application than the common law. This sort of answer would be heading for an average mark at the most. Instead, we have grasped the point at once: the real issue behind the question is whether the term 'conscience' can have any certain meaning and we then develop the essay to look at *unconscionability* and ask whether this really does depend on the whim of the individual judge.

[2] This is a good example of how knowledge of the history of equity can improve your answer. Although you may not get questions on the history of equity, you will be able to use your knowledge of history to add detail to this type of question – and of course gain those extra marks.

[3] This is an essential point to make and then leads you on later to look at how, in the context of actual cases, unconscionability has been grafted on to established equitable rules.

Watt (2009) makes the important point that unconscionability cannot be defined in the abstract but can only be understood in the context of particular cases. He adopts the words of Deane J in the Australian High Court in **Commonwealth of Australia v Verwayen** [1990] 170 CLR 394 at 441, who referred to unconscionability as 'involving the use of or insistence upon legal entitlement to take advantage of another's special vulnerability or misadventure . . . in a way that is unreasonable or oppressive to an extent that affronts ordinary minimum standards of fair dealing'. Watt himself also suggests the touchstone of conduct which is 'not routine' in the sense that it is 'non-routine reliance on a routine reading of law' (at p. 108).

[4] You really do need to include a concrete example at this point to explain how the theoretical ideas might work in practice.

He gives as an example the situation where a landowner evicts a non-owner from his land.[4] In routine cases this would be perfectly fair, as where the non-owner is simply a trespasser. Suppose, though, that the non-owner has built a house on this land in reliance on the landowner's promise to allow the non-owner to occupy the house for life? (See, e.g. **Inwards v Baker** [1965] 1 All ER 446 CA.) One could argue that the owner's conduct was 'non-routine' and in the formulation of Deane J (above) it would be 'unreasonable or oppressive to an extent that affronts ordinary minimum standards of fair dealing'. Thus, it brings the familiar equitable concept of estoppel into play.

[5] This approach will earn you a really good mark, as you are showing that you are thinking about the underlying idea of unconscionability by comparing the thought of one author with that of another.

This attempt by Watt to give clarity to the term 'unconscionability' can be set alongside the idea of Delany and Ryan (2008),[5] who feel that 'even the questionable approach of the Court of Appeal in **Pennington v Waine** [2002] EWCA Civ 227 appears premised on an understanding of the principle as essentially negative in character, a fallback weapon in the judicial arsenal to be used when harshness must be "tempered" rather than an instrument for inculcating any particular values of fairness'. This understanding of unconscionability as essentially negative is not inconsistent with Watt's analysis or that of Deane J. For example, where a non-owner in the example quoted by Watt (above) relies on the landowner's promise to allow him to occupy the house for life, the non-owner is using the unconscionable conduct of the owner in the negative sense of defending himself from a claim to evict him.

[6] You need to do this as well as outlining the theoretical discussion, as this essay requires a balance between both theory and actual cases.

With these theories in mind let us look at how unconscionability has actually been applied in equity.[6] In **Pennington v Waine** it was applied by Arden LJ in the context of a purported transfer of shares in a company which did not comply with the rule in **Re Rose** [1952] Ch 499 CA, as the transferor had not done all in her power to effect a transfer. She had told a partner in a firm who acted for the company that she wished to transfer some of her shares and later signed a share transfer form. Arden LJ held[7] that it would be unconscionable to allow the transferor in view of all that she had done to transfer the shares, to then change her mind and say that they were not the transferees' shares. The notion of unconscionability has been grafted onto an established rule but it is not clear if, in Watt's term, this was to deal with non-routine conduct or if it was unreasonable or oppressive conduct as outlined above by Deane J in **Commonwealth of Australia v Verwayen**. It could be argued that the conduct of the transferor was neither. In **Yeoman's Row Management Ltd v Cobbe** [2008] UKHL 55, the Court of Appeal applied unconscionability in an estoppel claim, but in the House of Lords Lord Scott held that the Court of Appeal had been influenced too much by the fact that it regarded the behaviour of the company as unconscionable without requiring the essential elements of proprietary estoppel to be present.

Thus, it is not clear whether unconscionability has played any real part in developing equity today or whether it simply confuses the law as it just adds to existing doctrines which are already capable of doing equity.[8]

[7] The point is that other members of the Court of Appeal did not use this term. If you hope for high marks it is vital to be precise.

[8] This essay obviously needs a conclusion but on the facts given and the arguments presented it can only be a tentative one. This will not lose you marks. Sometimes it is the very black and white conclusions which lose marks as they betray a superficial understanding of the law.

Make your answer stand out

- Look at the article by Delany and Ryan (2008) mentioned in the answer and note how the authors look at use of the term 'unconscionability' by the courts in a number of different contexts – research these.

- Consider the rejection of 'unconscionability' as the foundation of liability in cases of dishonest assistance in a breach of trust.

- Could 'unconscionability' be more appropriate where it is sought to develop the law rather than add a gloss to old doctrines as in the examples in this answer? Consider whether it could be the basis for unifying proprietary estoppel and constructive trusts.

Don't be tempted to . . .

- Fail to distinguish between 'conscience' and 'unconscionability'.
- Spend too long on history. A paragraph will be enough.
- Spend all of your time looking at cases – you must engage with the theoretical issues.
- Forget that when you do mention a case you make sure that you look at it from the point of view of how it illustrates the use of the term 'unconscionability'. This means that you will not necessarily be concerned with the actual decision.

Try it yourself

Now take a look at the question below and attempt to answer it. You can check your response against the answer guidance available on the companion website (**www.pearsoned.co.uk/lawexpressqa**).

The law of trusts has shown itself capable of solving an enormous variety of problems and has demonstrated great adaptability.

Consider what challenges it faces at present and how it might meet them.

www.pearsoned.co.uk/lawexpressqa

Go online to access more revision support including additional essay and problem questions with diagram plans, 'You be the marker' questions, and download all diagrams from the book.

Bibliography

Andrews, G. (2002) Undue influence – where's the disadvantage? *Conveyancer and Property Lawyer,* 66: 456.

Andrews, G. and Parsons, S. (2018) Challenging judicial presumptions when equity is not equality. 1 *Conv.* 10.

Baker, J.H. (1993) Land as a donatio mortis causa. *Law Quarterly Review,* 109:19.

Baker, J.H. (2002) *Introduction to English Legal History* (4th edn). Oxford: Oxford University Press.

Baughen, S. (2010) Performing animals and the dissolution of unincorporated associations: the 'contract-holding' theory vindicated. *Conveyancer and Property Lawyer,* 74: 216.

Birks, P. (1996) Equity in the modern law: an exercise in taxonomy. *University of Western Australia Law Review,* 26: 18.

Borkowski, A. (1999) *Deathbed Gifts: The Law of Donatio Mortis Causa.* Oxford: Oxford University Press.

Brook, J. (2014) *King* v *Dubrey* - a donatio mortis causa too far? *Conveyancer and Property Lawyer,* 78: 6: 525.

Brown, J. (2007) What are we to do with testamentary trusts of imperfect obligation? *Conveyancer and Property Lawyer,* 71: 148.

Brown, J. and Pawlowski, M. (2012) Testamentary trusts and the rule against capricious purposes: an underlying rationale? *Tru. L.I.,* 109.

Browne, D. (ed.) (1933) *Ashburner's Principles of Equity* (2nd edn). London: Butterworths.

Burn, E. and Virgo, G.J. (eds) (2008) *Maudsley & Burn's Trusts & Trustees: Cases and Materials* (7th edn). Oxford: Oxford University Press.

Carroll, E. (2018) "The assurances are only half the story . . . ": proprietary estoppel and testamentary capacity in James v James'. *Conveyancer and Property Lawyer,* 2: 192.

Chambers, R. (1997) *Resulting Trusts.* Oxford: Oxford University Press.

Chambers, R. (2013) Constructive trusts and breach of fiduciary duty. *Conveyancer and Property Lawyer,* 77: 3: 241.

Chan, B. (2013) The enigma of the Quistclose trust. *UCL Journal of Law and Jurisprudence,* 2(1): 1–39.

Charity Commission (2008) *Speaking Out: Guidance on Campaigning and Political Activity by Charities.* London: Charity Commission.

Clements, L.M. (2004) Bringing trusts back into the twenty-first century. *Web Journal of Current Legal Issues*, 2.

Conaglen, M. (2005) The nature and function of fiduciary loyalty. *Law Quarterly Review*, 121: 452.

Conaglen, M. (2007) *Fiduciary Loyalty*. Oxford: Hart Publishing.

Critchley, P. (1999) Instruments of fraud, testamentary dispositions and secret trusts. *Law Quarterly Review*, 115: 631.

Cumber, H. (2016) Donationes mortis causa: a doctrine on its deathbed? 1 *Conv.* 56.

Davies, D. (2004) The integrity of trusteeship. *Law Quarterly Review*, 120: 1.

Delany, H. and Ryan, D. (2008) Unconscionability: a unifying theme in equity. *Conveyancer and Property Lawyer*, 72: 401.

Dixon, G.L.M. (2009) Proprietary estoppel: a return to principle. *Conveyancer and Property Lawyer*, 73: 260.

Doggett, A. (2003) Explaining *Re Rose*: the search goes on. *Cambridge Law Journal*, 62: 263.

Dowling A. (2011) Vendors' application for specific performance. *Conveyancer*, 3: 208.

Duggan, A.J. (1996) Is equity efficient? *Law Quarterly Review*, 113: 601.

Dunn, A. (2008) Demanding service or servicing demand? Charities' regulation and the policy process. 71(2) *Modern Law Review* 247.

Emery, C.T. (1982) The most hallowed principle. *Law Quarterly Review*, 98: 551.

Etherton, T. (2008) Constructive trusts: a new model for equity and unjust enrichment. *Cambridge Law Journal*, 67: 265.

Finn, P. (1992) Fiduciary law and the modern world, in E. McKendrick (ed.), *Commercial Aspects of Trusts and Fiduciary Obligations*. Oxford: Oxford University Press.

Fletcher, R. (1996) Charities for the advancement of education. *Law Quarterly Review*, 112: 557.

Gardner, S. (1995) Two maxims of equity. *Cambridge Law Journal*, 54(1): 60.

Gardner, S. (2010) Reliance-based constructive trusts, in C. Mitchell (ed.), *Constructive and Resulting Trusts*. Oxford: Hart Publishing.

Garton, J. (2003) The role of the trust mechanism in the rule in *Re Rose. Conveyancer and Property Lawyer*, 5: 364.

Garton, J. (2007) Justifying the *cy-près* doctrine. *Trust Law International*, 21(3): 134.

Glister, J. and Lee, J. (eds.) (2015) *Hanbury and Martin: Modern Equity*. London: Sweet and Maxwell.

Gray, K. and Gray, S. (2003) The rhetoric of reality, in J. Getzler (ed.), *Rationalizing Property, Equity and Trusts: Essays in Honour of Edward Burn*. London: LexisNexis.

Green, B. (1984) Grey, Oughtred and Vandervell: a contextual reappraisal. *Modern Law Review*, 47: 385.

Griffiths, G. (2008) An inevitable tension? The disclosure of letters of wishes. *Conveyancer and Property Lawyer*, 4: 332.

Gummow, W. (2015) Bribes and constructive trusts. *The Law Quarterly Review*, 131(1): 21.

Hackney, J. (2008) Charities and public benefit. *Law Quarterly Review,* 124: 347.

Halliwell, M. (2003) Perfecting imperfect gifts and trust: have we reached the end of the Chancellor's foot? *Conveyancer and Property Lawyer,* 67: 192.

Hanbury, H.G. (2015) *see* Glister, J. and Lee, J.

Harding, M. (2008) Trusts for religious purposes and the question of public benefit. *Modern Law Review,* 71: 159.

Harris, J. (1971) Trust, power and duty. *Law Quarterly Review,* 87: 31.

Hayton, D. (2001) Developing the obligation characteristic of the trust. *Law Quarterly Review,* 96: 117.

Hayton, D. (2011) Proprietary liability for secret profits. *Law Quarterly Review,* 127: 487.

Hicks, A. (2011) Constructive trusts of fiduciary gain: Lister revived? *Conveyancer and Property Lawyer,* 1: 62.

Hodkinson, K. (1982) *Conveyancer and Property Lawyer,* 228.

Honoré, A. (2003) Trusts: the inessentials, in J. Getzler (ed.), *Rationalizing Property, Equity and Trusts: Essays in Honour of Edward Burn.* London: LexisNexis.

Iwobi, A. (2009) Out with the old, in with the new: religion, charitable status and the Charities Act 2006. *Legal Studies,* 29: 619.

Ker, B.S. (1953) Intermediate income. *Conveyancer and Property Lawyer,* 275.

Kodilinye, G. (1982) A fresh look at the rule in *Strong* v *Bird. Conveyancer and Property Lawyer* 46: 14.

Law Commission (1992) Consultation Paper, *Fiduciary Duties and Regulatory Rules* (No 124).

Law Commission (1999) Report, *Trustees' Powers and Duties* (No 260).

Lee, J. (2015) Constructing and limiting liability in equity. *Law Quarterly Review,* 131: 39.

Lee, R. (2018) Correcting mistakes in trust planning: a comparative post-Pitt analysis. 1 *Conv.* 45.

Luxton, P. (1997) Variations of trusts: settlors' intentions and the consent principle in *Saunders* v *Vautier. Modern Law Review,* 60: 719.

Luxton, P. (1998) Are you being served? Enforcing keep open covenants in leases. *Conveyancer and Property Lawyer,* 76: 396.

Luxton, P. (2007) Gifts to clubs: contract holding is trumps. *Conveyancer and Property Lawyer,* 274.

Mason, A. (1985) Themes and prospects, in P. D. Finn (ed.), *Essays in Equity.* Sydney: The Law Book Company.

Matthews, P. (1984) A heresy and a half in certainty of objects. *Conveyancer and Property Lawyer,* 48: 22.

Matthews, P. (1995) A problem in the construction of gifts to unincorporated associations. *Conveyancer and Property Lawyer,* 49: 302.

Matthews, P. (1996) The new trust: obligations without rights?, in A. J. Oakley (ed.), *Trends in Contemporary Trust Law.* Oxford: Oxford University Press.

McInnes, M. (2008) Charity and sport: a Canadian perspective. *Law Quarterly Review,* 124: 202.

McKay, L. (1974) *Re Baden* and the third class of certainty. *Conveyancer and Property Lawyer,* 38: 269.

Meager, R. (2003) Secret trusts: do they have a future? *Conveyancer and Property Lawyer,* 67: 203.

Millett, P.J. (1998) Equity's place in the law of commerce. *Law Quarterly Review,* 114: 214.

Mitchell, C. and Watterson, S. (2010) Remedies for knowing receipt, in D. Mitchell (ed.), *Constructive and Resulting Trusts.* Oxford: Hart Publishing.

Moffat, G. (2009) *Trusts Law* (5th edn). Cambridge: Cambridge University Press.

Nolan, R. (1996) The triumph of technicality. *Cambridge Law Journal,* 55(3): 436.

Ollikainen-Read, A. (2018) Assignments of equitable interests and the origins of Re Rose. 1 *Conv.* 63.

Panesar, S. (2013) Title deeds to land and donatio mortis causa. *Conveyancer and Property Lawyer,* 70.

Parry, N. (1989) Trusts for masses. *Conveyancer and Property Lawyer,* 53: 453.

Pawlowski, M. and Brown, J. (2004) Constituting a secret trust by estoppel. *Conveyancer and Property Lawyer,* 388.

Perrins, B. (1972) Can you keep half a secret? *Law Quarterly Review,* 88: 225.

Perrins, B. (1985) Secret trusts: are they dehors? *Conveyancer and Property Lawyer,* 49: 248.

Picton, J. (2011) *Kings* v *Bultitude* – A gift lost to charity? *Conveyancer and Property Lawyer,* 1: 69.

Ridge, P. (2008) Justifying the remedies for dishonest assistance. *Law Quarterly Review,* 124: 445.

Smith, L. (2003) The motive, not the deed, in J. Getzler (ed.), *Rationalizing Property, Equity and Trusts: Essays in Honour of Edward Burn.* London: LexisNexis.

Swadling, W. (2008) Explaining resulting trusts. *Law Quarterly Review,* 124: 72.

Swadling, W. (2011) The fiction of the constructive trust. 64 *Current Legal Problems* 1.

Thompson, M.P. (2003) Mortgages and undue influence, in E. Cooke (ed.), *Modern Studies in Property Law,* Vol. 2. Oxford: Hart Publishing.

Turner, P. (2006) The High Court of Australia on contracts to assign equitable rights. *Conveyancer and Property Lawyer,* 390.

Turner, P. (2015) The new fundamental norm of recovery for losses to express trusts. *Cambridge Law Journal,* 74(2): 188.

Virgo, G. (2003) Restitution through the looking glass: restitution within equity and equity within restitution, in J. Getzler (ed.), *Rationalizing Property, Equity and Trusts: Essays in Honour of Edward Burn.* London: LexisNexis.

Virgo, G. (2018) *The Principles of Equity and Trusts* (3rd edn). Oxford: Oxford University Press.

Watt, G. (2009) *Equity Stirring: The Story of Justice Beyond Law.* Oxford: Hart Publishing.

Whayman, D. (2018) Obligation and property in tracing claims. 2 *Conv.* 157.

Worthington, S. (2006) *Equity* (2nd edn). Oxford: Oxford University Press.

Index

account of profits 138–9, 238, 241, 267–8
account, taking an 248
administrators, appointment of 79
advancement, powers of 219–23
advancement, presumption of 120
Amnesty International 181
animals 199, 200, 209
appointment, powers of 53–5

beneficiary principle and purpose trusts 191–210
bona vacantia 206–9
breach of trust 217–18, 229–45, 269–73
bribes 133–4, 143, 150–1, 259–63

certainties *see* three certainties
cestui que trusts 203
Chancellor 10–11, 274–7
change of position 243
charitable trusts 138–9, 159–90
   administrative unworkability 175
   animals 199, 200, 209
   arts, culture, heritage or science 164
   benefit aspect 161, 163
   campaigning as political 165
   Charities Act 2006 171, 176
   Charities Act 2011 163–4, 169, 171–2, 180, 188–9, 198–200, 207–8
   Charity Commissioners 162, 163, 166–70
   cy-près 207–8, 210
   education and research 163, 164, 174, 177–8, 183, 189, 207–8
   failure of gifts 185–9, 207–8, 210
   general charitable intention 185–9
   guidance 180–4
   perpetuities, rule against 172–4, 201
   political campaigning or political activity 165
   political purposes 180–4
   poverty, relief of 166–7, 176–9, 187, 207–8, 209
   private trusts 172–4

public aspect 163
public benefit 10, 159–84, 199
purpose trusts 172–5, 198–201
religion 166, 169–70, 179, 200
research 162–5
spiritual or non-secular belief system 169
sport 172–5
surplus funds 207–8, 210
unincorporated associations 203–4
cheques 77–81
Clayton's Case, rule in 243–5
clean hands, he who comes to equity must come with 264
commercial trusts 249
common law
   equity 13–15, 83, 266–7
   fusion debate 10–11, 13–15
   land 9–10
   remedies 10, 14, 235–51
   unincorporated associations 203
compensation 142, 218
confidentiality 227
conflict of interests 137–44
consideration 266–7
constant supervision 21
constitution of trusts 71–90
   bribes 150–2
   declaration of trusts 61, 62, 75, 83–5, 256–8
   donatio mortis causa 74–81, 86–90
   enforcement 83–4, 256–8, 266–7
   formalities 74–5, 83–4, 256–8
   insolvent fiduciary 149–53
   intention 73–81, 256–7
   land 74–6, 256–8
   objects, certainty of 256, 258
   oral transactions 257–8
   perfecting imperfect gifts 82–5
   vesting 74, 79–80, 257
   volunteer, equity will not assist a 74, 83–5, 266–7

INDEX

constructive trusts 64, 66, 129–57, 150
  bribes 133–4, 263
  competing businesses 138–9
  conflict of interests, rule against 137–40
  donatio mortis causa 87
  family home 10, 133
  fiduciary relationships 10, 133–57
  formalities 62
  institutional constructive trusts 133
  intention 129–35
  knowing/dishonest assistance and knowing receipt
      138, 237–40
  land 132–5, 147–8
  mutual wills 110–12
  purchase of trust property 137–40
  remedies 10, 108, 137–40, 143, 156–7, 237
  secret and half-secret trusts 108, 132–5
  self-dealing rule 137–40
  writing 147–8
contract 24–6, 111, 154–7
covenants 14
creation of trusts *see* constitution of trusts; formalities
      for creation of trusts
cy-près 187–90, 206, 207

damages 13, 74, 259
declarations of trust 61, 62, 75, 83–5, 103, 256–8, 268
deeds 61, 75
definition/description of equity 2–7
delegation 215, 217
detrimental reliance 84, 155
disaster funds 208–10
disclosure 32, 138
discretion 14, 24–5, 39, 44–5, 51–5, 221, 258
dishonest assistance 239–41, 276–7
donatio mortis causa 10, 86–90
  cheques 77–81
  conditional on death 80–1
  constitution of trusts 74–8, 80–1
  contemplation of death 80–1, 87–9
  dominion, parting with 80–1
  intention 75–6, 80–1
  land 75–6
  proprietary estoppel 89
  unconscionability 88
  validating gifts 86–90
duty of care 215–18

education, advancement of 162–5, 174, 177, 183, 189,
      207–8
employment contracts 24–6

equitable interest, disposition 65–7
equitable remedies 14, 24–6
  see also specific remedies (e.g. specific
      performance)
  constructive trusts 10, 133, 138–9, 142, 237–40
  in personam, equity acts 9–10
  specific performance 19–20, 64
equity 269
  see also equitable remedies; maxims of equity
  acquisition issue 270–1
  common law 5, 13–15, 83
  context of limitation periods 269–73
  definition 2–8
  discretionary character 3
  discretionary system 4–5
  distinctive features 3, 4
  estoppel 76, 153–7, 276–7
  fusion debate 10–11, 13–15
  history 9–11
  principle of 66
  quantification issue 270–1
  unconscionability 10
equity follows the law 83, 266
estoppel 76, 153–7, 276–7
European Convention on Human Rights 209
exclusion clauses 259–63
executors, appointment of 79, 257
express trusts 61, 62

family home 10, 29–32, 133
family trusts 217, 241, 243
fiduciary relationships 10, 112, 133–57, 243, 263
fixed trusts 51–5
forfeiture clauses 231–2
formalities for creation of trusts 57–69
  see also oral transactions; writing
  constitution of trusts 74–5, 83–5, 256–8
  declarations of trust 61, 62, 75, 83–5, 106, 256–8,
      267–8
  donatio mortis causa 10, 73–81
  formalism 9–10, 64, 65
  intention 61, 265, 267–8
  land 61–2, 256–7
  objects, certainties of 256, 664
  presumed resulting trusts 61–2
  secret and half-secret trusts 106, 108, 147–8
  wills 96, 97, 99–103
fox hunting 198, 201
fraud
  breach of trust 240, 261–2
  constructive trusts 147–8

exclusion clauses 261–2
land 146–7, 267–8
mutual wills 113
oral transactions 146–8
secret and half-secret trusts 99, 104–7, 147–8
Statute of Frauds 1677 10, 106, 146
statute to be used as an instrument of fraud, equity
    will not allow 145–8, 265
writing 147–8
freedom of expression 165
freehold covenants 14
freezing orders 27
fusion debate 10–11, 13–15

half-secret trusts *see* secret and half-secret trusts
he who comes to equity must come with clean hands
    264, 266
history of equity 9–11
human rights 181, 209

illegality 201, 266
imperfect gifts, perfecting 82–5
implied trusts 62, 147–8
in personam, equity as acting 9
inalienability, rule against 173, 198–201
individual ascertainability test 39, 51–5
Inheritance (Provision for Families and dependants)
    Act 1975 90
Inheritance and Trustees' Powers Act 2014 220, 221
Inheritance Tax 66
injunctions 12, 26
insolvency 134, 261, 263–4
insolvent fiduciary 149–53
intention
    advancement and maintenance, powers of 221
    certainty of intention 38–9, 43–5, 98, 101–2, 255–8
    constitution of trusts 74–81, 255–8
    constructive trusts 129–35
    cy-près 187–90, 206–7
    discretionary trusts 39, 258
    donatio mortis causa 75–6, 80–1
    equity looks to the intent and not the form 265,
        267–8
    family home 10, 133
    formalities 61, 265, 267–8
    mutual wills 111
    purpose trusts 194
    resulting trusts 61, 119–20, 258
    secret and half-secret trusts 95–8, 101–2, 132–4
    tracing 243
    variation of trusts 228–32

investment powers of trustees 215–18
    account, taking an 227, 248
    advice, taking proper 217
    breach of trust 217–18
    care and skill 217
    delegation 215, 217
    diversification 217
    exclusion clauses 259
    negligence 261–2, 265
    remedies 215–18, 246
    restoration of property 218
    standard investment criteria 217–18
    standard of care 217
    suitability 217
    tracing 217–18

joint tenants, severance of 102
Judicature Acts 13
justice 9, 10, 275

King's Council, petitions to 9
knowing assistance and knowing receipt 133, 237,
    272–3

land
    common law 9–10
    constitution of trusts 74–6, 256–8
    constructive trusts 137–40, 147–8
    damages 74, 247–8
    declarations of trust 61, 106, 256–7
    deeds 61, 74–5
    donatio mortis causa 75–6, 87–9
    express trusts 61
    formalities 5, 61, 66–7, 256–7
    fraud 146–7, 266
    leases 13–14, 75
    oral transactions 147–9, 156, 257–8, 267–8
    proprietary estoppel 155–6
    purpose trusts 204
    registered land 86, 87, 89, 267–8
    resulting trusts 61–2, 123
    specific performance 14, 22, 74
    unincorporated associations 204
    vesting 74
    writing 74–5, 147–8, 255–8
leases 4, 13–14, 21, 75
letters of wishes 105, 107, 227
liquidation 67, 122, 125, 241, 243, 249, 251
lives in being plus 21 years 40–1, 173,
    199, 203
Lord Cairns Act 26, 251

maintenance, powers of 219–23
marriage consideration 266–7
masses, trusts for saying of 200–1
matrimonial home 125
maxims of equity 3, 4, 9, 64, 66, 264–5
  distinctive features 6
  equity follows the law 266
  equity looks to the intent and not the form 265,
    267–8
  equity will not allow a statute to be used as an
    instrument of fraud 145–8, 265, 267–8
  equity will not assist a volunteer 74, 83, 264–8
  equity will not perfect an imperfect gift 82–3, 85
  he who comes to equity must come with clean hands
    264, 265
  where equity and law conflict, equity shall
    prevail 13
memorials or tombs 195, 200
Milroy v *Lord,* principle in 74, 79, 84
misapplication of trust money 248, 251, 272–3
misrepresentation 29–31
mixing 245
monuments or tombs, trusts for 195, 200
mortgages and sureties 29–32
mutual wills 93–113

negligence 248, 259–63, 264
non-charitable purpose trusts *see* purpose trusts

objects, certainty of 38–46, 51–5
  constitution of trusts 256, 258
  discretionary trusts 51–5
  fixed trusts 51–5
  formalities 62, 256
  individual ascertainability test 39, 51–5
  list principle 54–5
  perpetuities, rule against 40–1
  private trusts 172–4
  purpose trusts 193–6
  resulting trusts 119–20
  secret and half-secret trusts 95–8, 101–2
oral transactions
  declarations of trust 257
  fraud 146
  land 147–8, 156, 257–8, 267–8
  proprietary estoppel 155–6
  secret and half-secret trusts 146–8
  wills 111

perfecting imperfect gifts 82–5
perpetuities, rule against

charitable trusts 173, 200
  inalienability, rule against 173, 199–200
  lives in being plus 21 years 40–1, 173, 199, 203
  objects, certainty of 40–1
  purpose trusts 173, 198–201, 203
  wait and see rule 173, 175, 199, 200, 203
personal services, contracts for 24–6
political campaigns 182
political purposes, charities for 165
poverty, relief of 163–4, 166–7, 176–8,
    207–9
prisoners of conscience 181
private trusts 49, 172–175, 192–5, 203, 206,
    210, 254
promissory estoppel 155–7
proprietary estoppel 72, 89, 130, 153–7, 276–7
protective trusts 231
public benefit 10, 138, 159–84, 174–84, 201,
    207–8
purpose trusts 174, 193–210
  administrative unworkability 175
  animals 194, 195, 198–201
  beneficiary principle 191–210
  cestui que trusts 203
  charitable trusts 172–5, 198–205
  Charities Act 1960 194
  disaster funds 208–10
  enforcement 192, 195, 197
  failure of trusts 203
  illegality 201
  imperfect obligation, trusts of 195, 198
  inalienability, rule against 200–3, 205
  interested adversary principle 193, 196
  lack of enforceability 194, 196
  land 204
  maladministration, reform 193–5
  masses 200–1
  monuments or tombs 195, 200
  objects, certainty of 195
  perpetuities, rule against 198–201, 203
  private trusts 188, 195
  public policy 193
  Quistclose trusts 115, 122, 125
  resulting trusts 173, 199–200, 208
  surplus funds 206–9
  testamentary freedom 196
  unincorporated associations 173–4,
    202–5
  void, as being considered 193–7

Quistclose trusts 122, 125

real property *see* land
religion
    charities 165, 166, 169–70, 179, 200–1
    forfeiture clause 231–2
    masses, trusts for saying 178, 200
remedies
    see also equitable remedies
    account of profits 138–9, 238, 241, 267–8
    account, taking an 246, 248–9
    breach of trust 5, 229–45
    bribery 261, 263–4
    common law 10, 14, 235–51
    compensation 142, 218, 246–50
    constructive trusts 10, 108, 133, 137–40, 142, 156,
       237–40
    contributions 238
    damages 14, 74
    dishonest assistance 239–41, 276–7
    injunctions 10, 13, 26
    insolvency 263–4
    investment powers 215–18, 246
    knowing assistance and knowing receipt 133,
       237–40, 272–3
    remoteness, principles of 240
    tracing 217–18, 241–5
research, charitable trusts for 162–5
restitution theorists 153
resulting trusts 115–20
    automatic resulting trusts 118–20
    certainty of objects 119–20
    charitable trusts 188, 189
    clean hands, he who comes to equity must come
      with 266
    company and family law 125
    contributions 266
    cy-près 188, 189
    declarations of trust 61
    fiduciary relationships 142–3
    formalities 61–3
    illegality 266
    intention 61, 119–20, 257
    land 59–63, 123
    liquidation 125
    perpetuities, rule against 173, 199
    presumed resulting trusts 61–2, 119, 120
    purchase price 238, 266
    purpose trusts 173, 198–200, 207–8
    Quistclose trusts 122, 125
    remedies 238
    secret and half-secret trusts 97, 106
    surplus funds 208–10

    unjust enrichment 120
    writing 147–8
Rose, *Re*, principle 79, 84, 258

Sale of Goods Act 1979 22
Sale of Goods (Amendment) Act 1995 50
Saunders v *Vautier*, rule in 230, 239
secret and half-secret trusts 9, 93–109
    acceptance of obligation 97, 98, 102
    certainty of intention 98, 101–2
    communication of intention 97,
      98, 102
    constructive trusts 108, 132–5
    declarations of trust 104–5
    dehors the will theory 104, 107
    extrinsic evidence 102
    formalities 106, 108
    fraud 98, 104–7, 147–8
    intention 95–8, 101–2
    land 100–3
    letters of wishes 106, 108
    objects, certainty 95–8, 101–3
    public policy 104–9
    resulting trusts 97, 106
    three certainties 95–8
    wills 95–8
    witnesses 96, 97
    writing 147–8
secret profits 262–3
self-dealing rule 138
shares 47–50, 79–80, 82–5, 258
signatures 29–31, 62, 103, 258
specific performance (SP)
    bars to 20, 21
    contract for personal service 20
    contracts for sale 22
    damages 26
    equitable remedy 19–20, 64
    fundamental principle 20
    fusion debate 14
    injunctions 26
    land 14–15, 74–5
    mutual wills 111
    personal services 24–6
    in personam, equity acts 10
    sale of goods 22
    supervision 26–7
sport, charitable trusts for 172–5
spouses and undue influence 29–32
standard of care 217
Statute of Frauds 1977 10, 87, 105, 146

statute to be used as an instrument of fraud, equity will not allow a 145–8, 265, 267–8
Strong v *Bird,* rule 77–81, 257
subject matter, certainty 38–41, 95–8, 101–3, 255–8
sureties 29–32
surplus funds 208–10

three certainties 35–55
    see also objects
    intention 38–9, 43–5, 98, 101–2, 255–8
    secret and half-secret trusts 113
    subject matter 38–46, 95–8, 101–2, 255–8
    trusts, creation of 35–55, 256
torture 181
tracing 217–18
trust and confidence, relationships of 30
trustees, duties and powers of 213–33
    see also investment powers of trustees
    competing businesses 138–9
    confidential nature of 226
    conflict of interests 137–40, 143
    constructive trusts 137–40, 143–4
    disclosure of trust documents to beneficiaries 224–8
    discretion, controlling trustees' 224–8
    fiduciary relationships 137–40, 142–4
    Inheritance and Trustees' Powers Act 2014
        220, 221
    limits of obligations 226–7
    misapplies trust money 248, 272–3
    Pitt v *Holt,* principles in 224–7
    self-dealing rule 137–40
    Trusts of Land and Appointment of Trustees
        Act 1996 226
trusts
    see also charitable trusts; constitution of trusts;
        constructive trusts; formalities for creation of
        trusts; resulting trusts; trustees
    breach of trust 217–18

and creditors 49
gifts distinguished 83, 85
Limitation Act 1980 272
private trusts 172–5, 203, 206, 210
rules on 48
subject matter of 46–7
variation of trusts 228–32

unascertained goods 46–50
unconscionability 7, 10, 78, 85, 88, 138, 155–6,
    240, 275–6
undue influence 29–32
    presumed undue influence 30, 143
    special relationships 29–32, 143
    sureties, spouses as 29–32
unincorporated associations 173, 202–5
unjust enrichment 120, 239

variation of trusts 228–32
vesting 74, 79–80, 257
volunteer, equity will not assist a 74, 83, 85,
    264, 266

wait and see rule 173, 199, 203
wills 95–113
    attestation 103
    formalities 96, 97, 106
    mutual wills 109–13
    oral wills 87
    witnesses 96, 97, 99–103
winding up 122–6
writ system 9
writing 65–6
    constitution of trusts 74–5, 256–8
    land 74–5, 146–7, 256–8
    mutual wills 111
    secret and half-secret trusts 147–8
    signatures 29–31, 62, 103, 258